T012203,2

POLITICS 101:

The *RIGHT* Course

YOUR HANDBOOK ON CURRENT POLITICAL ISSUES

JOSEPH M. WESTON SR.

abbott press®
A DIVISION OF WRITER'S DIGEST

Politics 101: The *Right* Course
Your Handbook on Current Political Issues

Abbott Press books may be ordered through booksellers or by contacting:

Abbott Press
1663 Liberty Drive
Bloomington, IN 47403
www.abbottpress.com
Phone: 1-866-697-5310

Because of the dynamic nature of the Internet, any web addresses or links contained in this book may have changed since publication and may no longer be valid. The views expressed in this work are solely those of the author and do not necessarily reflect the views of the publisher, and the publisher hereby disclaims any responsibility for them.

Any people depicted in stock imagery provided by Thinkstock are models, and such images are being used for illustrative purposes only.

Certain stock imagery © Thinkstock.

ISBN: 978-1-4582-0480-6 (sc)
ISBN: 978-1-4582-0482-0 (hc)
ISBN: 978-1-4582-0481-3 (e)

Library of Congress Control Number: 2012911857

Printed in the United States of America

Abbott Press rev. date: 10/04/2012

For my parents, who made it a priority to raise me
with the right set of values.

"The government should do for the people only what they cannot do better by themselves."

- Abraham Lincoln

Politics 101: The *Right* Course

Introduction

This is not just a book. It's a handbook, a tool and a reference manual. Women, put it in your pocketbook next to your lipstick and compact mirror. Guys, toss it in your toolbox. You'll never know when you have to hammer a point home. Drivers, put it in your glove box. Fliers, keep it in your carry-on. For those who wear camouflage or own a gun, stash it in your zippered pocket, compartment or duffel bag. You need to be prepared for altercations requiring you to make a point that is *dead-on*. Young mothers, put it in your baby bag. For all others, don't leave home without it. You'll never know when you need to defend life, liberty and the pursuit of happiness.

Everything you need to know about politics today is in this book. Details not enclosed are superfluous and need not be sought elsewhere. You'll want to read this book if:

- You were looking for *Politics for Dummies* and couldn't find it, so you're considering this one as a close substitute (and are relieved it has a less embarrassing title.)
- You want to be able to hold your own in any political conversation (and be able to end it with your sparring opponent left open-mouthed and speechless.)
- You want a tool to do a quick search without getting 367,142 results.
- You think conservatives are not cool, but want to give them a chance to make their case. (Maybe you could use this book to fan your liberal flames—you never know.)

- You know not to discuss sex or religion at a gathering, but will violate the rule of discussing politics, as you know it is vital to our nation's interest.
- You want to dazzle your friends and family with all the cool stuff you learned. (If you think the word *dazzle* is too dramatic, substitute *impress* or *antagonize*.)
- Your primary source of political knowledge is Jon Stewart.
- You realized your original idea of finding a new dating website won't be as exciting as reading a book on politics, which you'll find is more interesting and more challenging.
- You want to take the before and after political orientation test (enclosed) to see if you could be influenced. (And as long as you read the book, I won't mind if your score doesn't dramatically change.)
- You also want to give the questionnaire to others (friends don't let friends drive home politically deprived.)

You don't want to read this book if (My publisher told me not to include this section:)

- You're a committed liberal and never lost an argument about income re-distribution.
- You're a hard-line conservative and could make Rush Limbaugh look indecisive.
- You like reading political books put out by your favorite talk-show hosts, political pundit or presidential candidate. (And you're still looking for your next fix.)
- You like going under at a hypnosis demonstration and love being brainwashed by your favorite ideologue. (My tactics are honest and straightforward.)
- You thrive on strong language, verbal attacks and venomous partisan rhetoric. (Sorry, you won't find it between the covers herein.)

Some people are intimidated by politics the way I'm overwhelmed by watching sports. When relatives or friends start talking about their favorite team, I am clueless. So I understand that politics just doesn't interest everyone. But maybe more people would be interested if there was just one book out there that they could read so they don't have to read a half dozen or go to scores of websites to get the full scoop.

This is that book. It will explore both the liberal and conservative mind-set that creates the cultural chasm we see between the Occupy Wall Street demonstrators on the left and the Tea Party Movement on the right.

READER WARNING:

The contents of this book may cause serious side effects. I don't want to spoil the ending, but I can tell you this: Taking a full dose of *Politics 101: The* **Right** *Course* may cause you to improve your understanding of conservative, right-wing thinking. Please know it may permanently skew your political orientation. At the moment you finish this potion of common sense, your eyes will see more clearly. Cloudiness about the confusing world of politics will disappear. Nausea from listening to news will fade. Dizziness that once occurred from listening to the "No Spin Zone" will subside. Your preconceived notions will dissolve. No ingredients of hostility or harsh vitriol have been added to this unique medication. Political scientists have formulated it to point you to the *right* pathway.

Liberalism

Liberalism is like original sin: you are born with it. When I was young, I was a liberal. I was in good company, as many young people start out this way. You see, there is no course in elementary school that specifically teaches the philosophical differences between liberalism and conservatism. But if there were, we probably wouldn't really understand them at that tender age anyway. Parents don't generally sit down and teach their children about the political spectrum any more than we teach them about the birds and the bees before they are old enough. So when we are young, we form a basis for our political leanings based on what we hear our parents or relatives say to each other. Or it may be influenced from off-the-cuff remarks our elementary school teachers might make in history class.

As we grow, we are told things in very simple terms. The Democrats are for the poor and the working class, for helping those who need assistance, and for international diplomacy instead of war. They favor minority rights and want women to have the benefit of "choice." The Republicans are for the rich, are in favor of cutting government services to help people, are usually in favor of going to war, are against minority rights and are against abortion. During times of the Obama administration, the Republicans objected to gay marriage and expanding health care to those who can't afford it. This makes them mean. Who wants to grow up seeing himself or herself as mean? I think the need of young people to attain a certain level of self-esteem causes them to gravitate toward a compassionate view on life. This results in a nod to the left, as society teaches that Democrats have a monopoly on compassion.

From our beginning, our teachers instructed us to respect and tolerate people different from us. Liberals take the lead on tolerance of minorities. Television shows the starving children in fifth-world countries, underscoring the socioeconomic extremes in the world. We also learn how poverty can be close to home and see the benefits of income redistribution, a liberal tenet. Democrats, we are told, favor government funding to help the poor. In school, we learn the government should provide children with a great education so they can avoid the pitfalls into which these adults fell. The Democrats want more education subsidies than Republicans. We also notice many of the poor people are a minority, handicapped or mentally impaired. Although Republicans support noble causes, the Democrats take the credit because they supposedly are the champions for the helpless and downtrodden.

Our thinking processes about politics continue to form in our Junior High School years when we take history, geography and literature. It opens our eyes to a world of winners and losers, rich and poor, educated and illiterate, those living in peace and those who live in war-torn areas of the world. The cause of feeding the poor is identified more as a liberal than a conservative issue. In science class, we learn about global warming and the various endangered species and immediately identify with liberals, as they are the champions for ecological concerns. In history class, we learn about the struggle for civil rights in this country. The heroes for those who fought for minorities are often in the left to center camp. We also learn about the huge disparity in wealth. This breeds a temptation to appreciate income redistribution, a liberal tenet. You see how a view left of center seems to have an advantage in wielding influence to the young?

As we grow into adolescence, our desire for independence may result in minor skirmishes with establishment. First, we rebel against our parents for being too strict (e.g.: needing to finish our homework before watching TV or going out in the evening with friends.) We swear that when we become parents, we'll be more understanding of young people; be totally liberal and let them fully extend their need-to-learn-on-my-own-without-parental-guidance muscles. When we become old enough to drive, we might have a minor altercation with the law, perhaps a speeding ticket or two. Or, maybe the cops showed up at a party. As teenagers, we have a natural emotional reaction to whatever legal correction comes our way and we then put down law and order (a conservative tenet) as not cool. Then, you know someone in high school who gets pregnant and you are so thankful that person has the right to make the choice to have an abortion. *Wow,* you think. *I can't imagine having to be a parent at our age.* If I'm a guy, I'm thinking: *I sure would want my girlfriend to have that choice if I were the father.* If I'm a girl, I'm thinking: *I sure would like to have that choice if I got pregnant.* At that age, you cannot have the experience, perspective or wisdom to make an adult decision. In fact, the human brain does not fully mature until it is twenty-five years old. Unless you are attending a parochial school or unless you have already been raised pro-life by your parents, you probably adopt the liberal, pro-choice perspective on this issue. In fact, any concern about women's rights is linked to liberalism. Any young budding feminist will surely be voting for Democrats if that issue is important to her.

Our experiences growing up favor values that society associates with either liberalism or the Democratic Party. It's the same way with our associations of people. Everyone knows a policeman, fireman, teacher, government employee or blue-collar worker in a union. Often, their children will grow up Democrat since their platform is always more pro-union than the Republican platform. In many families, growing up Democratic is like growing up Catholic. You don't have a choice. You're born into it. And the penalties for defection are too high to even consider, at least until you are out of the house and on your own. By then, it might be too late. You could already be a hardened Democrat.

A friend of yours that graduated from high school gets involved with drugs and gets help from a government-funded program. Another classmate you know has grown up in a troubled family and they have benefited from a government-funded social worker that has intervened with serious family issues. You grow to appreciate the importance of how government programs may benefit people who at the moment just can't help themselves. Don't get me wrong. Conservatives are not for eliminating all government programs to help people with a need. Republicans have voted for government assistance in this country, but they generally are for a more efficient and less wasteful government that would result in less government spending. So, suffice it to say they are for cutting out the fat where possible. However, that's not what young people hear. They hear Democrats are in favor of compassionate, governmental assistance and Republicans are against it. The Democrats, therefore, are the compassionate ones and the Republicans are heartless. But the truth is in the details, not the generalities.

Consider this example: Young people might hear the Republicans want to intervene in a volatile situation in a politically unstable foreign country and this might result in American casualties. However, the

Democrats want to continue diplomatic attempts to solve the problem. Therefore, Republicans are warmongers and the Democrats are peacemakers. Is it any wonder that *anyone* in their teens would feel the need to be conservative or vote Republican when they turn eighteen?

Growing up with religious parents is extremely influential. Many social issues such as abortion, capital punishment, sentencing for violent crimes, gay marriage, sexual social issues and even healthcare are affected by the religious environment of a young person's family. However, most families don't attend a religious service on a weekly basis anymore. As a result, an overwhelming majority of young people grow up with minimal spiritual influence to affect their stance on social issues. This makes it more unlikely for these adolescents to adopt a firm emphasis on the preciousness of life. I had a strict Catholic upbringing and was the third of five children when my Mom was surprised with a pregnancy at the age of forty-six. It would have been unthinkable in our house to even consider terminating the pregnancy. This mindset carried over into my adult life. My sons both went to a fundamentalist Baptist church and had a solid spiritual basis to form values. But this kind of upbringing is not the norm in today's society.

The college experience is when the young adult can really fall into the crevice of liberal politics. This comes mostly through the influence of liberal-thinking professors who usually use their position to influence growing psyches. Journalists and other political pundits are predominantly liberal-minded and would naturally have an influence on anyone listening to the mainstream media. But young people generally concern themselves with social issues and don't spend a lot of time analyzing the details on the tax and spending habits of the Democrats versus the goal of minimizing such by the Republicans. To them, the Republicans and conservatives are an alien creature. It is my mission to shed light on this species "to the right" so the politically curious can see the merit of the overall conservative philosophy.

Conservatism

Conservatism is like club membership. You have to join. By this, I mean that adopting a conservative view doesn't happen naturally from familial socialization or subtle influences nearly as often as liberalism. And just as your successes or failures can be attributed to moments in your life, the awareness of taking on a conservative view may also be memorable. You could have experienced some of these events already and be qualified to bare the label. Each story behind the newly born conservative can be unique. As a child, municipal rules regarding lemonade stands, trick-or-treating or curfews might have impinged on your plans for having a good time. While a student, you may have been offended by discrimination in your school against Christians or Christmas in the name of "separation of church and state." Often, a significant moment occurs when you get your first paycheck and you are shocked at the amount of taxes that were taken out. As an adult, some news events or liberal commentary on TV may have offended your sensibilities. Sometimes the moment doesn't happen until you own your first home and get the feeling of being overly controlled by the municipality. If you start a business and experience the world of government regulation, you certainly will develop a resentment of various agencies telling you what to do. If you get divorced and the state steps in to tell you how exactly much you have to pay your ex-wife in child support, you surely will not be appreciating the extent of government intrusion.

In other cases, you may have started to become conservative when perturbed by facts:

- If your family managed their budget the way the federal government did, then you would have a debt of $460,000 based on a household income after taxes of $75,000 per year.
- The federal government spent $2.6 million to study how "AIDS" spreads among prostitutes in China. Another example of waste was when the Justice Department spent $16 a muffin during banquets for their conferences. The list of extravagance is almost endless.
- Obamacare took $500 billion in Medicare funds from seniors (who paid into health care their whole lives) and put that money towards freebies for people who don't pay for health care.
- As of March 2012, U.S. immigration officials were under orders "to provide abortion services for detained illegal aliens in some

circumstances and hormone therapy to those who say they are transgendered."

- "The food stamp program cost us $76 billion in 2011, an incredible jump from a $17 billion layout back in the year 2000. One explanation for the huge increase is that one of the rules for qualifying now stipulates the applicant qualifies if they have no income, regardless of their assets. This means wealthy millionaires qualify if they have no income. (Credit to Fox News broadcast July 10.)
- Even if Congress did pass a comprehensive income tax increase on the wealthy (a hot issue as of July during this election 2012 season,) the additional revenues probably wouldn't offset more than one percent of the annual fiscal deficit.

You may or may not have experienced one of the above moments that could shake your liberal-and-loving-it world. Perhaps this book could be that perspective-changing experience. Regardless, let's have some fun and chart where you think your sentiments currently would be plotted on a liberal vs. conservative spectrum. Pick a spot somewhere on the following two lines to describe your current political orientation and choose an actual number to represent the extent to which you consider yourself "conservative." The total of the scores coincide with "agree" answers to a total of 32 questions in a questionnaire at the end of this book. You'll fill out the questionnaire after reading the book, but I thought it would fun if you took a guess now of where your mindset is so that you can make a before-and-after comparison. I divided the conservative "spectrums" into two categories. Pick a number on the chart below or at least make an "X" someplace on the line.

First, make a guess how you rank in the philosophical areas.

Philosophical and Social Conservative Index

0	5	10	15	20

Hopeless Middle of the Road/Centrist   Conservative Very Conservative
Liberal

Now, take a guess at how you believe the country should handle money.

Fiscal Conservative Index

0	3	6	9	12

Hopeless   Middle of the Road/Centrist   Conservative   Very Conservative
Liberal

Now, add them together to get your total score on your current conservative position. Go ahead and make a note on this page of your social, fiscal, and total conservative scores. It will be interesting to see how close you came to your guess after you read this book and take the questionnaire. Even better, it will be neat to see if you underwent some enlightenment as a result of reading facts herein, resulting in an increase in your score. After all, I will be appealing mostly to your logic and common sense. I will make no attempt to use brainwashing techniques or mind-bending trickery.

I contrast the differences between liberals and conservatives regarding both their mindset and the policies they promote. Put on a pair of conservative lenses to see through the murky political waters of today. I hope to erase your incorrect, pre-conceived notions about the conservative political philosophy and enlighten you to the benefits thereof. Ready? Take a dive into my pool and refresh yourself with a closer look at the fish on the *right* side of the sea.

1.

Liberal Political Spectrum vs. Conservative Political Spectrum

L ET ME BEING by first stating the five basic concepts of conservatism:

1. Limited government
2. Free market
3. Individual freedom
4. Traditional American values
5. Strong national defense

Brit Hume, a former White House Correspondent, once summed up the struggle between the philosophies of liberalism vs. conservatism this way: "For the better part of a century, Americans have engaged in a seesawing debate over how to keep the United States strong, prosperous, just and free. Big government or small? Free markets or aggressive regulation? Should we protect our values abroad or meet our enemies halfway?"

Consider this quote by Rush Limbaugh, conservative radio talk show host: "The natural spirit of the human being is freedom and conservatism is simply freedom."

A famous quote very relevant to this book is by President Reagan while in the White House: "In this present crisis, government is not the solution to the problem, government is the problem."

This book highlights the differences between liberalism, which are the phrases to the left of each chapter vs. conservatism, which are the phrases on the right side of the "vs." This political divide can be based on the four spectra below.

Left	vs.	Right
Secular Progressivism	vs.	Traditionalism
Democratic Platform	vs.	Republican Platform
Government Control	vs.	Individual Freedom

Keep in mind the "left" and "right" sides are used interchangeably with "liberalism" and "conservatism," respectively. Liberalism has its philosophical roots in being "left" and generally favors the Democratic platform. A sub-section of Democrats and/or those on the left can also be "secular progressives" (to be defined and discussed later.) To be fair, Democrats can also be traditionalists. Conservatism has its roots in being "right," which generally favors the Republican platform and most often favors the "traditionalist" agenda.

Left vs. Right

Academically, *left* means more government and *right* means less government. It is as simple as that. An extreme left position means a central government will decide who owns what, (including the seizing of private assets,) who works where, what kind of schooling children get, what, if any, religion we can participate in, and what we can say and think. The most extreme left position is impossible to pull off because people are not robots. But a close example of a leftist government was the U.S.S.R. back in the mid-twentieth century. We called it a "communist" country, along with other countries like it in East Asia (like North Korea) during that time period.

The most extreme right position possible means there is virtually no real legitimate government and anarchy reigns. There is no government regulation and no political framework to create one. The extreme right position results in a totally dysfunctional society. The closest we come to an extreme right government is a "Totalitarian" regime—a group of illegitimate rulers that try to control citizens with violent and brutal tactics. A modern day example of a totalitarian regime would be Iraq before the U.S. invasion or some renegade African nations that are controlled by drug warlords. Theoretically, somewhere very close to the center between these extremes is the best balance on the average. I'm going to go out on a limb and say that underdeveloped societies probably need a strong central government to kick start development, gravitating more left of center. A mature, developed and economically accomplished nation such as the United States should be targeting a significantly right of center location on this spectrum, meaning less government than needed on the average. The very essence of this book is to show how our society will flourish with increased prosperity and freedom when government is less intrusive in our lives.

Secular Progressivism vs. Traditionalism

These opposite viewpoints are more recent in their evolution than left vs. right. Today, we have "secular progressives," who are dedicated to advancing an agenda devoid of any spiritual influence versus "traditionalists," who tend to think more like our founding fathers in incorporating religious beliefs into their politics. The word "secular" means:

1. worldly as opposed to sacred things; temporal
2. not concerned with or related to religion
3. not within the control of the Church

Secular progressives push a liberal agenda with fewer if any moral restraints or boundaries that otherwise would be traditionally adhered to. Politics to them should operate within secular guidelines. They prefer to concentrate on new, contemporary ideas and downplay ideals that have roots going back centuries. Traditionalists, on the opposite side of the spectrum, cling to values kept through the generations by parents and ancestors. They use their moral and spiritual compasses to provide guidelines for political opinion and participation. Traditionalists tend to prize their patriotism whereas secular progressives often subject the U.S. to more criticism by constantly comparing it to other countries. Traditionalists seem to balance government involvement against cost more than secular progressives, who generally have more tunnel vision in pursuing their agenda. Here's an example: Secular progressives generally believe the U.S. should have government-paid health care for those who otherwise can't afford it. In debates about this, they rarely are interested in drawing a balance between this goal and what it will cost the people. Rather, they just insist that we are overdue for providing this service.

A typical traditionalist regularly goes to church or is somewhat religious or spiritual, is pro-life, prefers to keep God alive in government affairs wherever possible, uses spiritual values to frame political views, doesn't believe in too much debt for either themselves or their country, is a Second Amendment advocate, emphasizes work ethic over quality of education, believes in balancing ecological needs with economic affordability, and tends to view political correctness as a fad that will hopefully recede. A typical secular-progressive may go to church on occasion but doesn't emphasize it as a priority, is pro-choice, doesn't believe God should have any presence in government, doesn't emphasize morality in politics, is not upset about our country's debt, is concerned about having enough gun control, emphasizes quality of public education over the work ethic, believes ecology is generally worth the cost to improve it, and is a firm believer in political correctness.

Democratic Platform vs. Republican Platform

The party platform sometimes is just a philosophical viewpoint and other times it can be a specific view on an issue. The Democratic Party is almost always chosen by liberals, those to the left and particularly the secular progressives. The Republican Party is almost always the choice for conservatives, those favoring right-wing policies and generally but not always the pick by traditionalists. The Republican website currently says this on the issue of *economy*: "We believe in the power and opportunity of America's free market economy." When you click on "courts," it simply says: "We believe a judge's role is to interpret the law." For "energy," it says only, "We believe in energy independence." Most fair-minded people regardless of their party affiliation would not argue with these points. The Democratic Party's website is wordier and has an emotional appeal. So, the real party platform is generally a rough conglomeration of whatever the leading candidates happen to say about the issue in question.

The determination of our viewpoints should come from listening to the candidates from both parties. It shouldn't be derived from what our parents' viewpoints have been or what our preconceived notions always were. We then have the choice to convert what we've heard into a decision on whether to favor the Democratic platform versus the Republican. This is where the rubber meets the road and you decide to vote Democratic or Republican. Many of you are thinking: "I vote for the candidate, not the party." That's a great way to go. I'm just talking now about how the two platforms would typically match up with voter philosophy. Regardless, I hope you will exercise your privilege and responsibility to vote.

A thorough understanding of the political spectra will enable you to plot each of the following positions on issues onto more than just the liberal vs. conservative framework. Remember, the left phrase of the chapter title is the liberal side vs. the conservative on the right.

Government Control vs. Individual Freedom

I list this platform contrast first because it is one of the most distinctive philosophical differences between liberalism and conservatism. Individual freedom is what historically has separated the United States from the rest of the world and certainly is the primary reason for mass integration here. Political philosophy over the years has labeled Democrats as wanting government to have more control than the status quo and Republicans as wanting government to have less control than the status quo. I thought I would start out with examples that are of a local nature and close to home so you can really relate to the impingement of your freedom as it is gobbled up by government control.

Local Taxes: If all citizens knew exactly where all their local tax money was going, there would be a revolt. Although it is public information, we just don't have the time to be vigilant watchdogs. How often do you see one or two construction guys doing the work while the other three or four observe? Why do these projects have to be babysat by policemen?

Sometimes you just don't know where your taxes are going. I just happened to be browsing our local newspaper one day when I saw a story about a lawsuit a local employee brought against the township to defend his termination. He was fired because he was caught having sex with a municipal employee in the records room. The cost to the township of defending the lawsuit had gotten into the hundreds of thousands and I was paying for it with my taxes.

The subjective assessment of the value of someone's house, even when compared to your neighbors, gives way too much power to the municipality. When you compare notes with other homeowners regarding what they pay in taxes, you hear all kinds of inconsistencies that seem to be unfair. If you request a re-assessment, municipalities can conclude that you are underpaying instead and start charging more property taxes right then and there. I'll read in my local newspaper that total municipal expense (after state contributions and adjustments) will increase 2% to 2.5% per year. But then my taxes go up about twice that much that year. Why? My property assessment should reflect about the same increase as the overall expense increase. How do I know those homeowners with connections are not getting assessment increases as high as mine?

A solution to resolving this unfairness would be to use a more objective way of assessing the land and property. Tax assessors could use a constant rate (published for all to see) for lot size and the exterior size dimensions of the house and other building structures on the property such as storage sheds. Each type of structure would have a set rate. The assessor would simply multiply the rate by the exterior size of the structure. This would give the homeowner more control over the tax issue and the freedom from being subjectively overcharged. It is bad policy by the township to penalize homeowners with higher taxes for making improvements to their house and property. This discourages the conscientious homeowner who wants to fix up and beautify their dwelling. Homeowners should have the freedom to increase the value of their property without having their taxes on it increased.

Permits: I'm not against all permits required by the township. They can be a good thing, of course. If you are building an addition onto your house, you want to ensure the electrical and construction work performed is up to standard. However, the purpose of the permits should be to protect citizens, not to raise revenue. I found the following two examples of this shocking: 1. Many townships require a permit for you to have a tree cut down on your property. In a North Jersey township, one homeowner decided to save money and cut down the trees on his property by himself. Although he did a great job, the township later charged him a $1,000 fine per tree for not applying for the necessary permit ahead of time. Wow. 2. A friend told me he paid $900 in permits last year just for the installation of a roof and vinyl siding. The amount was calculated as a percentage of the $25,000 he spent on the work. This sounds like extortion to me as the actual cost to expedite two simple permits is a small fraction of the $900 hold up. (Naturally, the permits on record will eventually trigger an increase in tax assessment on the house, so the homeowner will get tapped twice. Ouch.)

Planning Board Tyrants: I know one neighbor who owned multiple acres of property and chose to sell off five acres for the construction of one house. The next-door neighbor objected to the sale. He wanted to have those five acres of lovely woods remain untouched so he could enjoy his privacy and grow a garden on his neighbor's land. He tied up the sale with legal action although he had no legitimate beef. To settle the objection, the township actually took some land from the homeowner (the one selling off the five acres) and granted it to the complaining neighbor just to placate him so the sale could go forward.

Town Council Runs Roughshod: An ordinance to restructure the recreation department was passed by our town council in April 2010. Some citizens objected to the changes and launched a petition drive to repeal it. The council had a choice to either repeal the ordinance or let the whole town decide through a binding referendum. They did neither. To get their way and bypass citizen objections, they introduced a new ordinance that restructures the recreation department with the same major changes, but with a slightly different structure. In other words, they ignored the will of the people and expedited an "end run" around official policy by getting creative. No hurrahs here for the Democratic process.

Holiday Police: There are some townships telling residents what window of time they will allow to let their kids "trick or treat" on Halloween. A few towns over, they "cancelled" Halloween one year because it snowed and the oligarchs on their throne at the town hall decided trick-or-treating would put the little munchkins at risk.

There was at least one township in the general area where I live that created a law pinpointing the earliest date residents could first begin lighting up the seasonal decorations before Christmas and the latest date they could light them afterwards.

Christmas Grinch? Every year at this time, a local news TV channel will highlight a particular house decorated to the point where people from around the town will line up with their children to see it. You've seen them—their electric meter must be spinning so fast, it's a blur. Life-sized Santa Claus and his reindeer are on the front lawn, which is speckled with five-foot candy canes and sugarplums. You might have Mrs. Clause knitting stockings in her rocking chair or maybe a workshop for the elves on the porch. You get the picture. Sometimes, though, the newscaster will also tell you the township stopped by and inspected for electrical violations, giving the homeowner a summons for multiple extension cords connected to each other on the lawn. But if someone is making children's eyes glow with excitement and happiness, can't the township look the other way?

Condo Control Freaks? There was a new condo complex being built some years ago one town over and I understand that one of the many regulations was that you were not permitted to put anything outside of your property to decorate it. This would include flowerpots and flags, including the American flag. I realize that a condo resident doesn't own anything outside of his dwelling, but *come on.* This is just un-American. There always needs to be some flexibility with the minutia of legalities between two parties. After all, the condo owner will often do little things on the outside of his property to improve it without expecting a discount from the condo association, so I think the latter party should practice some flexibility as well.

Just before I had this book published, I was talking to a condo owner that *did* own the land in front of his house (a new type of condo arrangement.) I was complimenting him on his garden, and he told me that as of this year the condo association now lets them grow flowers of any color in *their own* garden, whereas heretofore they were only allowed to grow *yellow* flowers!

Greedy Lake Association: When my wife and I bought our house, we were told it was on a plot of land that gets billed $18/year for the beach club even though we don't live close to the lake. Homeowners using the lake are assessed the higher "active member" dues, $120. The plot thickens two years later when they started adding $50 surcharges for non-members too. As per the newsletter from the beach club, the purpose of the surcharge billing was to raise more money for the "lake fund." But it is wrong to charge homeowners that are non-members like us that would never use the lake. So, the lake association was billing outsiders extra to pay for goodies only those on the lake enjoy.

Betrayal by Historic Society: While this is not a municipal issue, one has to be careful of organizations like this one that take advantage. My church donated their old, vacant dilapidated church building to the Historical Society along with a mid-five figure sum for them to restore it. After five years of waiting to see restoration, all that has been done is a roof repair to keep the rain out.

Controlling Food: In 2011, a Chicago school tried to install a regulation forcing children to eat their "healthy" cafeteria food and preventing parents from providing bagged lunches to their children. Thankfully, the parents resisted the attempts of the school to do this. In February 2012, a four-year-old girl brought her lunch to school, which consisted of a turkey and cheese sandwich, a banana, apple juice and chips. Whereas this sounds like a well-rounded lunch to you and me, a school administrator in Raeford, NC believed the meal violated the U.S. Department of Agriculture's Guidelines. Overzealous school officials decided to give the child chicken nuggets. They originally charged the parent $1.25 for it, but retreated from their stance when they realized they had overstepped their bounds.

By the way, it's been a few years now that New York City restaurants have been told to take saltshakers off their tables. The food police there had decided the practice promotes bad eating habits. Adults eating in the big apple have to request salt from the wait staff if they want to sprinkle the white sodium particles on their cuisine.

The latest attempt by NYC to watch your waist line was reported by Fox News in the June 1 broadcast. Mayor Bloomberg has proposed a ban of the sale of sodas in any container larger than 16 fluid ounces.

No Toys for McDonalds? We've got state and local legislatures trying to prevent McDonald's restaurants from including "toys" in their "kids' menu" options. In 2011, a left-wing movement said the small toys entice and target kids by "playing on their emotions," making them wants to eat McDonald's food. So, left-wing zealots in San Francisco denied little children their toys at fast food places unless a meal met their nutritional requirements.

California is King of Control: The golden state needs to change their name to "the control state." Caffeinated beer is outlawed, the use of plastic bags is banned by shops in San Francisco and all CA children must remain in booster seats until they are eight years old. (Now, they're re-inventing safety?) In 2011, the city of San Francisco tried to ban goldfish from being showcased in aquariums as they felt doing so was contrary to their natural habitat.

Corporal Punishment for Children: A few years back, some leftist child advocates and their organizations were pushing for laws in New Jersey to prohibit the spanking of children by their parents. Is such a law really necessary? Our government currently offers services for abused children through the Division of Youth and Family Services (DYFS,) a part of the NJ Department of Children and Families. A synopsis of DYFS's current policy: Corporal punishment or spanking is not necessarily child abuse, but excessive corporal punishment may be child abuse. New Jersey DYFS is required by law to investigate all allegations of possible child abuse/neglect reported to the agency. Anecdotal evidence often indicates this organization oversteps its bounds.

Consider that there is an organization (NJ Parents Against DYFS) set up to challenge the decisions made by DYFS as it is seen by them as being far too over-reaching in their legal capacity to take children away from their parents. This is how they portray their mission on their website: "We see day after day that DYFS abuses and harms the children of our state by tearing them from the loving arms of their true families for little or no validated reason. This is a violation of both state and federal law. We here at New Jersey Parents Against DYFS seek to redefine the issues relating to child protection."

I find that this anti-DYFS organization is the perfect representation of the "individual freedom" or conservative perspective on this topic. Conversely, the splitting up of families by DYFS represents the liberal view. I do agree there are really bad parents out there that don't deserve to have children, but that others deserve to keep them despite a conclusion by DYFS. Naturally, each case must stand on its own. In conclusion, this topic strikes close to home and gives all of us an opportunity to decide where we are on this freedom issue.

Sex in the School Curriculum: Are you aware that the tax-paying parents of children for grades K-12 have absolutely no direct say regarding the curriculum? Although parents may provide input at meetings, the schools make the final determination regarding the subject of health and sex education. There have been many national news stories on liberal school districts promoting the gay agenda, sometimes pushing an "it's natural to experiment with sex" mindset onto young children. Check out this related story: California State Senator Mark Levine, who is openly gay, proposed a law in 2011 called "The Fair, Accurate, Inclusive and Respectful Education Act". According to Fox News, the law would compel public schools to present homosexual material to *grade school* students as part of their social studies curriculum. The gay studies would teach students about gay rights and gay leaders. The law would require the presentation of the material to have a positive spin on homosexuality, including gay marriage. Nothing adverse or negative about the gay agenda could be taught, including the mention of gay villains. No debate or criticism about the gay agenda would be permitted. As you might have guessed, the bill didn't pass into law.

Tenure is good for whom? I was shocked at the audio playback of a teacher and her aides in a public school autistic classroom as one could hear them bully the child. At times, they were shouting, cursing and in general disrespecting the young ten year-old autistic child. The father had finally planted the hidden wire on the child six months after his child reportedly was lashing out physically without an honest explanation from the administration as to why. This obviously means there had been continual unprofessional conduct by the teacher and/or aides in the classroom until the audio tape finally revealed the reason. As a result of the raw evidence implicating the teacher and two aides, one aide was fired but the teacher and other aid were reassigned, apparently because human resources and tenure guidelines overruled dismissal. A CNN News report on April 25 confirmed the facts from the "Shine from Yahoo" tell-all story.

Own a Small Business? I was in hotel and restaurant management for decades and I can attest to how rigid and intrusive overseeing agencies such as the Board of Health and Labor Board can be. Municipal and county regulations from the Planning Board to zoning and ecological regulations handed down from the EPA can be daunting, especially if you are trying to start a new business. Here are two minor but telling examples (not related to the hotel business) of how government abuses their power to pursue their own agenda and takes away freedom from a homeowner in the process.

1. Would you like to be able to direct market your product or service by targeting certain homeowners? Well, the post office outlawed the attachment of a flyer to the *outside* of a mailbox (which doesn't affect the homeowner's privacy as no one is opening their mailbox). This federal law obviously was passed to prevent businesses or organizations from delivering a marketing piece without paying U.S. postage. Moreover, consider the fact that the mailbox is owned by the homeowner and not the post office. Shouldn't the homeowner, then, have the freedom to

receive local literature, perhaps from a local club or church, through the use of their mailbox?

2. Some townships outlaw the placing of signs on a homeowner's front lawn advertising the contractor who is currently performing work at their property. Keep in mind the homeowner owns the property and pays a hefty amount of taxes to use it anyway they see fit (within reason). If homeowners prefer to allow the contractor to advertise on their property, they should not be denied this right by power-hungry planning board totalitarians.

"Getting Happy" Outlawed: Nineteen out of our fifty states currently outlaw the discounting of drink prices during time period traditionally nicknamed "happy hour." Don't you think this kind of government intrusion on private sector pricing is unconstitutional?

Like the Beach? If you do, you don't want to take your kids to a Los Angeles County Beach. Part of the fun of a beach is throwing footballs and Frisbees and digging holes in the sand with little kids, right? LA County authorities don't agree. The nerds there decided to levy a fine of $1,000 for digging a hole in the sand that is deeper than eighteen inches or for throwing a Frisbee or football. No word yet on how much a dance in the end zone will cost you.

A.D.A. Wants More: The American Disabilities Act will now require your local hotel and public swimming hole to have "a pool lift that is capable of being independently operated by a person with a disability or (have) sloped entry" by May 15, 2012. (Source: Recreonics.com) This requirement is for a bolted-in, permanent mechanical lift, not the portable version which had been required. Anecdotal evidence is that the portable versions were rarely, if ever requested, so why the need for the more expensive permanent lift?

Miniature Horses Not Welcome: Fresh horse droppings in our facility? "Hotels, restaurants, airlines and the like must now modify "policies, practices or procedures" to accommodate miniature horses as service animals. ... According to the Department of Justice (DOJ), which administers the ADA, miniature horses are a "viable alternative" to dogs for individuals with allergies or for observant Muslims and others whose religious beliefs preclude canine accompaniment." (Verbatim from: The Foundry website, April 13, 2011)

Picking on Little Kids? Here's the Biggest Contrast Yet: Kids across the country are getting their lemonade stands shut down by the local government for either not applying for a permit or for not obeying certain regulations. Meanwhile, the city of San Francisco allows its citizens to walk the streets naked. People can even go into restaurants and expect to be served naked, although they must bring a towel to sit on.

Concerned yet about the imbalance of our freedom and our upside down values in certain municipalities? There are tons of stories out there about the abuse of power at both the local and county level just as much as on the state and federal level. In fact, books have been written documenting government abuse and over-regulation. The ones I've shared are just a sampling from my personal experience and knowledge. My hope is that you have a homegrown feeling now of having some of your individual freedom sacrificed for governmental control.

2.

Leftist Tendencies vs. Right-wing Philosophies

I THOUGHT IT would be fun to start with philosophical contrasts between certain tendencies of the Democratic platform/secular progressive agenda on the left and the viewpoint of the Republican platform /traditionalists on the right. I'll start with issues related to the economy since that topic is key to the 2012 election.

Socialism vs. Capitalism

I'm not saying that socialism is an economic style that Democrats or liberals all want to adopt, but I would be remiss if I didn't acknowledge that the "socialist" word has been mentioned hundreds of time since President Obama started his campaign in 2008. Many journalists and Republican politicians have said President Obama has socialist tendencies and/or leanings. Re-distribution of income (through his proposed tax plan when he campaigned and his health care plan) can be categorized as such. Rather than get into a debate at this point on Obama's designs on re-distribution of wealth, I thought it would be interesting to first look at the efficacy of socialism. Communism (a political form of socialism) was practiced by the earliest settlers of this country and failed. Michael Frank published an account on this little known piece of Pilgrim history:

Joseph M. Weston Sr.

Recalling the story of the Pilgrims is a Thanksgiving tradition, but do you know the real story behind their triumph over hunger and poverty at Plymouth Colony nearly four centuries ago? Their salvation stemmed not so much from the charitable gestures of local Indians, but from their courageous decision to embrace the free-market principle of private property ownership a century and a half before Adam Smith wrote *The Wealth of Nations*.

Writing in his diary of the dire economic straits and self-destructive behavior that consumed his fellow Puritans shortly after their arrival, Governor William Bradford painted a picture of destitute settlers selling their clothes and bed coverings for food while others "became servants to the Indians," cutting wood and fetching water in exchange for "a capful of corn." The most desperate among them starved, with Bradford recounting how one settler, in gathering shellfish along the shore, "was so weak … he stuck fast in the mud and was found dead in the place."

The colony's leaders identified the source of their problem as a particularly vile form of what Bradford called "communism." Property in Plymouth Colony, he observed, was communally owned and cultivated. This system ("taking away of property and bringing it into a commonwealth") bred "confusion and discontent" and "retarded much employment that would have been to the settlers' benefit and comfort."

The most able and fit young men in Plymouth thought it an "injustice" that they were paid the same as those "not able to do a quarter the other could." Women, meanwhile, viewed the communal chores they were required to perform for others as a form of "slavery."

On the brink of extermination, the Colony's leaders changed course and allotted a parcel of land to each settler, hoping the private ownership of farmland would encourage self-sufficiency and lead to the cultivation of more corn and other foodstuffs. As Adam Smith would have predicted, this new system worked famously. "This had very good success,"

Bradford reported, "for it made all hands very industrious." In fact, "much more corn was planted than otherwise would have been" and productivity increased. "Women," for example, "went willingly into the field and took their little ones with them to set corn."

The famine that nearly wiped out the Pilgrims in 1623 gave way to a period of agricultural abundance that enabled the Massachusetts settlers to set down permanent roots in the New World, prosper, and play an indispensable role in the ultimate success of the American experiment.

A profoundly religious man, Bradford saw the hand of God in the Pilgrims' economic recovery. Their success, he observed, "may well evince the vanity of that conceit…that the taking away of property… would make men happy and flourishing, as if they were wiser than God." Bradford surmised, "God in his wisdom saw another course fitter for them."

Amen to that.

European Style Economics vs. U.S. Hybrid System

The extensive rioting in Greece and England that occurred in 2010 and 2011 is certainly alarming. During that time, the central government in many countries such as Greece, France and England broke down because the entitlements and services the government produces could no longer be financially sustained. The high taxes, low employment and excessive national debt in Greece caused riots in early 2010. Months later, the French government announced their version of social security won't be paid to citizens until they reach 62, raising the retirement age by two years. Again, there was rioting in the streets. When England significantly raised the tuition to universities there (also in 2010,) riots ensued again. Clearly, the citizens of these European countries take their entitlements seriously. Here's the point: Is it wise to create a society in which citizens are so dependent on their country to provide them with education, health care and retirement funds? I understand the global recession is hitting hard because national debts on a global scale have never been so critically high. But there hasn't been any rioting in the United States. It is more prudent for the services of education, health care and retirement funding not to be entirely state-based. I'm going to use the term "hybrid" to describe this, as this country uses a mix of government and the private sector to provide these services.

Education: Our publicly funded school systems K-12 and partially state-funded universities are augmented by parochial schools at every level including private universities. Students aren't guaranteed higher education but they can get government-backed loans to attend universities. The road to paying the high tuition bill can partly or fully be paid by scholarships.

Health Care: This service has been predominantly provided by the private sector with some government regulations. When Obamacare became the law of the land in 2010, governmental regulations were gradually increasing with the implementation of the new law. But our health care will continue to be a hybrid of involvement by both the government and private sector as there will not be a "single payer" for the health costs as there is in Canada and European countries. Judging from the anecdotal stories about the quality of state health care in these countries, it would seem that a health system in a competitive environment is best.

Retirement Funds: Few of us rely totally on the government for retirement funds. In fact, the age to collect social security was raised over the last decade, and there hasn't been any fallout. Investment and personal finance managers have been educating the public for some time about viewing savings for retirement as a three-legged stool. The first leg is social security. The second leg is tax-shielded funds we need to proactively invest in such as 401K plans. The third leg includes all other private investments such as our home, taxed investments and/or savings accounts. Someone very wise once said "Don't put all of your eggs in one basket."

For decades, our capitalist system was designed to have just enough government control to keep the free markets competing fairly and protecting the consumer from abuse. It has been successful for America since the Pilgrims took foothold. Admittedly, we are not totally pure in our capitalism as we have increasingly legislated government programs to redistribute wealth and provide opportunity to citizens needing a chance to succeed. For decades, this hybrid system has been serving us well. But since President Obama took office, he's been pushing the pendulum left by growing the government at an unprecedented rate.

Presidents Bush and Obama both took part in liberally throwing bailout nets. Then, Obama pushed through an $800 billion stimulus package filled to the brim with pork. Thirdly, he succeeded in getting the compromised version of the health care bill put through, but *had wanted* to implement the more socialist, European style of "single payer" health care. I'm the first to admit that Bush should have made top priority the rollback of the national debt when he first got into office. He is equally as guilty as he spent us into oblivion while America enjoyed his tax cuts. But we need to reverse what seems to now be an irresistible slide towards European style economics. As of 2011, Greece's debt is 150% of its GDP. The U.S.'s debt has now reached 100% of its GDP for the first time ever and is rising dangerously. When the overseas loans to the feds stop, there won't be rioting in the streets; just a slow, quiet collapse. After all, Americans are a very accepting and tolerant people.

Tamperism vs. Capitalism

"Tamperism" isn't a real word (yet)—I made it up. Since no one thinks that our economic style in this country will ever turn to a pure socialist one, we need a name for an economy overloaded with government oversee and regulation." That style would include chronic legislative pieces that are in essence instruments of re-distribution and regulations of the private sector that go beyond protecting the consumer. When government over-legislates and over-controls, it transforms the "free market" into a "freeze market." In other words, when government intervention tinkers with a balanced, competitive free market system; capitalism gets perverted into "tamperism." The most damaging government restrictions would include environmental requirements and extreme pro-union labor laws. I appreciate the need for unions in every economy, but there are some pro-union laws in America that take away the first amendment rights of the employer. E.g.: When a union is in the midst of trying to sign on a group of non-unionized employees, the employer is legally restricted from speaking to the employees about their decision to sign up. Another example of extreme pro-union legislation that didn't pass but was proposed during the Obama tenure: An employee would be denied the opportunity to cast a secret ballot on a decision to join a union, making it very awkward for them to cast an open ballot against unions.

Debate over what ails our economy often yields a liberal argument that claims the problem is lack of demand caused by a lack of disposable income from the consumer. But many fiscal conservatives cite the primary problem is a lack of ability to compete globally. Look at the amount of commerce that we have lost to the rest of the world in terms of factories and service centers. Economists say it is because companies take their capital beyond our borders as the business environment in the U.S. becomes less profitable as each decade passes. Environmental regulations, taxes, insurance, cost to build and tool, employee benefits and now health care have chased the American businessmen to greener pastures. It is all because our government has "tampered" with these business environment factors. Just as the game ends when the kid who brought the football goes home, the business game ends here when the big kid with the capital goes elsewhere.

Feelings vs. Logic

Are you feeling left or right today? I boldly assert those on the left side of the political spectrum become more embroiled with their feelings than the right. I believe the emotions behind their rhetoric is a natural outgrowth of their "nanny state" agenda. Promoting the protection of minorities, women, and the poor may require the tactical use of feelings and emotions.

From a policy standpoint, conservatives are able to make logical points about the national debt being too high to substantiate more government spending, ecology legislation being too restrictive to business operations, and the need for lower corporate taxes to stimulate business investment during a recession. These arguments can be substantiated with logic by showing how some government programs either are simply unaffordable or by using statistics showing business thrived more in a business environment with less regulation. Money and statistics are logical.

However, liberals need to "sell" their agenda using "feelings" the way that Madison Avenue tries to use emotion in its automobile commercials on television. Advocating any affirmative-action-type of legislation to benefit only minorities, pushing the gay agenda with controversial tolerance programs in the public school, and wanting the federal government to spend more despite our current fiscal debacle all cannot be done using logic alone. One must incorporate feelings to empathize with the groups benefiting from these policies in order to win these types of arguments.

In an effort to provide some documentation for my theory, I navigated my mouse to the Democratic National Committee website to take a peek at their agenda. I clicked on the tab "What we stand for" and viewed their list of thirteen items in this order: Civil Rights, Economy and Job Creation, Education, Energy Independence, Environment, Fair Elections, Health Care, Immigration Reform, National Security, Open Government, Retirement Security, Science/Technology and Voting Rights.

Intrigued, I clicked on "Civil Rights" and viewed at the top in bold a quote from John F. Kennedy as if we were in the late sixties and in the midst of fighting for civil rights. I truly hold Kennedy high as a hero, but there is no logic in making a case for civil rights as a major issue in Decision 2012. At this point, are not "civil rights" a mission accompli? In other words, I don't see any urgent needs for executive action or new legislation here. It isn't a major issue in decision 2012. But, it works as emotional appeal to those who feel vulnerable to a civil rights incident.

Next, I clicked on "Fair Elections" and read the following quote in bold at the top by President Barack Obama: "I don't think American elections should be bankrolled by America's most powerful (special) interests or worse, by foreign entities. I think they should be decided by the American people." This quote is indeed the height of irony. Election 2008 candidate Barack Obama received record amounts of money to bankroll his candidacy, from this country and abroad; so much that he couldn't even spend it all. Candidate Obama, then, was the epitome of his own description in the "Fair Elections" category. Regardless, it is still an emotional appeal to people who presume it will be the Republican candidate bankrolling the election.

The next tab I clicked on, "Open Government," also strikes an emotional appeal to those who feel un-empowered. At the top is another quote from Barack Obama about how government should be "transparent." The irony, again, is laughable. During his 2008 campaign, candidate Barack Obama promised the American people his administration would be "transparent." He later reneged with ***closed*** talks on pending legislative proposals after he took office. I then clicked on "Who we are" and found a lot of verbiage that I would sum up as "Democrats owning the party that sticks up for the little guy." Here's an example:

> Our party was founded on the conviction that wealth and privilege shouldn't be an entitlement to rule and the belief that the values of hardworking families are the values that should guide us. We didn't become the most prosperous country in the world by rewarding greed and recklessness or by letting those with the most influence write their own rules. We got here by rewarding hard work and responsibility, by investing in people and by growing our country from the bottom up.

Think about the phrase, "the wealth and privileged are writing the rules." What kind of *feelings* would that invoke? The writer included no substance to back this claim up, but did make a strong emotional appeal to the reader, assuming most were among the working class.

The essence of the liberal agenda is coupled tightly with emotional appeal to one's feelings. Very often, there is no substance or logic in their approach. When conveying the agenda of "the audacity of hope," the need to tap into "feelings" is of utmost importance.

Macro-Goodness vs. Micro-Goodness

This section dabbles in yet another worldview difference between liberals and conservatives. Consider these examples so I can explain exactly what I mean by the phrases "macro-goodness" and "micro-goodness." Example 1a: I take out the garbage consistently every week so the garage doesn't get smelly. If I forget one Monday morning, the garage will stink and my wife will get annoyed as she hates unpleasant odors. Being faithful to this chore is micro-goodness as it benefits a situation very close to me. Example 1b: When I faithfully separate the bottles/cans and the newspapers/cardboards from the trash/garbage category lest one glass jar accidentally get thrown into the garbage/trash section, I am being true to the ecological spirit of this practice. This is macro-goodness because society in general benefits from this action. Example 2a: John and Jane are equally charitable and both have $100 of disposable income to give. John gives it to local cause benefiting a poor family whose house burnt down. John's act of charity was micro-goodness because the benefit is very close to home. Example 2b: Jane donates it to the Sierra Club. This donation is macro-goodness because society in general benefits.

Legislation to improve the healthiness of the environment by reducing the carbon emissions from cars and factories is macro-goodness because it benefits all. The Obama administration decision to agree to not repeal the Bush tax cut on earners making more than $250,000 is micro-goodness because the benefit is personally realized. Legislation to require automobile manufacturers to make cars and trucks getting higher miles per gallon is both macro-good because everyone benefits from the lessening demand of oil consumption; but also micro-good because each car owner personally benefits from the savings. The reduction of benefits related to Medicare is a micro-good issue that is actually micro-bad for many seniors. A liberal thinks highly of the macro-good benefits of Planned Parenthood being able to reduce STDs and pregnancy among teenagers. Meanwhile, a father of a sixteen-year-old is worried about the micro-bad of his daughter becoming pregnant and getting an early term abortion, compliments of Planned Parenthood, without him ever knowing it.

Vote for Political Inspiration vs. Vote for Political Achievement

One of the key differences between liberals and conservatives is that the left are moved by the rhetoric of politicians who talk the talk and walk the walk of their ideology. Add a million dollar smile and sincere promises to lift up the downtrodden, and the Democratic candidate is halfway to the Oval Office from the outset. Those to the right of the spectrum are more apt to place their trust in the hard core facts of the candidate's voting record, actions and experience. Although the example is almost 4 years old, decision 2008 is a classical scenario of this wide chasm in voter decision making.

The electorate that chose Senator Obama as President said he is smart, eloquent, charismatic, good-hearted and looking to help the lower and middle class. We heard during the election in 2008 that his ethnic and cultural background could appeal to everyone and consequently would be a unifying force for this country. Apparently, he had the drive and the image people wanted to see in a president. Indeed, Americans are a positive lot and have achieved incredible things with the right mindset. I don't have to review all the "rags to riches" stories of Americans to demonstrate this.

Regardless, Americans hunger for leadership. Bernie Goldberg, a Fox News Analyst, said this about Barack Obama's campaign during the decision of 2008: "The problem with running a campaign based on words and little substance is that there is a tendency to overstate, to over-dramatize and to over-reach for something you can't actually live up to." The biggest problem with being moved by a politician's rhetoric is that it feeds into the naiveté of the American electorate. They actually believe the promises of a politician whereas in reality he secretly can only hope to achieve them. They buy the persona whereas in reality the campaigner is a skilled actor. They want to be led by a confident, charismatic leader who reflects their ideology whereas in reality the politician may trade his convictions in if changing them becomes politically expedient.

The naiveté of Americans is almost a proverb. We have a history of believing what the politician promises and then are surprised and angry when he does the opposite once he is in office. We buy things advertised on TV just because the person advertising them is one of our favorite movie stars, professional athletes or sexy supermodels. There is no Madison Avenue in any other country like the one we have here in which advertising successfully sells Americans. We believed we could win the war in Vietnam without even bombing North Vietnam. We believed we could bring a new government to Afghanistan and change their politics even though the Russians lost miserably after their invasion of Afghanistan back in 1979. The list of examples showing the naiveté of Americans is almost endless. Obama the campaigner tapped into this mindset of the American people with his promise of change and hope. It worked.

Now, let's talk about the political achievement side of the equation. Senator John McCain did not appear to be as smart, eloquent, charismatic or as committed to the poor and working class as his opponent. McCain is good-hearted, patriotic and a "compromiser." He has a distinctive reputation as a leader. His war record is stellar. His list of legislative achievement is impressive. He reached across the aisle to put together an immigration bill he co-sponsored. He was not as conservative as the media portrayed him and was even labeled a "maverick" by his own party. However, the Democratic machine successfully portrayed him as another "Bush." Rather than have the youth and drive of Obama, McCain sometimes appeared to be burnt out. Those liking John McCain isolated specific accomplishments, whether it was his military record, his legislative successes or specific times when he reached across the aisle to eliminate partisan bickering and make compromises. His experience was there in black and white and no trust factor was required. McCain was a known quantity. What you see is what you get. Typically, conservatives value these known quantities more than liberals. McCain ran on his record and his proposed policies. It wasn't enough. It didn't work.

Senator Obama showed little real achievements on his resume other than his formal education and winning elections. After all, being a state senator and Congressional senator just means you are good at getting elected. Americans bought Obama's message of hope and change. Political inspiration won over political achievement. I'm not grading Obama's performance as President here and now, but I think a good lesson to learn is this: Be aware of what degree you are blindly following a candidate based on his words, promises, charisma and smile.

Human Nature Can Be Altered vs. Human Nature Can't Be Altered

Can a leopard change its spots? Theory has it that liberals believe that human nature can be altered and conservatives believe it can't. Don't confuse this with the difference between the ability for individuals to alter their *behavior*. I base this statement, in part, on the fact that liberals have historically backed more lenient sentencing of convicted criminals whereas conservatives have scoffed at it. It is always a judge known to be liberal that will hand out absurdly short sentences to convicted violent criminals and always conservatives that express outrage about it.

The other basis from which I make this statement is the commonly held believe that liberals believe in "determinism." I have to give credit to Dan Nagasaki in his book, "The Beginners Guide to Conservative Politics" when he exposed this part of the liberal mindset:

> Determinism is the belief, espoused by liberals, that the environment, genetics or outside forces determine behavior. For example, liberals (the left) tend to believe that society, government, poverty and guns are primarily responsible for crime... Conservatives (the right) believe that crime is caused by people with bad values and bad judgment. In other words, conservatives place responsibility for crime on the individual.

Naturally, this would explain why conservatives favor much stiffer penalties than liberals and why they are staunch regarding Second Amendment rights. (Guns don't kill people; people kill people.)

Admittedly, Nagasaki separates the liberals and conservatives into two camps far away from each other, while I'm sure not all liberals have the viewpoints he claims. But I have to come full circle with his theory to make a point. "Liberals believe that human nature can be altered with enough education and government force," he wrote. He then describes the more traditional view on his theory. "Although people can be educated so that they know how to act good, polite or compassionate, their basic human nature must be controlled through the strength of church, family or social stigma."

I have observed that liberals have *not* relied on the church, family and moral values anywhere close to the extent that conservatives have to influence human nature and behavior.

This stark difference explains the liberal penchant for using government (like DYFS and various social service agencies) or large government funded organizations (such as Planned Parenthood) to step in for families that traditionally handled such issues on their own.

The ultimate manifestation of the theory that "human nature can be altered" occurred at the highest level after President Obama began his statesmanship in addressing our relations with the Muslim world.

Obama and his liberal supporters felt that a more congenial approach to addressing the Muslim world is a better one than the position of strength and rigid military tactics used by the Bush Administration. Obama signed legislation to close Guantanamo Bay, declared water-boarding would no longer be practiced (even on terrorists that have killed Americans,) and made drastic changes in CIA personnel/culture to expedite his soft approach. The basis for his reasoning was that the Arab World, specifically the Islamic terrorists, were being antagonized by Bush—who supposedly created more incentive for the extremists to wage their war. Obama said that Bush's tactics were being used by the extremists as "propaganda tools to recruit more terrorists."

Making nice to the billion-strong Muslim world is one thing, but softening rhetoric and altering policy to try to affect the mindset of the terror operatives is quite another. The President and his party believed, at least in this case, that human nature could be altered. Now that Obama's first term is nearing the end, there has been absolutely no evidence that the intentions of Islamic extremists have simmered. I tag this as "Evidence A" that no one can alter their nature, except with the occurrence of divine intervention.

Politically Correct vs. Tell It Like It Is

I remember being at the lunch table with young friends and colleagues a few years back and in a conversation I casually used the word "gay." One of my colleagues sitting across from me gasped and advised in a low voice that I'm not supposed to use that word. Puzzled, I questioned this; as I wasn't saying anyone was gay or that there was anything wrong with being "gay." She replied, "I know. But somebody within earshot could be gay, just hear *that* word and think you are saying something offensive." Admittedly, the setting was in a corporate environment where we all use a professional demeanor. But I knew at that moment that political correctness had taken a leap up into a level beyond my understanding and, quite frankly; my personal level of acceptance.

A news story broke in 2011 about a court decision to grant an untenured teacher the right to take four weeks of school off in the middle of the school year to go on a pilgrimage. The school administration had denied such a request prior to the law suit as it was rightly against their policy. The teacher was Muslim. Experts in this area said the courts would never have granted the same request to someone if they were Jewish, Catholic or Evangelical. Apparently, it is politically correct for judges to grant certain minorities more rights than others.

The most blaring contemporary example of political correctness gone amuck is President Obama's response to the terrorist attack on Nov. 5, 2009 by a Muslim extremist who was functioning as a U.S. Army psychiatrist at the time. Without apparent provocation, Major Nidal Malik Hasan rampaged about the Army facility while on the job at Fort Hood, TX and shot up scores of his colleagues there at the site. Thirteen people were murdered in the massacre and twenty-nine others were wounded. The subsequent investigation by the Army showed that the incident was not one of someone who was just angry or mentally disturbed; but a real, homegrown jihadist terrorist attack. The evidence: He had a history of making inappropriate jihadist remarks to his colleagues, he had e-mailed an Al Qaeda recruiter on numerous occasions, and was found after he was arrested to be carrying a card with the letters SOA (meaning Soldier of Allah.) You don't get more proof than that to show the world this was an *Islamic* terrorist attack.

Regardless, President Obama and everyone in his administration never described the tragedy as a jihadist or Islamic terrorist attack. They never identified the killer to be a suspected jihadist and never even pointed out the evidence in question, so at least the public could make their own conclusion. It was almost like Obama didn't want the incident to be labeled as an *Islamic* terrorist attack so the record wouldn't show such an act occurred on his watch. This refusal to face up to the facts was actually beyond political correctness; as I would consider it political *manipulation.*

Shortly after Obama took office, he and his administration decided they were not going to use the phrase jihad, jihadist or Islamic terrorist—period. We can only surmise *this* was the ultimate act of political correctness; lest any Muslims be offended. The problem with this thinking is that it actually precludes the construction of a strategy to a real solution to Islamic terrorism. Why? You can't solve a problem unless you will identify it first. It is like an alcoholic who can't solve his addiction because he won't admit to himself he is an alcoholic. After all, wasn't the culture of political correctness the biggest factor that led to the September 11 tragedy in 2001? Had the U.S. ignored political correctness and aggressively pursued a policy denying potential Islamic terrorists access to this country based on their profile and background; the two twin towers would still be standing. Even if some of them gained access to our country, a culture refusing to be politically correct would not have resulted in training these terrorists to fly the aircraft that they cleverly used as bombs against us. I could have subtitled this section as "not offending anyone" vs. "survival." Think about it.

Attack the Arguers vs. Attack the Argument

Both Democrats and Republicans are guilty of attacking the arguer. I have to admit that Republican on Republican bashing in TV spots and speeches during the 2012 primary season, which many journalists have said was the most negative interparty campaigning they've ever seen, gives credence to the fact that both parties engage. But I think you'll agree that the examples below of liberals attacking conservatives were most newsworthy, most offensive, and without merit.

A big story broke in February of 2011 about the state of Wisconsin having to elicit givebacks from union state workers in order to manage the state's fiscal crisis. The newly elected Republican Governor and his Republican dominated state Congress came under strong, emotional fire by the union leaders and workers who rallied and picketed to voice their objection. Fox News aired the state's point of view from their conservative analytical contributors as well as the union's in keeping with their fair and balanced coverage. But because Fox News was the only channel that thoroughly explained the governor's viewpoint in detail, the union had a little demonstration against Fox News as well. Rather than go head to head on the issues, the union workers simply said with their signs and voices that Fox News journalists are "liars" and "fascists." No one came forth from the union to express why they thought the Fox News coverage was unfair or skewed in favor of the governor's repeal of some union rights.

A most unseemly and eyebrow-raising example of a totally unnecessary attack is as follows. A few years ago, a late term abortion doctor in Kansas named George Tiller had become infamous for the sheer volume of patients he was servicing. In 2007, Kansas Attorney General Phil Kline led a case against Dr. Tiller, charging him with nineteen misdemeanors. Although the abortion acts themselves were legal, the Attorney General was charging him for not reporting certain abortion cases that have to be reported by law. The court acquitted the abortion doctor on all counts.

The medical board in Kansas was so disturbed by the outcome; they launched their own investigation after the decision. The plot thickens. In May 2009, Dr. Tiller was murdered—a tragic event. The medical board's decision to investigate further becomes moot. However, the board that oversees all the attorneys in Kansas decided they want to revoke the license of the Attorney General who led the case against Dr. Killer for the seventeen misdemeanors. It is apparent there were enough members on this attorney oversee board that still wanted vengeance against a lawyer that was too pro-life for their politics. I view this as a very unseemly example of someone attacked only because he was the "arguer" for his point. The merits of the case had already been won by Dr. Tiller's defense. There was no need to seek to ruin the career of someone that had just been doing his job.

Even more disturbing than this example of "attacking the arguer" is a story regarding on-going intimidation reported by Fox News Analyst Laura Ingraham in April, 2012. A far left group called "Color of Change" apparently is in business to threaten to inflict economic woes onto corporations that engage in the financial support of a specific legislative advocacy group. American Legislative Exchange Council (ALEC) is that organization, which has backed conservative legislation such as voter ID laws and "stand your ground statutes" (pro-Second Amendment legislation that supports using arms for people to defend themselves.) Several major corporations have dropped their support for ALEC because operatives working for Color of Change have apparently convinced these companies that it would not be in their economic interests to maintain their association with ALEC. McDonalds corporation was the most recent to withdraw their membership, coming out and stating they did so under pressure from Color of Change. Ingraham reported this organization is well-funded by George Soros, a far left billionaire who generously funds other far left concerns such as "Media Matters" and "Move On.org." According to Ingraham, "the goal (of these organizations) is to shut down conservative speech." After hearing this Fox News report that the Color of Change organization "will hurt you" and "do anything they can" if you act against their ideology, I winced to think that such fascist tactics were being practiced in our 2012 America.

We all need to be keenly aware of attacks on persons and organizations in the fray of political battle. Tactics like those discussed merely deepen the divide and embitter the opponents. Only a discourse on the merits of each side will ever come to resolve the many issues in this country.

Disrespectful Vitriol vs. Respectful Dialogue

"Those Republicans are demons....And the Tea Partiers can all go to hell." These are the words of sitting congresswoman (as of 2012) Maxine Waters (D.) They are just a bit dramatic, in my opinion and unseemly for a person representing the electorate. But the most broadcasted examples that fit both the "Attack the Arguer" and "Disrespectful Vitriol" categories are the attacks from the left on former vice presidential candidate and former Alaska Governor Sarah Palin. Although Palin currently holds no office, she is an icon in the right-wing world. As I write this in June, 2012, she is still the most prominent spokesperson of the Tea Party movement. Palin has used her fame to bring the common sense message of *smaller and less intrusive federal government* to the country and she has done so in a very down to earth style.

The insipid attacks from the left on her and her family (particularly her daughter who got pregnant at seventeen) have been unprecedented in their uncouth nature. Many journalists noted the liberal media believes women who are climbing their way to the top are supposed to be liberal, pro-choice, a feminist and a secular progressive. It would seem the left fears that her traditional, ultra-conservative perspective on politics, if elevated to the maximum level possible, could set back their agenda. Regardless, Palin became a target and the vitriol began. CNN anchor Chris Mathews and other well-known journalists on his "news" program even stooped to calling Palin "stupid" and "ignorant" without substantiation. These fifth-grade level names contribute nothing to the political discourse.

Mathews also called Mitt Romney "The Grand Wizard" when commenting on a video of Romney in mid-April 2012 (about the time it had become apparent he was the presumptive Republican nominee.) There was no preface or explanation for the remark other than the fact that Mathews was rooting against him and hoping the comment would cost Romney votes. (Romney has never been accused of saying or doing anything bigoted.) Mathews apologized for the inappropriate comment the next day.

Fox News Analyst Monica Crowley, Ph.D., said this back in 2011 about the criticisms from the left about the Tea Party (the arguers for a smaller federal government.)

> We have a 14.6 trillion dollar national debt. The Tea Party emerged in early 2009 to try to bring the nation's fiscal health back in to order. That meant calling for restraints on spending and bringing down the deficit and the debt. For their efforts, they have been routinely smeared as racists, sexists, homophobes and terrorists (metaphorically,) even by the Vice President of the United States… Here's the double standard. For the left, when they go out and protest and agitate, whether it is against the Vietnam War, the Iraq War; you name it—that's a beautiful exercise of the First Amendment. But when conservatives and regular Americans go out and exercise their first Amendment rights; all of a sudden they are a racist, unruly, hysterical, irrational mob.

Another extreme and un-American example of a disgraceful action was perpetrated repeatedly by fanatics that call themselves the Westboro Baptist Church. (They aren't really a church, but a very small group of relatives and friends calling themselves this in an attempt to appear legitimate.) They have on more than one occasion used the funeral of a fallen war hero as a venue to oppose the acceptance of homosexuality in America. I believe few have been able to really understand the link between their proselytizing and God's supposed decision to take it out on the troops. Their actions of spewing hateful speech and carrying signs indicating how Americans will go to hell were intended to disrupt the funeral as well as get free advertising for their cause. Their signs read, "God Hates America," "America is doomed," "Israel is doomed," "God hates the world," "God is your enemy," "Fags Doom Nations," "Thank God for Dead Soldiers," "Thank God for Maimed Soldiers," "God Blew Up The Troops," and "Soldiers Die, God Laughs." The videos showing the vileness (their screaming was obnoxious) of this misguided group could actually make someone sick to the stomach.

Disrespect and hate speech discredits one's viewpoints, negating one's efforts so no fair-minded person will consider the message. Always be respectful and as logical as possible when making your viewpoints known.

Left Leaning Media and Slant vs. Reporting with Balance

The "free press" as we know it in America is now defunct. By this, I mean freedom from spin and slant, freedom from ideological constraints, and freedom from conflict of interests through ownership concerns—all no longer exist. Gone are the days of an honest, objective, uncorrupted media; at least for the most part. It is common knowledge that the mainstream media today is significantly slanted towards promoting leftist ideology and Democratic candidates. I'm not providing you with any news flash here. A Pew Poll taken during decision 2008 showed that only eight percent of the press themselves say they are conservatives. So, this means news gets reported and commented overwhelmingly through the eyes, ears, mouth and pen from journalists plotted left of center. The assertion that the liberal media slant influenced "Decision 2008" is supported by a Pew Poll. It said that seventy percent of Americans believed the media was slanted towards supporting Barack Obama on the campaign trail and only nine percent said it was not.

Fox New Analyst Bernie Goldberg wrote a book titled, *A Slobbering Love Affair* to document what he subtitled *"The True (And Pathetic) Story of the Torrid Romance Between Barack Obama and the Mainstream Media."*) This New York Times bestselling author argues that the left-leaning mainstream media crossed the line during the 2008 presidential election campaign and helped to determine the outcome. Goldberg has been joined by a wide array of journalists and politicians to the right that do give the mainstream media credit (or blame) for being "in bed" with the candidate in "Decision 2008" that had the "audacity of hope."

Even late into Obama's tenure, the media was still pulling for him. In April 2012, the Associated Press Chairman of the Board, Dean Singleton, spoke to the American Society of Newspaper Editors. When he introduced President Obama, he gave a glowing performance appraisal of Obama's efforts in office. Singleton's praises of Obama were so "over the top," one would have thought Obama had just gotten married and the Singleton was the best man giving a toast. Keep in mind the Associated Press is the most widely distributed news service in the country. It is a given that the reports are assumed to be *objective*. So when the Chairman of a *hard* news service makes subjective remarks to his peers about Obama's job approval, what does that mean? You tell me.

Consider the following examples of a different kind of spin, an over-dramatization to put the Tea Party in a negative light. Read below how it is almost laughable how the journalists use over-the-top metaphors and borderline emotional panic. The time period (2011) was just before the country was in danger of going into default in paying loans if both parties of Congress did not agree on the terms of raising the debt ceiling another $2 trillion. The first two quotes were written by journalists describing the Tea Party's influence on negotiations determining the outcome.

"It's like a form of economic terrorism. These Tea Party guys are like stripped with dynamite and standing in the middle of Times Square at rush hour and saying "You either do it my way or we will blow you up and the whole country with us. You tell me how these kind of stand offs end."

This one is from another liberal journalist, Margaret Carlson (Bloomberg News Columnist,) who was quick to parrot the previous metaphor. "They have stripped explosives to the Capitol and think they are immune from it. The Tea Party caucus wants this crisis."

The third is a quote from MSNBC anchor, Chris Matthews, about the Republican Party: "The GOP has become the Mahatis of the American government. They are willing to risk bringing down the whole country to service their anti-tax ideology.

I have to give credit to Fox News Analyst Bernie Goldberg for nailing this issue cold. Goldberg sets the table with the options on how to describe a Tea Partier: "A journalist could portray them as either principled Patriots that care about their country or dangerous, scary stupid wackos. A lot of liberals have portrayed them as the latter." Goldberg then provided us with the following examples:

Tina Brown, Editor in Chief, Newsweek, called the Tea Partiers suicide bombers.

Tom Friedman of the NY Times compared them to Hezbollah (a Shi'a Muslim militant group and political party based in Lebanon.)

Peter Goodman, Business Editor of the Huffington Post, said they are acting like terrorists.

William Yeoman, who teaches law at American University, said on Politico, "The Tea Party faction of the house has now become full-blown terrorists."

Fareed Zakaria, CNN anchor, said they want to blow up the country.

Paul Krugman, New York Times columnist, said they want to blow up the economy.

David Brock at the NY Times said the Tea Partiers had no sense of moral decency.

The Vice President of the United States, Joe Biden, said they are acting like terrorists.

Why have I cited many examples using the same type of metaphor? It obviously makes these journalists all look like a bunch of "copycats." But it also indicates to me that, not only are they unoriginal in copying the same metaphor, they are copying the same thought process. How can it be that about forty percent of people describe themselves as conservative, yet only eight percent of journalists describe themselves as conservative? Why wouldn't the merit of the conservative viewpoint win the mindset of more journalists? I think it's because they catch the *liberal disease* when they become a journalist; and there's no cure.

During the midterm elections of 2010, the Republicans had used metaphorical terms such as "target," "hit," "rifle," "fire," and "bulls eye" to dramatize their campaign platform. Here's the ironic twist: The liberal media objected to the use of these metaphors by the Republicans. Fox News Analyst Bernie Goldberg pointed out that the left said it was supposedly "unseemly in a political debate to use violent words to help the listener visualize your point. Isn't it ironic and also hypocritical that (the same liberal media) that criticized the use of violent metaphors are now comparing the Tea Partiers to terrorists? These are people that don't even call *real* terrorists "terrorists."" The next part is where I laughed out loud. Bernie goes on to mock what a liberal journalist might say in reporting a real terrorist attack: "these are misguided individuals… they didn't mean it when they shot up the Army Base…it was just an accident."

I now ask you to remember the Norway terrorist attacks that occurred in July 2011, killing 77 people. Various internet sources say:

- It was the deadliest attack in Norway since World War II.
- Breivik was right-wing extremist and an Islamophobe.
- He was highly critical of Muslim immigration into Christian societies.
- Breivik stated that "myself and many more like me do not necessarily have a personal relationship with Jesus Christ and God." in his manifesto, he "did not see himself as religious," but he did identify as a cultural Christian and wrote about the differences between cultural and religious Christians…"

Ready for the spin? Here is The New York Times headline for their story on this attack: AS HORRORS EMERGE, NORWAY CHARGES CHRISTIAN EXTREMIST

Understandably, citizens (and also journalists that do not make a practice of criticizing Christianity) were outraged at the New York Times for telling the world that the terrorist was a Christian. This simply was not true. He did not go to church or even was affiliated with a church, did not carry or even own a Bible, had no Christian education and did not practice Christianity in any way. Breivik even stated that he did not have a relationship with Jesus Christ and did not see himself as religious. So, where does the New York Times get off headlining this terrorist is a Christian? A person is not a Christian solely because he writes on Christianity and looks at Christian websites.

Fox News Anchor Bill O'Reilly explained the spin by saying that media liberals are looking for a Christian parallel to Muslim extremists so the emphasis on Muslims can have an example to counterweight it. A simpler theory is that the media today just can't wait for the opportunity to put Christians in a bad light to reciprocate for their general disapproval of the secular progressive agenda. So when the opportunity comes *close* to presenting itself, they will make the stretch to bridge the gap between truth and fiction. This headline was most definitely fiction.

A classic example of media slant is the comparison between the reportage on the Tea Party versus the Occupy Wall Street movement. The comparisons between the two are that they were both exercising their First Amendment rights. But it pretty much ends there. The Tea Party was truly a grassroots movement, was well organized, had regional spokesmen, was expedited to abide by laws pertaining to demonstrations, was peaceful, respectful of others' rights (by and large with some exception) and had a single, cohesive motive and purpose. They demonstrated during the day and ended before night. Their message was clear. Their impact influenced the Congress. They changed the tone of negotiations and increased the urgency of debate to decrease the deficit.

In contrast, the Occupy Wall Street movement was reported to be a grassroots movement, but in actuality was not. Research indicated that big liberal money organized the event and advertisements had been placed in Craig's list offering to pay protestors $600 a week for their participation. The movement was not well organized, had no *real* spokesmen, was not peaceful, did not abide by laws, was not respectful to others' rights and did not have a pointed message. In fact, their intent was muddied by so many different anti-establishment signs; it was difficult for the media to report on the movement's purpose.

Signs they carried complained about everything from Wall Street to unemployment to Pro-Lifers to the "one percenters" (who they said need to pay more tax.) Their campaign was not focused and they ultimately seemed to influence no one either at Wall Street or in Washington. Admittedly, the original Occupy Wall Street movement was reportedly hijacked time and again by little known, peripheral groups that used violence as their currency. Although this was unfortunate for the original Occupy Wall Street group as it destroyed their legitimacy, no spokesman emerged from the "true" Occupy Wall Street group to set the record straight. No attempt was made to separate the pure message of the original movement with all the violent actions by the groups that spontaneously emerged with them. Overall, their message was muddled. Some say the original protestors objected to the cozy, questionable relationship between Wall Street and Washington; others say the group was venting in general about the horrors of our current economy as it affects those lowest on the food chain. Regardless, the final perception was that all the abhorrent activity was condoned by the original "Occupiers."

The movement was described by some as a "collective counter culture." They illegally camped out in city parks for weeks, living there and making their tents their homes. They were sleeping there, having sex outdoors and creating a sanitation nightmare that later cost the host cities millions to clean up. There were reports of widespread drug use and drug trafficking out in the open among the protestors. However, you wouldn't at first find reports of this from the mainstream liberal media, such as ABC, NBC or CBS. After a while, though, news channels eventually did show clips of the rioting and deliberate destruction of private and public property. Admittedly, the mainstream media finally reported on the rioting in the streets of Oakland, CA in early 2012 that was aimed at the destruction of government buildings downtown. In fact, rioters broke into City Hall there and burned American Flags. The police arrested four-hundred protestors. More than one-thousand were involved in the melee.

Here's the bottom line: In spite of all the differences, the left leaning journalists tried to compare the Occupy Wall Street movement to the Tea Party, providing the former with far more legitimacy than they were entitled to. Tim Graham from the Media Research Center provided us with the following statistics on the issue, which were gleaned only from the mainstream stations of ABC, CBS and NBC:

- Graham reported these mainstream channels were so smitten by the Occupy Wall Street Movement; they aired on the average one story on it per day per news channel. Compare this obsession with the airing of only thirteen stories on the Tea Party movement, equating to only four stories per network on the average for the entire year. This calculates to these mainstream channels reporting on Occupy Wall Street about *ninety times* more often than the Tea Party. Yet, you tell me which movement had more political significance?
- Graham counted the number of times the media had placed labels on the Tea Party ("corporate AstroTurf," "conservative," "racist,") which were numerous. Contrast this to the Occupy Wall Street movement, which virtually had no labels attached to them during the reporting.
- Graham also assessed the positive vs. negative spin the media placed on the two movements. He said the Tea Party received overwhelming negative spin while 93% of the sound bites aired about the Occupy Wall Street movement were positive.

I think these statistics really sum up the slant of the left-wing media. They were promoting the message of the Occupy Wall Street Movement as it represented the media's liberal agenda, whereas the Tea Party message was one that they were against. One would need to ask, after truly assessing the nefarious deeds and activity of the Occupy Wall Street mob, how such a consistent, positive spin could genuinely be reported. A late 2011 poll on approval of Wall Street occupiers was as high as fifty percent. What TV channels were *they* watching?

The Trayvon Martin tragedy is an example that portrays the gradual decline in traditional journalistic practices and ethics by the mainstream media. Many TV and cable stations were literally trying the case from the TV anchors' desk as if they were an eyewitness to exactly what happened. What's worse was the commentary, which sensationalized the story to the point where the anchors' comments ran contrary to the indisputable facts that had already been established by the police and the aired 911 tapes. For example, police had reported a physical scuffle and altercation, but commentary implied the seventeen-year-old African-American boy had been shot while simply walking to the store. In one case, a mainstream TV channel aired a cleverly edited version of the original 911 tape to make the racial profiling component appear more egregious than the correct, unedited version that had originally been aired by other stations. These various overly dramatic commentaries by mainstream news journalists trumping up the race factor in the Trayvon Martin incident deepened the divide between blacks and whites for months. Specifically, it resulted in rogue vigilante demands by black groups and most probably influenced one high profile assault against two white reporters by a mob of angry blacks in a Norfolk, VA.

The metamorphosis of the press to an ideologically based medium continues as it steps down from under-reporting significant stories to completely omitting them. Someone could write a whole book on the decline of media integrity today and provide hundreds of examples of omission alone. In the interest of brevity, I will provide just two telling examples that occurred within weeks of each other in May 2012.

On May 22, a significant story broke about Catholic organizations filing dozens of lawsuits against the Obama Administration's requirement for health insurance companies to pay for contraception and sterilization, both practices against Catholic doctrine. The lawsuits were extremely newsworthy at the time as their end result could have affected Obamacare legislation and the rights of 65 million Catholics. In addition, the cost to defend them could have been in the tens of millions, perhaps even hundreds of millions. Moreover, the lawsuits affected voter impressions of the Obama Administration and had the potential at that time to influence the upcoming election in November, 2012. Amazingly, ABC and NBC news ignored the story completely while the CBS evening news devoted 19 seconds to it. (Source of this example: Fox News "The Factor," May 24, 2012.) The only explanation for the omission by the two mainstream news stations is that the story rubbed against their ideology and, quite frankly, shined an unfavorable light on the Obama Administration. After all, the electorate was in the process of making up their minds for the big election.

The second example, picked out by the Media Research Center, confirmed that ABC, NBC, CBS, and CNN nightly news did not report on a vote in Congress to outlaw "gender based abortions." (This is a decision by a mother to terminate a pregnancy if the fetus is not the gender she prefers). Although the bill passed in the House of Representatives by 221 to 144, the "yes" vote tally failed to meet the two-thirds majority needed to trump an eventual veto by a pro-choice President. (Source: Fox News, Bill O'Reilly broadcast on May 31, 2012.) If prime time TV airing of what amounts to an anti-abortion referendum in the House of Representatives had occurred, damaging exposure for President Obama would have resulted. As it is, the most pro-choice President the Oval Office has ever seen is struggling to compete in the polls with a pro-life Republican challenger. So, the ideologically driven media looked the other way.

Journalistic ethics get trumped by corruption when one looks at General Electric, owner of both NBC and their cable news channel MSNBC. GE's CEO, Jeffrey Emelt, reportedly made large campaign contributions to Obama and went on to develop extensive business entanglements with him. During decision 2008, MSNBC was literally a cheering section for the President and had overwhelmingly portrayed Obama in a positive light during his campaign. You tell me why. Compare this to Fox News, which had a perfect record of airing fifty percent positive stories and fifty percent negative stories as related to Obama when he was on his campaign trail. The cozy association between Jeffrey E-Melt and Barack Obama dims the idea of a free press in this country being able to report objectively. Obama promoted E-Melt from economic advisor to head of his job council. Moreover, Emelt's standing as the number one guy to grow jobs did not wither when he sent GE's entire aircraft division (taking with it all the jobs therein) to China. In response, even Democrats and many liberals were beating the conflict of interest drum. The example of MSNBC having a strong partiality in promoting Obama is actually beyond media "spin" and enters the un-pioneered territory of "media control" due to a conflict of interest at the highest level.

While we are on the subject of "media control," a Fox News report in February 2012 revealed the following: Media Matters, a left-wing organization, was pledging to spend $20 million to influence news coverage in favor of President Obama. Tucker Carlson, Fox News Contributor, said that sources from that group told him that Media Matters virtually "writes" the script for the liberal cable news channel, MSNBC. He reported this as a damaging revelation, showing MSNBC violated serious journalistic ethics:

- No credit has been provided for the source of news (Media Matters) that the station did not learn first-hand.
- MSNBC is obviously aware that Media Matters is a committed left-wing propaganda outlet and blindly taking their copy as their own is incredibly irresponsible.
- No reported fact-check is being made.

Fox News added that many columnists that write for the Washington Post get their information from Media Matters. In conclusion, the state of the media today has moved on from mere bias, slant and spin and pioneered into the territories of corruption and irresponsible plagiarism.

Here's a story that is almost in a category by itself. It gives new meaning to the phrase "airing dirty laundry." It's not media spin, but a sordid intrusiveness from a well-known anchor for a mainstream TV channel.

A media assault on the personal life of Newt Gingrich occurred during the Republican presidential debate directly before the South Carolina Republican primary in January, 2012. First, I'll fill you in on the back-story. Newt Gingrich had admitted in years past that he had cheated on his wives in previous marriages. Since that time, he had said he amended his ways and even recently converted to Catholicism. Subsequent to this and sometime before the debate, an ABC journalist interviewed Newt's ex-wife regarding the details of their emotionally charged divorce, which occurred ten years ago. Newt's ex-wife was understandably angry as she was jilted while Newt went on to marry his mistress. Regardless, this ABC journalist airs the recent interview about this ten-year-old story on the basis it has news value because the ex-wife implied something she had never mentioned in public before. It was that Newt had *intimated* that his ex-wife participate in an "open marriage," although she admitted he had never used those words. The video clip of the interview makes the rounds on the internet and becomes the latest, hottest gossip to fire up the vitriol about a Republican candidate's most personal interactions.

Getting back to the debate, CNN anchor John King kicked off the South Carolina Republican presidential debate with the topic of the video clip. Newt's response to the moderator was a lambasting of the press that I believe remains unmatched in our lifetime:

> I think the destructive, vicious, negative nature of much of the news media makes it harder to govern this country, harder for decent people to run for office and I am appalled that you would begin a presidential debate with a topic like that. To take an ex-wife and to make it two days before the primary and to make it a significant question in a presidential campaign is as close to despicable as anything I can imagine...My daughters wrote the head of ABC and made the point that it was wrong, that they should pull it and I am frankly astounded that CNN would take trash like that and use it to open a presidential debate...Let me make it perfectly clear the story is false; every person and friend we know during that time said it was false and we offered several of them to ABC to prove it was false. They weren't interested as they would like to attack any Republican...I'm tired of the elite media protecting Barak Obama by attacking Republicans.

Both Democrats and Republicans stood, applauded and cheered for the lacing that Newt gave the press. The people had spoken. I understand that a presidential candidate's character can be called into question at any time as the electorate needs to have them examined every which way, but there was foul play here regarding adherence to proper journalistic ethics. First, the venue for this kind of character vetting should not be a debate where the candidates are competing against each other on the issues, their ideas and their past voting records. Secondly, I join the critics who felt that a video clip about a jilted, angry ex-wife talking about a ten-year-old conversation with her ex-husband should not be considered as fair game without proper collaboration that her accusation was true. After all, ABC news declined the input of sources willing to argue that her insinuation was baseless. They refused to report both sides of the story. But responsible journalism would have silenced the bomb that the mainstream media couldn't wait to drop in Newt's lap in front of millions. I believe this story is classic in that it showed a mainstream media attacking the character of a Republican candidate with a hunger that was a bit over the top.

Unjustifiable Anger vs. Justifiable Anger

What do the holocaust, the 1960s' civil rights era, Vietnam War, anti-abortion rallies, the Tea Party Movement and lenient sentences for child molesters all have in common? They rightly incite justifiable anger. This common emotion is not only a part of the human condition, it is often necessary for positive political change. Although this seems obvious, I'm going to take my discussion one step further by stating that the force of anger has become increasingly lost in the sauce at times over the last several decades. Where was this vital ingredient when life and liberty-changing decisions were being made? During decades of the removal of many religious rights by the courts, we murmured under our breaths rather than protest. When the Supreme Court joined the feminist movement and decided to give women the right to abortion, we said: "*Well, I guess these intellectually gifted men in black robes know what they are talking about. Who are we to argue?*" When justice is not served for convicted criminals who commit heinous crimes, we throw our hands up in the air and merely complain there is nothing we can do about it. We are too accepting as a people when injustices befall us. I believe it is a byproduct of apathy and tolerance run rampant.

As a nation, we seem to wait for that "tipping point" before protests begin. It took the dramatic gesture of tossing large amounts of tea overboard at the original Boston Tea Party to generate momentum for the Declaration of Independence. Consider that it took our national consciousness about two-hundred years before we recognized that our treatment of blacks was unacceptable. Change did not occur until African-Americans got angry and protested. How many years of senseless deaths in Vietnam and Iraq did it take before Americans finally stood up and made some noise? The outrageously large fiscal deficit and national debt kept the economy from growing for years before the Tea Party movement finally evolved. Even then, their impact still didn't result in enough change (yet) to reverse the course of fiscal history. We need to get angry when change for the better hangs in the balance. Here are my six rules of thumb (all need to apply) for when anger is an appropriate political ingredient:

1. Action has occurred that has offended our sensibilities and is not politics as usual.
2. The motivation is for either promoting positive change (that fair-minded people would agree on) or condemning unacceptable practices or decisions.
3. The object of the anger is a specific party that is deserving of it because of actions committed or failure to act when appropriate.
4. The issue is vital to life or liberty and not a minor issue or a trite belief of a group of people.
5. Anger is used as a last resort as unemotional rhetoric to affect change has not worked.
6. The anger is not meant to motivate action that is unjust, immoral, unethical or illegal.

Here are some examples in which I don't think anger was appropriate or just:

1. Columbia University students flip out on an invited speaker whose vision was to bring the ROTC program back to the campus. (This is not a vital issue and anger was not used as a last resort. Moreover, the students' actions posed a physical threat to the presenter.)

2. Mainstream media news anchors get angry at Sarah Palin for making conservative political commentary. (This is ideological politics as usual.)

3. Occupy Wall Street Movement anger motivates protestors to commit unjust, immoral and illegal acts as part of their modus operandi. In addition, the object of their anger was projected (for the most part) onto the wrong group. Wall Street is not responsible for the inequity of wealth, the poor economy or the tax policy in this country. The group guilty of these problems work in Washington, D.C.

You get the point and I'll spare you further examples. Here's an example using anger productively that struck me as book-worthy (note it fulfilled all six requirements:)

After Whitney Houston died, the reaction from the press that another Hollywood icon died from drug abuse was the same as usual when this type of tragedy occurs. By that, I mean most of the emphasis is on remembering the superstar's greatness and contribution to the arts. Journalistic efforts to draw attention to the senseless *cause* of the death of a young star are virtually hidden in the shadows. This time, someone stood up and made a point of it, using anger and a corrective tone. A superstar himself, this news anchor went onto both the Today Show and the Fox and Friends Show and carried this message to a large audience, saying:

> *When was the last time you saw a public service announcement to say to the American public, 'you know, you don't want to be like Whitney Houston. Don't be like Elvis or Janis Joplin.' They (the public announcements) don't exist."* On the Fox and Friends Show, he was noticeably angry: *"There's nobody in the media saying, 'you know what, this could lead to death and if it doesn't lead to death, 75% of all child abuse neglect is done by substance abusers. Let's tell the truth. And not only that, when you buy this garbage, who are you helping? The Mexican cartel, which killed 40,000 human beings. Every time you buy a marijuana cigarette, it goes to them. Are we*

getting this? Where is it in the media? Who's saying this? Nobody.

After he finished, you could hear a pin drop. Then, the talk show host agreed. No one disagreed. The message got through. His anger was justified.

3.

Democratic Perspective vs. Republican Perspective
(as expressed through actual policy and party platforms)

Bigger Government vs. Smaller Government

SINCE OUR DEMOCRACY formed, we've always had the back and forth debate between the two perspectives. The bigger government not only means more taxes and spending, but less individual freedom as a bigger government translates into more laws and regulations. The Democrats, historically, were always looking out for the little guy and the Republicans seemed to favor the well-to-do by always rallying for the interest of business. After all, those businesses only could afford raises, bonuses and promotions for the employees if their companies did well. Typically, the Democrats argued that underprivileged and middle class citizens benefit from the wonders that big brother can deliver. I remember listening to conversations my parents had about the many benefits they enjoyed from Uncle Sam. My dad came from humble beginnings in downtown South Philadelphia. A World War II veteran, he went to the Wharton School of business at the University of Pennsylvania on the GI bill. The advantages of a provisional government brought us social security, welfare, Medicaid and Medicare, unemployment insurance, the most capable military in the world, quality education and government-backed loans to enable financially challenged students. Most of us agree these were all needed programs. But as government continued to increase its spending, smaller government advocates pointed to the rich entitlements provided to government employees, excessive spending on various programs and the loads of pork barrel brought home by your local congressmen. Conservatives believe the benefits that government provides us have to be limited to the revenue coming in to support them.

When President Obama campaigned in 2008, he promised to cut the deficit in half by 2012. It was about 10 trillion when he began his administration. It turns out that by the end of his term, Obama will have increased the fiscal deficit by more money than all of the previous presidential administrations **combined**. By mid-year 2011, the national debt exceeded fourteen trillion dollars and by end of year 2011, it exceeded fifteen trillion dollars. At mid-2012, we're looking at sixteen trillion.

To be honest, both parties are to blame for the size of the national debt. Now our nation is at the point where we wish we could have the debate of bigger government vs. smaller government. But that's history. Today, it is a question of *how much* smaller will Congress agree to make it. So, the debate of smaller government has been won, but not soon enough. The next debate will be on which tool to use to trim the overblown size of the government: the Democrats' scalpel vs. the Republicans' machete. Perhaps Obama hasn't yet imagined the Republicans getting out the chainsaw.

Scalpel vs. Machete

National Debt increases have been:

- $ 547 million a day during the Clinton administration
- $ 1.6 billion a day during the Bush administration
- $ 4.1 billion a day during the Obama administration

In 2010, President Obama ordered a bi-partisan commission to look into how the budget can be balanced over the next ten years. Not surprisingly, the recommendations the commission returned were sobering. During President Obama's first solo press conference of 2011, he spoke on his budgetary intentions and how he plans to balance them against the feedback from the commission, which emphasizes the need for bitter medicine to subdue the federal appetite. Although Obama went on record as saying he agrees much of the commission's framework, he flat out ignored their findings. In his April 2011 speech, Obama announced he will incorporate into his budget large amounts of money for economic stimulation, using as an example, funds for students to attend college. He didn't even say he wanted the government to be smaller.

Fast forward to the fiscal budget for 2012. The enacted budget contained $2.469 trillion in receipts and $3.796 trillion in outlays, for a deficit of $1.327 trillion. (Courtesy of United States Office of Management and Budget, retrieved 13 February 2012.) As you can see, the country has reached a dire need to slash spending as our overall fiscal situation is so serious, it is expected any year now to crash our way of life as we know it. But why will it crash? Read on.

Blind Folders Are Still On vs. Doomsday Really is Here

"No generation has a right to bind the succeeding generation with vast public debts."

-Thomas Jefferson

Fiscal conservatives assert many on the left haven't yet understood the enormity of the looming crisis. The interest on the debt we are paying is such a large percentage of federal money expended, it is crowding out the ability to fund other more worthwhile projects and programs. In fact, our country had to borrow thirty cents on the dollar to meet our spending needs in 2011. Furthermore, the feds have resorted to "printing money" since March 2009 to pay down the national debt and make cash available to lend to banks. This is artificially generated money beyond what the government honestly takes in. Every dollar has value because it represents a dollar's worth of goods for services that has already been traded and converted to money, which is tradable in turn for other goods and services. But when a government injects into an economy a large amount of money that ***wasn't*** "earned," it eventually will weaken the value of those dollars that ***were*** earned. We can't print "fake" money in our basement the way the feds can, so an overabundance of the fed's unearned dollars let loose into the free market will eventually bid up the cost of goods. This contributes to inflation as the dollar will be able to buy less.

An April 29 Money News website article (by Newsmax) quoted the following from Robert Wiedemer, financial commentator and author of the best-selling book, *Aftershock*: "I think the Fed is making huge mistakes in what they are doing with the amount of money printing that they are doing. It's one of those things that are not going to show up right away, but when it does it's a massive problem… I think we are going to see much higher inflation over the next two to four years."

Indeed, many economists concur that our weak dollar makes gas at the pump more expensive as the dollar is continually becoming worth less in the global economy as compared to other monetary units. In fact, our current dollar is only worth one penny of the 1913 dollar. The picture gets even worse when one considers the international ramifications of the continual fall in the worth of the dollar versus other foreign currencies. In 2011, the countries of China, India, Russia and Brazil called to replace the U.S. dollar as the international reserve currency with a monetary unit that provides more "stability and certainty." Many economists predict that if this does happen, the resulting ramifications will be sobering.

This country experienced a mortgage crash in 2008 that paralyzed our banking system, devastated the holders of mortgage-filled investments and cost the feds big money to stabilize by paying for bailouts. For the first time in 65 years, our national debt has exceeded our Gross National Product (GNP.) Do we really want to take a chance so soon on another crash that could result in even scarier consequences? Plus, the damage to the economy from lagging investments because of the distrust of Wall Street going forward can never be calculated. What up until now was the unthinkable has finally happened in 2011. The federal government's credit rating was reduced by agencies that determine such. This sentiment was echoed by Wall Street numbers dropping as well after the "powers to be" in Washington failed to significantly cut the deficit. In fact, the loss of confidence in the stability of our dollar and our economy is probably the biggest impediment for cash rich corporations to take risks in investing capital in our country. Many of them opt to invest it overseas.

The obvious conclusion I am drawing here is that the U.S. federal government is slipping slowing towards disaster. Unless we reverse gears, the death of our economic success will be imminent. We will be like a frog that was placed into a pot of water on the red hot stove just as the temperature was getting to a comfortable lukewarm. He stays there and enjoys the warming water as it turns into an exhilarating hot bath. The water is soothing; the frog falls into what he thinks is a relaxing nap. The water boils and kills him while he sleeps. As Americans, we are virtually napping as we enjoy our governmentally provided benefits. We live in denial while we assume they will always be there. To avoid getting burnt, Americans need to wake up and vote in those candidates who resolve to significantly cut the deficit. In fact, the ultimate goal would be to pass a constitutional amendment that requires the federal government only spend what it takes in, making federal deficits unconstitutional.

Re-Distribute Wealth vs. It's Redistributed Enough Now

Myth buster alert—Re-distribution of wealth has in fact always been a part of American legislative history, and Republicans have voted for it. Consider these facts:

- Federal government programs considered to be *"re-distribution"* of wealth are welfare, food stamps, Medicaid and some provisions of Obamacare.
- Our tax code has always been a *"progressive"* one in that increasing amounts of income per household are coupled with increasing percentages of taxes they pay. Households making more than one million per year will pay an average of 29% in taxes to the feds. Households that make between $50,000 and $75,000 per year will pay an average of 15% in taxes to the feds. Households that make between $20,000 and $30,000 per year will only pay an average of 6% in taxes to the feds. (Tax money from the bigger earners gets *re-distributed* to fund the programs above.)

- The top 1% of earners contributes 41% of the total revenue sent to the IRS. (Ten years ago, the top 1% only contributed 22%.) The top 5% of earners pay 64% of the federal income tax that Uncle Sam collects. Aren't these examples of *extreme* re-distribution?
- 47% of American households pay no federal income tax. (Admittedly, this statistic would include those who are retired, not working or don't have to work.) This means that *re-distribution* of government funds comes from only 53% of Americans.
- State sales taxes are considered *"regressive"* in that they do not apply to basic food or clothing in many states. By only taxing items beyond the basics, the sales tax burden is *re-distributed* to those that can afford to pay for luxuries.
- Municipal tax money is *re-distributed* to local schools. How? Let's say a family with 3 children and a couple who can't have children both live in houses that is taxed the same amount. Some of the money from the taxes paid by the couple with no children will go to educate the 3 children in the other family from K through 12th grades. That's a form of *re-distribution* as the township is taking money from the childless couple (who pay without benefiting) and putting it towards educating the family with 3 children.
- Sometimes corporation taxes come up in a discussion on re-distribution as those on the left often say they don't pay enough to the I.R.S. Here's the latest facts on that: Consider first that the top federal rate for U.S. Corporations is 35 percent and when additional state rates are added, the average tax rate for U.S. corporations rises to 39.2 percent. Only Japan's rate has been higher, 39.8 percent. But on April 1, 2012 Japan's rate dropped to 36.8 percent. This means the U.S. now has the highest corporation taxes in the world. (Source: Newsmax alert April 1, 2012.) So, by what standard are they not paying their "fair share?" Admittedly, tax loopholes significantly reduce the effective total corporation tax revenue collected by the I.R.S., so corporate tax reform is definitely needed.

So, America is indeed a land of income and tax money re-distribution. An internet informational piece by Newsmax in April 2012 gave us the latest statistics on re-distribution of monies by Uncle Sam. Here's where it all goes:

- The federal government will spend more than $668 billion on anti-poverty programs this year, an increase of 41 percent or more than $193 billion since President Barack Obama took office. State and local government expenditures will amount to another $284 billion, bringing the total to nearly $1 trillion — far more than the $685 billion spent on defense.
- Federal, state and local governments now spend $20,610 a year for every poor person in the United States or *$61,830 for each poor family of three.*
- The federal government alone now funds 126 separate and often overlapping programs designed to fight poverty.
- There are 33 housing programs run by four different cabinet departments, 21 programs providing food or food-purchasing assistance administered by three different federal departments and one independent agency and eight healthcare programs administered by five separate agencies within the Department of Health and Human Services.
- The largest welfare program is Medicaid, which provides benefits to 49 million Americans (that can't afford health care) and cost more than $228 billion last year, followed by the food stamps program, with 41 million participants and a price tag of nearly $72 billion. Other programs range from Federal Pell Grants ($41 billion) down to lower-cost programs such as Weatherization Assistance for Low Income Persons ($250 million) and the Senior Farmers Market Nutrition Program ($20 million.)
- At least *106 million Americans receive benefits* from one or more of these programs. (That is just over a third of 313.4 million Americans as of April 22, 2012.) Including entitlements such as Social Security and Medicare and salaries for government employees, more than half of Americans now receive a substantial portion of their income from the government.

The information I just provided clearly shows that income and tax *re-distribution* has been around for a while. Therefore, just using the term *income re-distribution* itself doesn't take the conservative argument very far by trying to show, for example, some provisions of Obamacare as lopsided. So, conservative pundits can gasp in horror when mentioning the phrase "income re-distribution" or they can make faces when using the term as if they are staring down Karl Marx. But the drama needs to be augmented with a more detailed analysis or creative arguments to convince those left to center that additional freebies compliments of Obama are just too generous. After all, Americans expect goodies from the government.

Evidently, that expectation is being met; and cash for the poor may even be easier to come by according to a report in mid-July, 2012, by Dick Morris, Fox News contributor. Morris said President Obama wants to do away with the "work" requirement to receive welfare; whether it is a private sector job or work the government provides so you can earn your check Morris went on: "When President Obama took office, 43% of Americans got checks (any type, including social security or unemployment) from the government. Now, 50% are. His goal is to expand entitlements to expand his base."

The appropriateness of further re-distribution of wealth is subject to opinion, which is probably in accordance with where you are placed on the socio-economic ladder. A relevant question at this point is to what extent re-distribution of wealth has helped the "have-nots" graduate to the "haves." Consider this: Since Lyndon Johnson declared a war on poverty during his presidency; the U.S. spent $15 trillion on anti-poverty programs. Back in 1964, about 19 percent the U.S. was considered to be in poverty. After 45 years, that percentage dropped only to 15.1 percent (although rising.) The point is that government entitlements have their limits in affecting poverty. (Statistics from Newsmax.com)

The failure to bring down the poverty rate more than four percent begs the question "why." Conservatives point to a variety of statistics that show factors contributing to poverty are poor parenting/poor role models, dropping out of school, drug addiction and bearing children out of wedlock. From a liberal vs. conservative perspective, I will end this topic with one statistic: If a person graduates from high school, doesn't abuse drugs/alcohol and does not have children out of wedlock, they only have a five percent chance of being poor. All of these three factors are personal choices that come from free will. Moreover, the statistics regarding the problem of having children before marriage are very unsettling as 41% of babies born today are out of wedlock. No matter how much money the federal government throws at poverty, they can't prevent anyone from making bad decisions. (Statistics from Fox News broadcasts.)

A controversial proposal discussed in 2011 takes the drug abuse link with poverty to the next level. The legislation dictated mandatory drug screening for recipients of welfare and food stamps. If you fail, you don't get the entitlement. That sounds pretty harsh. But the thinking behind it is that the federal government is now unwittingly supporting drug abuse as welfare, cash and food stamps get traded for drugs and alcohol. Ideally, the drug-screening requirement going forward would curb drug/alcohol abuse and ultimately reduce addiction statistics. Hopefully, the new policy would reduce substance abuse as a factor in holding people back from escaping the vicious cycle of poverty. Theoretically, the idea has merit. In the name of compassion, though, I would think such a piece of legislation would provide medical assistance, drug counseling and non-cash living support for those that continually fail the drug screening.

Too Big to Fail vs. No Bailouts

To bailout or not, that is the question. The issue of bailouts is typically a liberal vs. conservative one with the latter group being the hesitant ones to spend our money on a situation gone sour. Conservatives say free market principles will eventually solve the problem (at the risk of sounding cute) *for free.* The 2008 bailouts beg the questions: "Is it right to bailout banks, insurance companies and related private concerns when they were at least part of the blame for the crash? Is it fair to bailout the big three auto companies when there are hundreds of other companies just as deserving for bailout money? How big is too big to fail?

These questions started to be asked during the last months of the Bush Administration right after the banking-mortgage-housing industry collapsed in 2008. Various internet sources reveal that Bush's first response was to bailout The American International Group (AIG,) a large insurance corporation. (This company had to pay out when "insured" mortgages were defaulted on.) The original bailout terms provided AIG with an $85-billion bridge loan. AIG was considered to be a "systematically significant institution." In other words, its failure could cause a domino effect of consequences. The bailout was enhanced in November 2008 through the Troubled Asset Relief Program (TARP) of the $700 billion Emergency Economic Stabilization Act, which rescued the mortgage/financial industry. Citigroup, a financial-services company which is much bigger than AIG, was also bailed out. Citigroup was considered too big to fail, especially after the federal government's failure to save Lehman Brothers earlier in the year.

The U.S. Government does have a history of bailing out concerns that are considered to be vital to the economy. To provide an objective perspective on this topic, I provided the following chart on the U.S. history of bailouts, compliments of ProPublica.org. Notice the huge difference in the amount of money provided for previous bailouts versus the unprecedented debacle of 2008. I also researched whether the taxpayers collected 100% of the funds back—against the government loans or share purchases of each company. A check in the right hand column will indicate the feds recouped 100% of their investment or loans (in some cases with a profit from interest, dividends or increased net worth of shares they were given in exchange for funds). An X in the right hand column will indicate the government (and taxpayers) took a partial loss on the deal. I put a "?" in the column to the right to show that we're not sure if we'll ever collect 100% of the disbursement.

Year	Company	Amount	Returned?
1970	Penn Central Railroad	3.2 billion	✓
1971	Lockheed (aircraft builders)	1.4 billion	✓
1974	Franklin National Bank	7.8 billion	X
1975	New York City	9.4 billion	✓
1980	Chrysler	4.0 billion	✓
1984	Continental Illinois Bank and Trust Company	9.5 billion	X
1989	Numerous Savings and Loan Associations	293.3 billion	X
2001	Airline Industry	186 billion	X
2008	Bear Stearns (global investment bank/brokerage firm)	90 billion	✓

2008	Fannie Mae and Freddie Mac (government enterprises	400 billion	?
	That enabled consumers to get affordable mortgages	(Included in TARP)	
2008	American International Group (international insurance	180 billion	?
	company for mortgages and other policies).	(some Included in TARP)	
2008	(and 2009) The big three auto makers	25 billion at first	✓
	(Included in TARP)		
2008	Troubled Asset Relief Program (TARP)	700 billion	?

(In addition to including concerns above, funds went to various banks and lending programs)

2008	Citi Group (large bank)	280 billion	✓
2009	Bank of America	142.2 billion	✓
2009	Additional bailout for GM and Chrysler	New total 82 billion	?
	(This listing not from ProPublica but according to a	(all with TARP $)	
	Mar. 18, 2011 website article by Stanford Knowledgebase)		

So, the history of bailouts shows a mixed bag of results in terms of payback to the feds. A quick analysis shows that bailouts were most productive regarding concerns not involving banks. Bailouts regarding banks (with some recent exceptions) and the government enterprises of Freddie Mac/Fannie Mae were the dry sponges that absorbed most of the un-recouped bailout money the feds spent over time. Although the majority of the 2008 bailout money was returned to the feds (after interest and dividends are added in,) Fannie Mae and Freddie Mac asked for more money in 2012 to stay in business. ***This bailout chart is further evidence that most unreturned funds were to fix problems the***

government itself created. Chalk this section up to more documentation that the federal government's penchant for control eventually causes them to trip over themselves.

The most controversial bailouts in 2008 and 2009 were the funds loaned to Chrysler and GM. Pure free-market conservatives said that General Motors and Chrysler deserved to go bankrupt because of mismanagement. Assertions from experts in the field said that they had neglected to become innovative and competitive with their products and didn't control costs, giving into strong labor union demands. Various website articles said that many in Congress accused the auto-makers of not operating competitively for years. The companies had delayed making alternative energy vehicles, instead reaping profits from sales of SUVs and other large vehicles. When sales declined in 2006, they launched 0% financing plans to lure buyers. Union members were paid $70/hour on average. GM had twice as many brands as needed and twice as many dealerships, thanks to state franchise regulations. Bankruptcy would actually help them, critics claimed, as it would force them to come to terms with their issues and force labor unions to back down from their bargaining positions. At that point, they contended, the government could step in to assist ***managed bankruptcy*** to ensure eventual success.

Ironically, Chrysler and General Motors did in fact go bankrupt, *even after **two** bailouts*. Various website articles state that in December 2008, U.S. President George W. Bush agreed to a $4 billion bailout for ***Chrysler*** followed by an additional $8.5 billion bailout extended by President Barack Obama early in his administration. In total, the government granted a $12.5 billion dollar bailout for Chrysler using Troubled Asset Relief Program funds provided by Congress and Canadian government funds. Chrysler received loans for three months in order to come up with specific plans to restructure into viable companies. An additional $1.5 billion was loaned to Chrysler Financial, its credit affiliate. On June 10, 2009, Chrysler LLC emerged from Chapter 11 bankruptcy reorganization and substantially all of its operations were sold to a new company—Chrysler Group LLC; organized in alliance with the Italian automaker Fiat.

A CNN Money website report on June 2, 2009 said this about the ***General Motors*** bankruptcy: "In the end, even $19.4 billion in federal help wasn't enough to keep the nation's largest automaker out of bankruptcy. The government will pour another $30 billion into GM to fund operations during its reorganization."

Given the above facts, here's my take on the whole debacle: ***Although Democratic pundits today give praise to President Obama for "rescuing" GM and Chrysler as they are now successful, I'm hoping this brief history of what happened will show this is not exactly the case.*** To recap, Obama poured unprecedented amounts money into GM and Chrysler to keep them from going bankrupt, but failed to achieve the objective. The two car companies emerged as eventual successes again ***only after*** they went bankrupt. The key to regaining strength was through the bankruptcy more than the bailout, specifically ***managed and funded bankruptcy***. So, it would appear the free-market conservatives were right after all to let two of the "big three" go bankrupt from the beginning.

Another conservative observation that arose after Obama took office regarded a new take on the bailout issue, which raised this question by those on the left side: "What about assisting the victims like the homeowner, who gets stuck with a mortgage he can't pay and is facing foreclosure?" After all, the private concerns that had caused all the trouble were getting bailed out. Why not the individual homeowner? This last question was answered by Obama with an FHA Re-Finance Program allowing $8.1 billion of the fed's money to back it. The ProPublica.org website cited:

> The program, announced in March of 2010, is aimed at helping homeowners who are underwater, meaning they owe more on their mortgage than their house is worth. The homeowner would end up in a mortgage insured by the Federal Housing Administration (FHA) with a new mortgage balance adjusted to the house's current worth. The plan is limited to homeowners who qualify for a refinance (those who are current on their mortgage). The $8.1 billion will be used to provide loss protection for investors on the refinanced first liens.

Another part of the TARP, to directly assist the homeowner, was the Housing Finance Agency Innovation Fund. The ProPublica.org website described it this way:

> This program will provide up to $7.6 billion to fund "innovative measures" to help families in the states that have been hardest hit by the aftermath of the burst of the housing bubble. Ten states received a total of $2.1 billion for plans targeted at steep home price declines and unemployment. Those states are California, Florida, Arizona, Michigan, Nevada, North Carolina, Ohio Oregon, Rhode Island and South Carolina. In order to receive funds, each state's housing finance agencies had to submit plans to the Treasury Department for evaluation.

Predictably, these federally funded benefits to homeowners annoyed some free-market conservatives. I remember a sound bite aired on TV from a Wall Street trader who didn't like President Obama's generosity with these taxpayer funds. ***"Homeowners, do you want to pay for your neighbor's mortgage as well as your own? Mr. President, are you listening?"*** This wrinkle was classic conservative rumblings about a solution perceived to be too liberal.

Overall, prevailing wisdom dictated that the bank industry bailouts had to be expedited to rebuild the crash. Only the pure free-market conservatives had principled objections to giving the feds keys to the private sector. In fact, a CNN Money website article written on Oct. 2, 2008 reported that the Senate version of the $700 billion bailout bill passed by 74 to 25. But the song that claimed to save America went flat after banks took the money and kept it. Consumers soon found that banks were singing a tune different than the feds had put their money on. Burnt by government-induced policies to lend money freely (read why and how in the section "more regulation vs. less regulation") bankers decided they were going to think long and hard before letting go of the dough. Anecdotal complaints of consumers and small businesses not being able to get loans ran rampant through 2009. It causes one to take pause to think about how government can only have so much control over banks and needs to stop their penchant to do so. Banks eventually came around and normal lending resumed. Take note they did so on their own without further governmental arm-twisting.

Stimulate Through Government vs. High Costs and Excessive Waste

The real controversy regarding liberal vs. conservative conflicts occurred after President Obama came into office in January of 2009. The Bush Administration had already invested $700 billion to finance loans for the banking industry to rebuild. Soon after he took office, President Obama and his democratically controlled Congress decided they were going to pass another piece of legislation of unprecedented proportions to stimulate an economy that was shaken up and stalled. Obama's fix for our economic woes was legislation of unprecedented proportions. According to various websites, the $787 billion economic stimulus package approved by Congress in February, 2009 was designed to quickly jumpstart economic growth. Supposedly, it would save between 900,000 and 2.3 million jobs. The package allocated funds as follows:

- $288 billion in tax cuts.
- $224 billion in extended unemployment benefits, education and health care.
- $275 billion for job creation using federal contracts, grants and loans.

To Obama's credit, the Stimulus Package added 140,000 jobs to government payrolls and is also credited to saving state and local government jobs that would have been lost. It was difficult to assess how many. But let's take a look at some examples where the government used "stimulus" money to create jobs (credit to Fox News:)

- Johnson Controls received $300 million in federal grants for green jobs. 150 people were hired. That equates to $2 million per job created that the U.S. taxpayer will owe.
- California was awarded $186 million to weatherize homes. 538 jobs were created as a result. That equates to a $346,000 tab to us per job created.

- California was awarded $59 million to train people for green jobs. 719 jobs were created. That's a much better result, but still equates to $82,000 per job that we are paying for.

You get the point. How efficient is it for our tax money to pay for government jobs vs. using that tax money to subsidize private sector jobs? Proponents of the package say it kept the economy from getting worse and opponents of it say it felt short of reaching its goal of keeping the unemployment rate under eight percent. The unemployment rate never fell below eight percent during the Obama administration and was as high as ten percent in October, 2009 (CNN Money website: April 9, 2012.) I think a purely objective statistical assessment of the state of the nation one thousand days into Obama's tenure tells the story (credit to Fox News:)

- The national debt had increased $4.2 trillion (to put this into perspective, the national debt was about $10 trillion when he took office, so Obama increased it 42% in only 2.7 years.)
- Although his stimulus package added a lot of government jobs and some private sector jobs, the net loss of jobs was still over two million.
- Three million more Americans live in poverty (as of Oct., 2011) than when Obama took office.
- Four million bankruptcies occurred.
- 2.4 million houses were foreclosed on by banks.
- Gasoline prices (as of one thousand days in, not now) had risen more than 80%.
- Health insurance premiums were up thirteen percent.

Judging from raw results, the effectiveness of Obama's economic policies (or lack of them) is at best questionable.

Conservatives herald that stimulating the private sector is the key to economic improvement for everyone on the socio-economic ladder. Here's how I view it: putting stimulus money into the hands of the private sector is a more efficient use of stimulus money. Why? The government is like an employment agency that takes a cut or commission to do the hiring. In addition, they have a huge bureaucracy that costs money, even if they are operating at optimal performance. The federal government just doesn't have a good track record in managing their capital. Look at the post office, which was $5.5 billion in debt as of the end of 2011. I remember it wasn't until about mid 2011 that they announced Saturday delivery might have to end. Big deal. What were they waiting for? Do something about the problem. Raise the cost of a stamp. Cut expenses. In this electronic age, we probably only need postal mail delivered three days a week at best. Although I think it is great they don't want to lay off workers, they are supposed to be a self-sustaining agency. Is this an indication of the carefree, nonchalant attitude of the rest of the federal government?

I'm not an economist, but the prevailing wisdom is to find ways to incentivize capital to be spent, reward investment, reward job creation, strengthen the dollar, find ways to compete against international competition, adjust taxation where needed to improve trade, and improve confidence in the future.

Here's Mitt Romney's seven-point plan for the economy that he campaigned on:

- Make sure our corporate tax rates are competitive with other nations.
- Ensure that our regulation and bureaucracies work not just for the people in Washington, but for the businesses that we are trying to grow.
- Have trade policies that work for us, not just for our trading partners or competition.
- Have an energy policy that enables us to become "energy secure."
- Abide by the rule of law.
- Get institutions to build human capital because capitalism is about people, not just money and physical goods.
- Have a government that doesn't spend more than it takes in.

We are far away from accomplishing that last objective. In fact, conservatives viewed that the impact on the national debt from the $787 billion dollar stimulus package overshadowed the extent of real economic growth that it would seed. I contend that excessive waste and/or corruption in government exacerbates the problem and adds another reason not to trust the feds with stimulus money. Here are a few startling examples of the way governments spends our money (credit to Fox News:)

- The federal government spent $1.5 million studying the immune system of the shrimp.
- They spent $1.5 million developing a laundry-folding robot.
- They spent $2.6 million studying how AIDS spreads among prostitutes in *China.*
- The feds increased their limo fleet 73% at $60,000 per car since Obama took office.
- According to Karl Rove, former Deputy Chief of Staff for President Bush, the Stimulus Package passed by the Obama Administration in 2009 included the spending of tens of millions for a commission to study the use of animated characters to sell breakfast cereals and other foods to children.
- In September, 2011, an audit of the Justice Department showed wasteful and extravagant spending on their employees. Between October 2007 and October 2009, ten conferences cost American taxpayers $4.4 million. In August, 2009, $4,200 was spent on 250 muffins, equating to $16 a muffin. In July, 2008, two coffee breaks cost the taxpayers $15,600 or $52 per person.
- In April 2012, the General Services Administration (GSA) spent $820,000 for a conference for 300 people. That figure includes $130,000 to scout the location for the event. Regardless, the cost to the taxpayers here equates to $2,733 per person that attended.
- One GSA Regional Commissioner took more than one hundred trips, many involving lavish parties in Las Vegas suites, on our dime by disguising them as work related when in actuality they were personal.
- Tom Schatz, president of Citizens Against Government Waste, augmented the April 2012 Fox News reportage on federal government waste and prefaced his report with this statement: "The culture of waste is alive and well in Washington. In the

past five years, spending has gone up 27%...record deficits and record debt and no one is watching how the money is being spent. Schatz provided, as an example, federal monies that were allocated towards providing homeowners a weatherization credit. He said that the Inspector General at the Department of Energy told the Secretary of Energy, Steven Chu, that they can't keep track of the $225 million that had previously been set aside during the Bush Administration for this purpose. Despite this, the Obama Administration increased the allotment to $5 billion (22 times the amount they couldn't keep track of) as part of the Stimulus Package that was passed. Consequently, Schatz reported, the potential for abuse extends proportionately.

I could provide reams of documentation to show government waste and corruption if needed, but I will assume you're convinced government waste is like a runaway train. Given a choice on where to inject stimulus money, isn't it best spent by the taxpayer rather than those that make their living off taxpayers?

Obamacare Thumbs Up vs. Obamacare Thumbs Down

The Supreme Court ruled by a slim 5-4 vote at the end of June 2012 that, with the exception of some minor clauses having to be thrown out, the Obamacare program was constitutional. This means this section is more relevant than ever in terms of a voter making up their mind to vote for or against Obama's re-election; which translates to a vote for or against Obamacare. But, don't worry. I'm not going to tackle the impossible task of debating the merits of this piece of legislation, as it is way too complicated. What I will do is to capsulate the intent and content of it just enough to give you a general understanding of its merits, its downside and why it was so hotly contested. After you've read all the facts, you decide thumbs up or down.

To keep it simple, I am going to list the major benefits of the program to Americans. Then, I will provide a brief, general method of how revenues will be generated to help pay for the cost of the program. Next, I will review the objections to Obamacare. The two twists—the constitutional challenge and the religious freedom flap—have already passed constitutional muster. I won't re-hash these issues here as they are a moot point. However, I took apart the Supreme Court decision from a legal standpoint at the beginning of chapter 4. In the meantime, I'll start with the back story of how Obamacare legislation came to be.

Americans for years have been complaining about health insurance companies. Their policies were too expensive and the limitations for coverage were sometimes unfair or hidden. There was no coverage for pre-existing conditions and the cost for getting extended coverage (Cobra) while in between jobs was prohibitive. These were just the most talked about complaints. Even Republicans admitted health insurance reform was needed. But we went from one extreme to the other. Obama actually was hoping to achieve government-paid health care not unlike that in Canada and European states, one in which the U.S. government would be the "single-payer." This didn't materialize. The bill that was ultimately voted on was actually a compromise and more of a "government controlled" program rather than a "government paid" system. The specifics of the legislation consumed over a thousand pages. Word on the street was that no congressman that voted on it either read it in its entirety or even completely understood it. The Republicans had a problem with that because the devil was in the details, and accused the Democrats of blindly following the lead of the blind. Nancy Pelosi, who was Speaker of the House at the time, was quoted during the tumult as saying, "just vote for it and we'll find out what's in it later."

Admittedly, there are lots of great reform ideas that came to fruition. Here's the synopsis, according to various internet sources, of what the fuss was all about:

- Thirty million Americans not having insurance will now be covered.
- Insurance companies can't deny coverage. There would be "guaranteed issue."
- "Community rating" would require premiums to be consistent in accordance with the same age and locale.

- Individuals and small businesses without insurance could now buy it at a "Health Insurance Exchange" at an affordable price as they would be federally subsidized.
- Eligibility for Medicaid (current government paid insurance for the poor) would be expanded to include those at 133% of the poverty level.
- Low income families up to 400% of the poverty level will receive subsidizing on a sliding scale when purchasing their "individual/family" insurance at the "Health Insurance Exchange."
- Minimum standards for health insurance policies were to be established and coverage caps would be banned. Additional requirements were added, like children can be on their parents' policies until they turn 26.
- Lots of requirements (I'll avoid the boring details) regarding expense ratios, transparency and administrative processes also were placed on insurance companies.
- The plan included lots of "freebies" with no co-pay in many instances, especially regarding women's preventative health care.

A variety of taxes and fees were set up to pay for the extra "goodies." Those affected:

- Individuals of a certain income paying Medicare contributions.
- Individuals having "Cadillac" insurance policies.
- Indoor tanning salons.
- Health insurance providers.
- Manufacturers and importers of drugs and medical devices.
- Individuals using medical expense tax deductions.

Conservatives maintained the cost and disruption to health care will far outrun benefits:

- Obamacare would ruin the quality of health insurance. The overall expansion of medical services would cause the supply of health care to fall short of the increased demand, creating long waits and poor service just like the anecdotal stories we hear about in other countries with government-run health care.

- Premiums for those of us footing the bill would skyrocket. (Premiums have in fact gone up dramatically since the inception of the legislation with forecasts of even higher rates.)

- The increased taxes and fees mentioned above would dampen economic growth and be an accelerant to increased medical costs.

- The costs would contribute to the increasing national deficit as conservatives believe the insufficient revenue stream to pay for it will require more money.

- The Republicans have an ideological problem with it as the plan is clearly skewed to taking money from the "haves" and giving it to the "have-nots" to provide them with free or very low cost health care. Example: Obamacare would take $500 billion in funding to Medicare and use it for "freebies" and low cost care to low income patients.

- The program makes us all pay for women's contraception, who will now get it for free.

- Remember the inflammatory phrase "Death panels?" Most probably coined by Republicans, (and labeled by Democrats as propaganda,) the term applied to a committee that would make decisions on who gets health care and who doesn't. Many conservatives interpreting Obamacare said that the doling out of health care services would be plotted against the age of the patients receiving them. Theoretically, patients who were aging would be at risk of not qualifying for certain tests, procedures or operations because they would be too old to warrant the expense to Obamacare insurance. E.g.: Will they pay for an eighty-year-old to get expensive cancer screening?

- "One size doesn't fill all" is the mantra of some doctors that have come on TV to talk about how the bureaucratic processes of Obama care will in fact determine what diagnostic and cancer screening tests will and won't be paid for. Many doctors today are emphasizing the individual differences in treatment needed as one's individual medical history and that of their parents should be the determining factors of what tests a patient should get, not the statistical conclusions of number-crunching oligarchs sitting at a desk in Washington, D.C.

- Even though the religious objection by Catholics passed Constitutional muster with the Supreme Court ruling at the end of June, there is still a bad taste in the mouths of many Catholic based institutions. Here's why: They were not included in that category of Catholic run facilities that were exempted from having to provide to its employees insurance that included coverage for contraception and sterilization. These practices are against the Catholic doctrine, and those running these Catholic facilities had claimed their religious rights were being trampled on.

In conclusion, the conservative view is that many people don't trust the government with the scale of responsibility and control that Obamacare would require. Moreover, Obamacare doesn't incorporate the following two ideas that would lower health care costs without costing Americans money. First, we need legislation creating more competition among health care providers, allowing *inter*state as well as *intra*state competition. Secondly, we desperately need tort reform to lower medical insurance for the professionals, which carry a large part of the continually increasing costs.

What a saga! Obamacare truly represents the perfect storm between the left and the right. It's one of "re-distribution of wealth" vs. "no more re-distribution of wealth." It underscores "government control" vs. "individual freedom." It is the classical struggle of "socialism leanings" vs. "capitalism." It is yet another issue underscoring "secular progressiveness vs. religious rights." The vote on it was clearly Democrats vs. Republicans. These divides will continue to frame politics in America.

"No Child Left Behind" vs. Localize Education Dollars

President Bush's administration passed an act designed to control education across our land through a uniform, regimented, centralized approach using federal dollars and emphasizing national testing standard to all schools across America. President Obama subsequently adopted this centralized approach, although he made many changes to it.

During the Republican national debate that occurred on January 15, 2012, Newt Gingrich asserted the "No child Left Behind" program has been an abject failure. He pointed out that the feds can't possibly determine the best course of education for every school in the country. He added that the standardized testing that the law dictates doesn't take into account the large cultural, language and scholastic differences among students. Consequently, the results of the testing can be self-defeating. He then proceeded with a convincing argument to scrap federal dollars and control altogether. "Take that money and that control and give it to the states," he proposed. "Then, if the states are smart, they in turn will take the money and the control and give it to the local municipalities," he said during an election 2012 debate.

Gingrich contends, and I agree, that local control of education will have tremendous advantages that federal control will not. Parents will become more engaged in their children's education as they will have more input in it. Schools will be able to tailor the needs of the students in their community and appropriate money where they see fit. Newt's answer to the question summed up the right-wing perspective on this issue of federal control of education (on the left) vs. local control of education (on the right). His sentiments were also echoed by other Republican candidates. It seems to me that out of all institutions that would benefit from local control, education stands out among them.

Ecologically Green vs. Economically Green

Which type of "green" do you prefer? It seems the left is more concerned with the green outdoors and the right wants the green in their wallet. The more regulations to protect the environment, the more the policies are on the left side, favoring government control. Conversely, policies with less regulation are generally favored by the right or the Republican Platform, as they allow business to grow and be more profitable. Conservatives are quicker to object to regulations when the benefits to our ecology are relatively small in comparison to the cost.

Joseph M. Weston Sr.

Here's a personal anecdote about how severe EPA regulations have become in the Obama administration. It involves a new process to remove lead that is now being enforced onto contractors by the EPA. I couldn't believe my ears when a building contractor I know told me in 2010 about these lead eradication classes he had to take, which cost him several hundred dollars. Basically, the EPA was requiring contractors to take responsibility for determining if lead exists on the surface they are working on and removing it at their expense. For example, if a contractor is removing a crumbling, plastered wall in an old house and replacing it with sheetrock, he will have to send out samples of the paint to get it tested before he begins the work. If analysis determines lead is in the paint, even if it is only in the bottom layer of paint on a wall that has been repainted with non-leaded painted fifteen times over, the environment is considered contaminated. The contractor will then have to engage in a protracted process with certain equipment to remove the contamination and dispose of it in accordance with the strict EPA requirements. The fine for being caught not strictly adhering to the procedures is $6,000. He told me the EPA was hiring agents to spot contractors that are in the midst of a job without abiding by the regulations. All expenses will be at the contractor's cost (who will have to pass it on to the customer.) But from what I understand, the EPA procedures are *so* daunting and *so* costly; they are a "deal-breaker" and most likely will rarely be abided by. So, let's get this straight. The feds are spending the taxpayer's money to enforce lead removal regulations that are so strict, they will either kill the project altogether or be ignored.

Even more bizarre is what the contractor told me about power washing. Vinyl siding, he said, has some lead in it. The EPA theorizes that this lead could be sprayed off the vinyl during power washing and go into the ground, thereby contaminating it. Therefore, a contractor who power washes a house has to follow the following EPA procedures: Sheets of heavy plastic have to be placed on the ground tight against the house in such a way as to catch all the water that bounces off and drips down from the vinyl during power washing. Then, the water has to somehow be collected into buckets and poured down the homeowner's toilets. Anyone who has ever power washed a house would agree that this whole concept is just laughable. My business acquaintance estimated this procedure would probably triple the cost to the homeowner of power washing. (I strongly doubt any contractor followed these power washing regulations.)

But let's think this through to completion.

Let's say the homeowners with the crumbling, plastered wall and the dirty, vinyl-covered house gets estimates for plaster removal and power washing. They are two to three times what the work would normally cost. The homeowner says, "forget it," and finally does the work himself, getting his brother-in-law to help him. Here's the punch line: If the homeowner does the work himself, the EPA does not require the lead identification and removal procedures to be done. The regulations are only for contractors. Now, one has to think about how exaggerated the health hazard *really is* if the EPA is okay with the homeowner doing the work. We also need to ask ourselves: Is it the government's responsibility to protect everyone from every possible bad thing such as a remote possibility of lead poisoning? No. Do they have the right to force private contractors to be responsible for a fixing a problem they did not cause? No. Shouldn't the owner of the house have the personal freedom to decide how they want to deal with the problem and then call a company that specializes in lead removal? Yes.

In my quest to see to how much EPA regulations had become tougher since President Obama took office, I searched the website and did find articles with headlines announcing newer, stricter regulations:

- A September 2011 headline from EPA Abuse.com read "U.S. EPA Proposes Stricter Regulations of Air Emissions From Hydraulic Fracturing and Other Oil and Gas Operations"
- A March 2012 Oil and Gas Investor.com headline read "EPA Fracking Rule May Cut Gas Drilling"
- A March 2012 Huff Post Green website headline read: "EPA Power Plant Regulations to Limit Heat-Trapping Pollution"
- A March 29, 2012 headline from EPA Abuse.com read: "EPA Usurping Privately Owned Land For Agenda 21 Buffer Zones"
- An April 2, 2012 website article from the DesMoines Record. com started out: "The U.S. Environmental Protection Agency

last week issued a proposed rule that truly could be a game-changer for the electric-power industry in this country. If the industry's predictions are to be believed, the United States is on its way toward the eventual demise of the coal-burning power plant as old plants are phased out and not replaced."

Finally, here's some documentation that is a commentary of the EPA's actions during the Obama Administration according to James E. McCarthy, Specialist in Environmental Policy and Claudia Copeland, Specialist in Resources and Environmental Policy in a "Congressional Research Service" publication. It can be found on fas.org.

> In the two years since Barack Obama was sworn in as President, the Environmental Protection Agency (EPA) has proposed and promulgated numerous regulations implementing the pollution-control statutes enacted by Congress. Critics have reacted strongly. Many, both within Congress and outside of it, have accused the agency of *reaching beyond the authority given it by Congress* and ignoring or underestimating the costs and economic impacts of proposed and promulgated rules. Republican leaders have promised vigorous oversight of the agency and the House has already voted to overturn specific regulations and to limit the agency's authority. Particular attention is being paid to the Clean Air Act, under which EPA has moved forward with the first federal controls on emissions of greenhouse gases and addressed conventional pollutants from a number of industries.

I rest my case that Obama's EPA is acting too aggressively for us to maintain and grow our energy resources without significantly increasing costs to the industry and the consumer.

Oil Flow Up During Obama Tenure vs. Obama's Real Record on Oil

What's the real deal on oil production during the Obama administration? "The administration says its policies have supported more development and that oil production is rising, but most of today's production increases relate to projects begun before it came into office as well as to what is happening on state and private lands (the latter of which is beyond the president's control.) Moreover, from 2009 to 2011, production from federal lands and federal waters combined declined significantly for both oil and natural gas." (Source: scribd.com website) The same source also provided the following facts on Obama's actions regarding oil exploration in the years he was in office:

2009 Obama Administration

- Cancels leases on 77 parcels of land in Utah. It (later) revisits Utah leases, continuing suspension or permanently withdrawing most.
- Delays new off shore leasing plan.
- Proposes billions in new taxes on oil and gas industry in FY 2010 budget proposal.
- Announces new rounds of oil shale research and development leases in Colorado, Wyoming and Utah with significantly reduced lease acreage and unattainable lease terms.
- Shortens lease terms for upcoming Central Gulf of Mexico lease sale.

2010: Obama Administration

- Proposes additional regulatory hurdles for development on Federal lands.
- Proposes billions in new taxes on oil and gas industry in FY 2011 budget proposal.
- Cancels the remaining Alaska lease sales in the Beaufort and Chukchi Seas offshore and withdraws Bristol Bay from the program.
- Cancels the Virginia offshore lease sale, despite bipartisan support from Virginia's governor and congressional delegation.

2011: Obama Administration

- Proposes billions in new taxes on oil and gas industry in FY 2012 budget proposal.
- Proposes a ban on horizontal drilling in the George Washington National Forest.

- Issues an ANPR regarding new regulations for gas gathering lines that would substantially impact development of the Marcellus Shale.
- Proposes one-size-fits-all new source performance standards that may significantly hamper oil and gas operations.
- Again proposes billions in new taxes.
- Issues new 2012-2017 five-year plan that fails to open any new offshore areas to oil and gas development.
- Releases study plan on potential impacts on ground water from hydraulic fracturing that fails to address concerns regarding the transparency and scientific validity of the study approach.
- Raises the minimum bid amount for offshore lease blocks in water depths of 400 meters and greater from $37.50 per acre to $100 per acre.
- Produces a draft report on its groundwater investigation in Pavillion, Wyoming and receives extensive criticism for questionable scientific methodology. Administration cancels a planned auction of public lands in the Wayne National Forest.

2012: Obama Administration
- Proposes billions in new taxes on oil and gas industry in FY 2013 budget proposal.
- Rejects permit for Keystone XL pipeline.
- Begins testing water wells in Dimock, Pennsylvania despite having no new information from laboratory results to justify doing so.
- Recommends removing from leasing availability over 1.8 million acres of oil shale and tar sands energy resources in Colorado, Utah and Wyoming.

Every event above either stopped, reduced or limited oil drilling or was part of a plan to give higher priority to environmental concerns over oil exploration. It would be fair to summarize Obama's policies as being anti-oil exploration. Here's more evidence of an anti-oil drilling administration as per the following April 25, 2011 website article from "The Foundry:"

There are an estimated 27 billion barrels of oil waiting to be tapped in the Arctic Ocean, off the coast of Alaska. But after spending five years and nearly $4 billion, Shell Oil Company has been forced to abandon its efforts to drill for oil in the region (because of environmental agencies.)

As it turns out, Shell was finally able to resume oil drilling, but not until the company waded through over two years of obstacles from the EPA and other environmental groups. But at this point, I'm thinking, *"No wonder this country is behind in oil production."*

But there's more—the original April 25, 2011 article in the Foundry about Shell continued with additional commentary:

President Barack Obama said in his weekly address on Saturday that "there's no silver bullet that can bring down gas prices right away," but that one thing America can do is pursue "safe and responsible production of oil at home." Too bad his words and his actions are not one and the same. Aside from the EPA's decision on Shell, the Obama administration has imposed a months-long moratorium on deep-water offshore drilling that curtailed domestic production and sent some seven drilling rigs elsewhere.

Indeed, Obama's policies are highly skewed towards protecting the environment as opposed to increasing the supply of energy in this country. Overall, the Obama administration initiated regulations calculated to result in the shutting down of about ten percent of coal-generated electricity. At the end of 2011, Obama's EPA finalized tough new rules on emissions by power plants. They will inevitably result in higher electricity rates to consumers. (Source: April 25, 2012 "The Foundry" website article)

A significant opportunity to increase domestic oil supply arose in late 2011. It involved a proposed pipeline from Alberta, Canada to various points in the U.S. to provide raw materials to refine oil into gasoline. Unfortunately, Obama killed the project in January 2012 (actually tabled it until 2013) because of pressure from environmentalists. Various internet sources reported November 7, 2011 that several thousand environmentalist supporters, some shouldering a long black inflatable replica of a pipeline, formed a human chain around the White House to try to convince Barack Obama to block the controversial Keystone XL project. Then, on November 10, 2011, President Obama announced after months of protest that "the decision on the pipeline permit would be delayed until at least 2013, pending further environmental review."

Various internet sources say that the initial capacity of the Keystone Pipeline is 435,000 barrels per day, which will be increased up to 590,000 barrels per day. The Keystone XL will add 510,000 barrels per day increasing the total capacity up to 1.1 million barrels per day. Wow. That's a lot of oil and a lot of jobs that would be needed to build the pipeline. But Obama has different priorities. I understand there was a lot of environmental disagreement on the possible ecological risk that the pipeline could create. There were also reports that some environmental studies were not objective and skewed in favor of the environmentalists' agenda. Reading the back-and-forth arguments as to which organization was exaggerating their claims more than the next one is frustrating because one doesn't really know who's telling the truth. ***But we do know this—environmental influence won over Obama's resolve to increase the oil supply in the U.S. and decrease U.S. reliance on Middle East oil.***

We all want clean energy, Mr. President, but until we have the luxury of turning our noses up on the environmentally challenging fuel, we need to power this country somehow without paying $5 dollars per gallon at the pump. In early 2012, many journalists and congressmen even speculated that President Obama didn't even want to curb high gasoline prices. When Steven Chu, Secretary of Energy was asked at the end of February 2012 if the administration wants to lower gas prices, he said, "No. The overall goal is to decrease our dependency on oil." In the spirit of balanced coverage, he recanted the remark the next day; but most of us believe his first answer was the truthful one.

To be fair, Obama did compromise on some action at the end of 2011 which would have resulted in more oil exploration in the U.S. However, even the kindest assessment of his actions are best summarized as "too little, too late." At this point in the president's tenure (mid 2012,) it's not a question as to what a president can do to lower gas prices at the pump; but what President Obama can "undo" that he's done already.

President Can't Control Gas Prices vs. What the President Can Do

"The President can't control gasoline prices at the pump," I have heard from TV journalists all throughout 2011 and 2012 as they defend the President against suggestions he isn't doing anything about them. Is this really true or is it just rhetoric to keep this item off of the campaign attack list by Republicans readying for election 2012? Just off the top of my head, I came up with a list that I later augmented after listening to an informative talk on the subject at the end of March 2012 by Dick Morris, Fox News Contributor.

- First, we just finished talking about how the U.S. has not maximized its potential to drill and increase the domestic supply of oil through the proposed Keystone Pipeline. If every administration was successful in maximizing domestic oil exploration and flow, we would have a greater domestic supply of oil, resulting in lower prices at the pump at this point. (I'm not just blaming Obama and I do realize the pump prices don't get affected overnight.)
- I understand that ongoing political developments in the Middle East constantly affect oil prices. However, isn't it the President's job to use our political clout in the world to stabilize situations that might affect oil prices? I understand most times this may be impossible and other times difficult at best. But I think it is a cop out to say *"he can't do anything."*
- Currently, investors can buy and sell oil easily without receiving delivery of the actual oil. This causes price instability. Many solution-minded journalists and politicians have suggested legislation to keep profit-hungry investors from oil speculation by requiring them to take delivery. Dick Morris claims "59 cents on the gallon is due to speculation."
- Because of the warm weather during the winter of 2011 into 2012, companies have exported record amounts of oil due to an over-supply here in the U.S. This caused oil prices to go up despite the warm winter and over-supply. Why don't

we propose legislation to heavily tax the oil exporting or to even end it? I know this would sound drastic to free market conservatives, but these oil exports have really tinkered with the natural law of supply and demand here in the U.S.

- I mentioned earlier that the dropping value of the dollar against other international monetary units is reflecting an increased cost at the pump. The pursuit of an economic policy to stabilize the dollar can be affected by the powers to be in Washington (and therefore to some extent by the president,) but this is not being done. Dick Morris contributed the very telling fact that the U.S. has tripled the money supply since Obama has been in office (which weakens the dollar.)
- Federal tax at the pump equates to $.18/gallon according to Dick Morris. Three quarters of this is for highway construction and one quarter is for maintenance, he says. What about a temporary ban on the construction portion of this tax so we can give back to the consumers 13.5 cents per gallon from this tax?

I'm not alone at holding any President somewhat accountable for gas prices. A Reuter's poll of 606 Americans taken from March 26-27, 2012 showed the following results for this question: "How do you feel about the way President Obama is handling gas prices?"

Disapprove   68%
Approve   24%

This answer would not be surprising considering the fact that the average price for a gallon of regular gasoline on the day Obama began his tenure (January 20, 2009) was $1.84 and the average price on March 8, 2012 more than doubled in three years to $3.91.

> *I'm not in the position to say exactly what the President should have been doing about gas prices at the pump, but I do know it isn't to bow before the King of Saudi Arabia.*

Investing in Green Companies vs. Money Out the Window

We all want this country to migrate to clean energy as soon as possible to improve both the cleanliness of the environment and significantly decrease our reliance on foreign oil. But the Obama administration's rush to use your tax money to fund "green" companies proved to be imprudent. During the earlier days of the Obama administration, it lent over $500 million to a solar power company (Solyndra) to subsidize and advance their efforts to bring their product to market. A year later, the company declared bankruptcy. Since $500 million is an awful lot of money to lend to a tiny company, the FBI is investigating what happened to it. They raided the headquarters in Fremont, CA and the homes of three executives, seizing their computers. I guess we'll wait and see what comes of their findings. In the meantime, let's check out the backstory.

Karl Rove, a former advisor to President G. W. Bush, reported to Fox News in 2011 that a committee of career employees at the Energy Department unanimously advised the Bush administration to reject Solyndra's application to receive government loans. The staff under Bush had checked out the company using due diligence and had red-flagged it. Yet, the Obama administration approved it just a few months later. Karl Rove succinctly captured what happened when he said, "It would appear the White House put their thumb on the scale of this thing." The company's supporters gave significant amounts of money to Obama's 2008 campaign. In fact, George K. Kaiser, a billionaire, is a huge benefactor of Solyndra. Kaiser is an Obama donor who made sixteen visits to the White House during the period of the loan's approval. You finish the story. Needless to say, it is at the very least the epitome of "crony capitalism."

Regardless, the loans that the Obama Department of Energy handed out to ecological companies didn't stop here. The year 2012 saw more green companies having financial trouble, even with large infusions of cash from the Obama administration. A French company bought one of them out. (How do we get *that* money back?) Whereas we understand Obama's commitment to clean energy includes subsidizing these companies with seed money, he and the Department of Energy get failing marks for due diligence in investigating the recipients.

Even the fed's investment in a battery-operated car, the Chevy Volt, has yet to be successful. From its beginning, the car was wrought with problems from spontaneously bursting into flames to falling short on the mileage goal (from a charged battery) during wintery months. A March 5, 2012 website article by The National Legal and Policy Center spoke on GM's announcement of halting production (at that time) of the vehicle due to lack of demand. The article included harsh commentary saying "you would think that the evidence would finally be conclusive that the over-hyped, over-subsidized vehicle is a flop...taxpayers have been bilked out of billions of dollars to produce a car that does practically nothing for the environment or foreign oil dependence while being unwanted by the 99% of consumers that cannot afford, nor want the car." The Chevy Volt lists at about $40,000 (give or take depending on options) before the $7,500 tax rebate. Every bottom-line-for-what-you're-paying comparison I've seen recommends other various hybrids on the market instead.

Industry experts say the U.S. still needs twenty to thirty more years of reliance on oil before clean energy can replace it. One can summarize from the Obama administration's overall record that concern for the environment is clearly a priority. Unfortunately, his concern is much lower for the implementation cost to industry, the supply of energy and the cost to both the consumer and taxpayer.

More Regulation vs. Less Regulation

The left favors more regulation of Wall Street, banks, the environment, and of businesses in general to protect the consumer. The right favors less. You just read that an emphasis on funding green companies is costing us big money. You've also read that environment regulations are reducing oil production and increasing costs to the consumer. Let's talk now about regulations on businesses:

The Small Business Administration says the costs to comply with Federal Regulations on an annual basis are $1.75 trillion. This equates to twelve percent of our $14.5 trillion dollar economy. Consider these facts about how regulations have grown since Obama took office (as per Fox News:)

* Regulation policies have increased about 25%.
* Jobs at regulatory agencies are up thirteen percent.
* Regulatory budgets are up sixteen percent.
* Regulations cost small business owners $11,000 per worker.

Moderate regulations are important, but the pendulum has swung too far in over-regulating. Upon inheriting a crashed economy, Obama would have done well to re-examine regulations upon entering office and water them down to advance economic growth. Let's look at what caused the banking, mortgage, and housing industries to collapse in 2008 and to what extent over-regulation was to blame. Of 3 major factors, the first was CRA (according to Ron Paul, former member of the U.S. House Committee on Financial Services.)

1. The Community Re-Investment Act (CRA) of 1977 was originally designed to end discrimination by banks of people living in poor areas. Banks had been "red-lining;" not lending in accordance with where you live (e.g.: depressed neighborhood.) CRA ended up being revised in 1989, 1991, 1992, 1994, 1995, and 1999. More regulatory changes occurred in 2005, 2007, and 2008. That's a lot of regulation. Consider these commentaries (at the time) on the economic impact of the CRA on the 2008 housing crash:

   * Economist Stan Liebowitz wrote in the *New York Post* that a strengthening of the CRA in the 1990s encouraged a loosening of lending standards throughout the banking industry. He also charges the Federal Reserve with ignoring the negative impact of the CRA. (Feb. 5, 2008 article was titled, *The Real Scandal – How Feds Invited the Mortgage Mess*.)
   * In a commentary for CNN, Congressman Ron Paul, who serves on the United States House Committee on Financial Services, charged the CRA with "forcing banks to lend to people who normally would be rejected as bad credit risks." (Source: *CNN*. Retrieved 2008-09-23.)

  *   In a Wall Street Journal opinion piece, Austrian school economist Russell Roberts wrote that the CRA subsidized low-income housing by pressuring banks to serve poor borrowers and poor regions of the country. (*How Government Stoked The Mania,* Wall Street Journal, October 3, 2008.)

So, CRA ended up having an affirmative action effect, causing banks to loan money to people who couldn't afford the mortgage in the end. Conventional wisdom is that banks need to require a down payment, are allowed to use due diligence to see if a family can truly afford the purchase, and can require a conventional mortgage. But, the CRA twisted the arms of bankers to exchange their conventional practices for creative ones that only led to upside-down equity and eventual foreclosures. This over-regulation actually created an environment of under-regulation in some respects in that banks traded in their conventional practices for free-wheeling, liberal style lending that didn't have the usual safeguards built in.

Admittedly, the over-regulation of banks was only part of the problem. When Wall Street sold investment vehicles consisting of a relatively high percentage of bad mortgages for far more than what they were worth, the whole house of cards fell. Companies that rated the investments were guilty as well. Theoretically, the proper regulations might have prevented Wall Street from doing this. So, I have to admit there is a telling story here about how **under**-regulation of Wall Street was the second act of the play that caused the curtains to drop.

To prevent Wall Street's involvement in the banking-housing debacle from re-occurring, the Obama administration passed a regulation heavy bill in 2010 called the Dodd-Frank Wall Street Reform and Consumer Protection Act. But, unfortunately, it appears the banking industry was thrown into the same prison cell as the "Wall Streeters," and unfairly got sentenced with equally stringent regulations. The banks were truly declared guilty by association. A summary of how the legislation falls short is succinctly captured in an article by Michael Simkovic, titled *Competition and Crisis in Mortgage Securitization* published in the *Indiana Law Journal, Vol. 88, 2013* as follows:

As with other major financial reforms, some legal and financial scholars on both sides of the political spectrum have criticized the law, arguing on the one hand that the reforms were insufficient to prevent another financial crisis or additional "bail outs" of financial institutions, and on the other hand that the reforms went too far and would unduly restrict the ability of banks and other financial institutions to make loans.

Critics of the legislation say the additional red tape and costs to keep up with the Dodd-Frank regulations restricted banks, particularly small banks, from making loans. Since the Wall Street collapse, banks have indeed been reluctant to lend according to many journalists and economic pundits. One of the anecdotal reports even included Donald Trump himself going on TV saying that even he couldn't get a loan he wanted.

The second and third major factors in the downfall of the housing industry, according to Ron Paul during an election 2012 Presidential debate, were (quotes for points 2 and 3 are Ron Paul's words and the commentary below them are mine:)

2. "The federally supported lending agencies of Freddie Mac and Fannie Mae were given a seemingly unlimited amount of credit from the Federal Reserve."

This ultimately contributed to the subsidizing of an inordinate amount of mortgages. Although first time homeowners will thrilled to get mortgages they might not have gotten in another era, the American Dream was short lived for many of them after houses values dropped and put them into negative equity territory. The housing market spiral continued downward as millions of homeowners were forced to stay put, sell at a loss, or face foreclosure. This downturn affected the moving industry, then the home improvement industry, and the ripples went on continuously.

3. "The Federal Reserve held interest rates too low for too long."

This contributed to the supply of money available for mortgages, making them affordable to those who otherwise would not have been able to buy. At first blush, this sounds like a good thing; but the mortgages were *too* affordable, *at first*. You know the end game: an unprecedented number of foreclosures.

These three factors that were to blame for the housing industry downfall ***involved some type of over-regulation***, (although the problem with Wall Street, admittedly, was *under*-regulation.) The increase of mortgage money available and the increased supply of houses eventually created a bubble, which burst. House values plummeted. Consequently, it became commonplace for homeowners to end up owing more than what the value of their house was worth (being up-side down.) This kept people from selling their house, which prevented the housing market from re-cooperating. Job losses resulting from the housing industry downturn increased the number of foreclosures. Four years after the 2008 crash, sales of homes and prices of them in 2012 are at an all time low. The average house has decreased in value 30 to 35 percent between 2006 and 2012. In 2011, new home sales were the lowest in history.

To wrap up this section on regulation, various types of government ***over***-regulation:

- Became a prohibitively large expense for companies.
- Retarded growth.
- Stifled oil production in the U.S.
- Caused the crash of the housing market.

With increasing regulations going forward, it is no wonder that economy has been very slow to re-cooperate. The unemployment rate only documents those that are actually receiving an unemployment check. Many economists speculate that the actual percentage of those unemployed is in the high teens. In January 2012, Fox News Anchor Sean Hannity reported the following statistics:

* Thirteen million people are out of work. 4 million have been out of work for more than a year.

* We've lost a net of two million jobs since President Obama took office in January 2009.
* 49 million Americans live in poverty.

Mitch Daniels (D), Indiana Governor, said this on the day of the State of the Union speech on January 2012: "One in five men of prime working age and nearly half of all persons under thirty did not go to work today." He also cited the following facts:

* The federal government spends one of four dollars in the entire economy.
* The federal government borrows one of every three dollars it spends.

These are sobering statistics, and have relevance to may sections of this book. But, they scream for a sense of urgency. Some Republican Presidential candidates in the 2012 race were rightly suggesting the rolling back of regulations. We need to reverse their crippling effect on capital investment in this country and to keep the jobs from being shipped overseas.

Freebies vs. Freedom

Many of the financial issues we've discussed in this Democratic Platform vs. Republican Platform section can be summed up as a struggle between those wanting "free stuff" from the government and those wanting the "freedom from having to pay for it." I'm thinking most Americans would want:

* Freedom from having to pay for women's free contraception and other Obamacare freebies.
* Freedom from having to buy health insurance or pay a penalty if we don't.
* Freedom from having to pay for subsidies to green companies, especially when they fail.
* Freedom from having to pay for bailouts.

- Freedom from having to pay for food stamps to people who have considerable assets and are milking the system.
- Freedom from having to pay interest on money loaned to the federal government.
- Freedom to keep our children and grandchildren from being overburdened with an unprecedented weight of an un-payable national debt.
- Freedom from legislation that continues to redistribute our income.
- Freedom to be generous on our terms without the government taking our money and being generous with it on their terms.
- Freedom from being sued when there has been no negligence by the defendant. (See tort reform in the next section.)

These issues during 2011 and 2012 moved to front and center as President Obama ramped up the cultural war against the "haves" and divided the nation by emphasizing the need to redistribute to the "have-nots." Whereas our country has always been a generous one, conservatives believe their sensibilities are being pushed to the limit. Unfortunately, the decision of 2012 will be largely determined by those who want the freebies versus those that want the freedom from having to pay for them.

Protect Freeing of Secrets vs. Protect National Security

Which do you think is more important—protecting the "right to know" or national security? The perfect contemporary example to demonstrate the penchant among liberals for wanting to publicize security sensitive information is the Julian Assange sensation. It's a story about a hacker that published volumes of material on the internet, much of which put the U.S. in a compromising position.

Assange published classified details in 2010 about American involvement in the wars in Afghanistan and Iraq. This would include highly sensitive material that could affect U.S. relations with other countries and compromise U.S. security. Many politicians, conservative journalists and pundits asserted this act violated espionage and/or U.S. security laws. Contrast this to the left point of view that the U.S.

government should practice transparency and openness, condoning the publishing of U.S. national security secrets. Some on the far left are even calling Assange a hero.

The Obama administration played down the Wiki leaks debacle. Since Obama could do little about the information already leaked, many pundits believed he didn't want to call undue attention to the fact that U.S. national security could have been severely compromised. Regardless, this contemporary event is only the latest in a long philosophical battle between the conservative viewpoint and a largely liberal media. The latter, according to conservatives, has been publicizing information for decades that puts Americans, particularly our military, in jeopardy. One of the earlier examples of a media run amuck with information is when the New York Times printed detailed instructions (decades ago) on how to assemble an atom bomb.

A more recent example of the media publicizing sensitive material that could put U.S. soldiers at risk occurred in April, 2012. U.S. servicemen had found dismembered corpses of Taliban operatives and posed with them in photographs taken by military personnel. The bodies had been ripped apart by the explosives these Taliban suicide bombers had self-detonated. The LA Times published two of these photos with a story contending that U.S. military discipline was breaking down in the Afghanistan War. Conservative leaning journalists and pundits criticized the actions of the LA Times, saying it would likely endanger U.S. troops as Muslim tempers could flair and stir violence. Today, photos are not just considered to be journalistic art, but images which can easily be reproduced on the internet and quickly downloaded onto any electronic device. Sensitive photos such as these are the perfect currency for abuse, specifically propaganda. Indeed, this is not the first time a media outlet has done this. Regardless, the LA Times certainly placed their business interest above the country's security interest. U.S. Secretary of Defense Leon Panetta spoke on April 18 in a very sobering tone: "We had urged the LA Times not to run those photos. The reason for that is these kinds of photos are used by the enemy to incite violence. Lives have been lost as the result of publication of similar photos in the past. We regret that they were published."

A more troubling example of the release of documents of a national security concern is when the Obama administration released documents that embarrassed our country and virtually indicted it for Bush's hard line tactics to fight terrorism. Read an account of what happened on August 24, 2009:

> The federal government handed over to the American Civil Liberties Union dozens of documents from the Justice Department Office of Legal Counsel (OLC) related to torture under the Bush administration. The documents, which comprise hundreds of pages, were made public in response to two ACLU Freedom of Information Act (FOIA) lawsuits for documents related to the treatment of detainees in U.S. custody overseas." (Source is ACLU.org.)

The questions I hope you are asking yourself are: Why would citizens of the United States need to see publication of information that the CIA, pentagon and presidential administration would want to keep to themselves? Why would the President of the United States sacrifice his country's image before the world just to make a claim to "transparency?" One answer is that Obama and his team had a political motivation in this case to embarrass the Bush Administration and build a case that they were guilty of war crimes. The more general answer is that many citizens on the left traditionally don't trust decisions the U.S. makes regarding foreign policy. They therefore take pleasure in seeing the "powers-to-be" embarrassed and having their objectives foiled.

I believe this inclination began during the Vietnam era. The conflict became increasingly protracted as years passed and the country became split on whether we should pull out before our objective was accomplished. Emotional debates raged among the populous questioning the benefits of continuing a war that seemed only to be successful in bringing home body bags. Then, military actions taken such as the bombing in Cambodia was kept secret from the media until the leaks began. The CIA and other departments over the decades have been suspected of spinning their intelligence to reflect the President's agenda. After all, it was the CIA that advised the Bush administration to believe that Saddam Hussein was hiding weapons of mass destruction. Of course, this proved to be false. The Iraqi invasion was indeed another war that split the country in terms of support, and more distrust followed. Now that the U.S. is comprised of so many citizens from other countries that have a more international viewpoint on foreign policy decisions, I don't see this distrust for the government's foreign policy decisions ending anytime soon.

Behold the Poor Immigrant vs. Close the Borders

Give me your tired, your poor, your huddles masses yearning to be free, the wretched refuse of your teeming shore. Send these, the homeless, tempest-tost to me, I lift my lamp beside the golden door!

This insignia etched in stone at the base of the Statue of Liberty truly is poetic and tugs at emotional, patriotic heartstrings. Since all of us with the exception of Native Americans trace our roots back to immigrating ancestors, we all agree with the sentiment. However, immigration today is different now for many reasons. First, I want to say that I highly respect the honest, hard-working immigrants coming into this country. Nevertheless, I must write on the issues brought to the table by those who choose to arrive illegally.

The biggest difference between today's flood of immigrants and the days of Ellis Island is that most of it is done illegally. In the era of terrorism, the problem with letting in people from other countries without checking with the INS (Immigration and Naturalization Service) can lead to security issues, and it has. The trafficking of drugs and people at alarming rates over these borders has been occurring for decades. Criminal illegal immigrants have been committing violent crimes. Irresponsible illegal immigrants have been caught driving while intoxicated, injuring and killing Americans. Moreover, the issue that has become increasingly problematic is that we can no longer afford immigrants who don't pay income taxes but use government services. Many states like California have gone bankrupt because the cost of providing health care, education and other government services to illegal immigrants far outweighs the revenue from tax payers. Consider this extreme example of taxes being used to provide services that most would consider to be a bit over the top: A March 7, 2012 Newsmax website article said U.S. immigration officials were under orders "to provide abortion services for detained illegal aliens in some circumstances and hormone therapy to those who say they are transgendered."

Illegal immigration was once a minor issue in which the feds looked the other way as small businesses hired illegal workers willing to do tasks most Americans weren't. But it now has become the number one cause for many "border" states to bust their budget. Add to that all the money the feds are spending to keep the flow of incoming immigrants down. If there ever was an issue in America that took a 180-degree turn, this is it. Here are statistics to back up my comments regarding the crime, tax evasion and costs of the immigrants. The following ten facts were reported by the Los Angeles Times in 2010:

1. 40% of all workers in L. A. County are working for cash and not paying taxes. This is because they are predominantly illegal immigrants working without a green card.
2. 95% of warrants for murder in Los Angeles are for illegal aliens.
3. 75% of people in the most wanted list in Los Angeles are illegal aliens.
4. Over 2/3 of all births in Los Angeles County are to illegal aliens or Mexicans on "Medi-Cal," whose births were paid for by taxpayers.
5. Nearly 35% of all inmates in California detention centers are Mexican nationals here illegally.
6. Over 300,000 illegal aliens in Los Angeles County are living in garages.
7. The FBI reports half of all gang members in Los Angeles are most likely illegal aliens.
8. Nearly 60% of all occupants of HUD properties are illegal.
9. 21 radio stations in L. A. are Spanish speaking.
10. In L. A. County, 5.1 million people speak English, 3.9 million speak Spanish. (There are 10.2 million people in L.A. County.)

It has also been reported that less than two percent of illegal aliens are picking our crops, but 29% are on welfare. Over seventy percent of the United States annual population growth (and over ninety percent of California, Florida and New York) results from immigration. In addition, 29% of inmates in federal prisons are illegal aliens.

In 2011, Fox News reported the following statistics:

- There are 11.2 million illegal aliens in the United States.
- They comprise 5% of the labor work force.
- 57% of legal and illegal immigrant households used at least one welfare program in 2009. (Source: Center for Immigration Studies.)
- In 2010, authorities detained 445,000 aliens crossing the Mexican border.
- 59,000 immigrants came from countries other than Mexico, with some from the Middle East.
- The U.S. Border Patrol seized more than four million pounds of drugs coming across it in 2010 alone. They also seized 147 million in cash during the same time period.
- Only 650 miles of border are fenced with 1300 miles remaining open. Only 1200 National Guard troops back up the border patrol. (Some journalists and politicians believe at least 12,000 are needed.)

So, why doesn't our government resolve to close our porous borders? After all, there are fierce drug battles taking place along the Mexican border. The problem is that the Hispanic population of the United States, which has grown to be very large, is a significant potential block of voters. Conservatives argue the problem is that politicians didn't want to lose the Hispanic vote, as preventing their Mexican comrades from coming here is offensive.

Politically, Hispanics don't want to hear that the message Lady Liberty speaks doesn't apply to "illegal" immigrants. It took years for President Bush to finally assign 5,000 National Guard troops to patrol border areas that were fallen victim to crime. It would seem he didn't want to alienate the Hispanic vote during his 2004 re-election campaign. In fact, he outlined a plan in January 2004 to revamp the nation's immigration laws and allow illegal immigrants to obtain legal status as temporary workers. Regardless, the assignment of the National

Guard troops was effective where the men were stationed, so one could conclude that another 10,000 men would seal up the problem.

When President Obama came into office, he withdrew the National Guard troops. Politics strikes again. But after the state of Arizona started to become overwhelmed with the flow of immigrants, particularly from a security standpoint, Obama finally buckled under the pressure and assigned a measly 1,200 troops. This small amount was seen as only a token while those politicians serious about border patrol were calling for a troop presence ten times that.

The political wrinkle in 2011 regarding this issue that split liberals vs. conservatives is the controversial Arizona law that allowed the state and local police to detain suspected illegal aliens. The law only applied to those involved in a police matter already. In other words, the police cannot arbitrarily decide to detain someone simply based on the fact that someone looked Latino in skin-color. In fact, the federal laws regarding the detaining of suspected illegal immigrants are even stronger and stricter than the state's new law. So, the case cannot be made that those in Arizona advocating the law (such as sheriffs, police and citizens concerned for their security) are mean or bigoted, as the federal law is even more intrusive. Conservatives assert the Obama Administration wanted to be the only team that can play the game. However, the feds had been doing absolutely nothing in Arizona to keep the drug violence, car accidents and other crime near the border in check. Why not let the locals protect themselves? It's not as if they're going to send the feds a bill for services rendered. Larry Dever, the AZ Sherriff of Cochise County, went on Fox News in May of 2011 and said this:

> A lot of the crime is below the radar screen and not reported, not reflected by what Janet Napolitano (Director of Homeland Security) would have you believe when she says 'crime is down.' There are cut fences, water sources that are destroyed, livestock that dies from ingesting plastic bottles that are left behind and roadways that are damaged. There is a multi-million dollar fire still burning that has been set by drug and human smugglers. The same fire burned last year. This year's fire is called 'Horseshoe Fire 2.' There are murders, rapes and home invasions with homeowners being tied up. After

invaders deliver their contraband, they will often burglarize homes as they head back towards the border and they will steal guns, jewelry and cash. In spite of what is claimed by the administration, the border is more dangerous than it has ever been. A lot of fence is called 'Normandy fence.' It stops vehicles, but not people. There is fence called 'no-climb' fence, but experiments show it takes the average eighteen to twenty-five year-old male about fourteen seconds to climb it.

Even states that don't border another country are passing immigration laws. Georgia found they were spending $2.4 billion of their 18 billion dollar budget on issues regarding illegal immigration. The problem is that illegal immigrants were getting educated, but paying no taxes. They were using emergency rooms free and not paying for a health care plan. The Georgia law says:

- Employers have to check the applicant's immigration status when they are being considered for hire.
- A citizen is not permitted to transport an illegal immigrant after he/she commits a crime.
- Any illegal immigrant who uses false documentation to get a job is committing a crime subject to a severe penalty.

The feds are saying these laws might lead to racial profiling, but there haven't been any accusations of this on record since the police (at least in Arizona) have been using the laws to patrol. So, the racial profiling argument is not based on fact, but speculation. (Regardless, the Ninth Circuit Court upheld the "stay" on the Arizona law in 2011 pending further review. Then in June 2012, the Supreme Court ruled most of the legislation passed by border states as unconstitutional. See my remarks on this at the end of this section.) It is easy for someone comfortably removed from the local situation and not experiencing these problems to dismiss the urgency of it. The Attorney General and Democratic politicians in Washington, D.C. can for the sake of keeping to leftist ideology say that this law is offensive to minorities. However, until they live in the shoes of an Arizona resident by the border, they should defer to the state's judgment on this issue.

Consider the Secure Communities Program as reported by Fox News, also in May 2011:

It is a comprehensive federal plan to identify and remove criminal aliens from the community. It is based on the severity of the crimes they commit and are prioritized accordingly. This federally funded program is *not* optional. The program requires the cities to cooperate with the U.S. Immigration and Customs Enforcement (ICE), which locates and fingerprints undocumented aliens. In other words, when a local authority arrests an undocumented alien, they are required to send the fingerprints to the feds, who keep a fingerprint database. ICE pulls the records out of the computer system and then notifies the city and county authorities. They then may tell the city that they are putting a detainer (order to detain) on a specific alien who is being held in a local or county jail for a specific crime.

Here's the rub—many cities refuse to cooperate with this federal program. They are called "sanctuary cities." As an example, Michael Hennessey, Sheriff of San Francisco, is telling the feds he is not going to cooperate with them as San Francisco wants to remain a "sanctuary city." Isn't that lovely? A conservative's best guess for the reasoning is twofold: First, there's this link with the liberal philosophy of protecting minorities. Secondly, there is clear political motivation to get the Hispanic vote. To me, this is politics at its worse.

But the plot thickens and border states suffer a setback as the Supreme Court ruled in June 2012 that most of the teeth in the border states law are outside state rights parameters set forth in the Constitution. A one sentence synopsis of the ruling is that the states cannot by themselves enforce state-legislated immigration laws as this role is reserved for the feds; but that states can participate in processes pertaining to the verification of a person's immigration status (mostly because the states' participation in this comes from a federal edict to begin with.)

This ruling knocked the wind out of police personnel trying to protect citizens in their state who get no help from the feds in fighting illegal immigration crime.

A June 26 Fox News report released more disturbing news coming from the federal powers-to-be immediately after the Supreme Court ruling. The Obama Administration's reaction to the one ruling that held states could continue to verify immigration status for the purpose of sharing information with the feds was this: Homeland Security announced that it suspended its agreements with Arizona police regarding the detention and reporting of illegal aliens. The feds went on to detail that they will refuse to deport these individuals except under certain extreme circumstances, which are:

1.   The suspect has a felony record.
2.   The suspect has previously been removed from the country.
3.   The suspect is a recent border crosser.

This means that illegal immigrants who have been convicted of driving under the influence (DUI for both first and second offenses) in Arizona will no longer be subject to deportation as this crime is considered a misdemeanor. I was truly shocked and disturbed to see that the feds took this opportunity to renege on their own soft enforcement of the deportation of criminal illegal aliens. One could conclude that November is coming shortly and that this new stance by the Obama Administration to protect criminal illegal aliens smacks of "get the Latino vote" politics. Unfortunately, this new policy comes at the cost of putting at risk the personal safety of Americans who live by the borders.

Enhanced Image vs. Enhanced Interrogation

Left-wingers are the first to say that torture, being an immoral act, is not acceptable by a country such as ours that has the responsibility for moral leadership. "We are better than that," I've heard many news anchors on liberal news stations say. I believe most conservatives would agree that "torture," (the dictionary uses the words "pain," "anguish," and "grotesque" to define the word) should never be considered by U.S. interrogators. However, President Obama's administration asserts that "water-boarding" is torture. Most conservatives and many centrists disagree. Water-boarding has been demonstrated on television. It is the forcing of water into the throat until the person interrogated takes on the sensation of drowning. In fact, the U.S. military has used this process on their own recruits for training purposes. So, is it really so terrible to use water-boarding on a known terrorist who has taken many lives for no reason other than pure hate? Before you take a solid stance on this, pass the following test by applying the following scenario to your life. If you knew for a fact that enhanced interrogation by a known terrorist would lead to information that would save the life of a loved one, would you still be against it?

The fantasy that the Obama administration has about ruling out water-boarding is that the moral leadership image and moral credibility of the U.S. will be restored. It was Obama's hope the U.S. would receive more cooperation from NATO countries and other allies in our battle against terrorism if we fell in line with their moral standards. (It's easy for other countries to sit high in their tower of morality when they were not the ones that were attacked.) However, the record shows that there was absolutely no increase in the contribution other countries made as a result of Obama's "Apology Tour" and his actions to reverse Bush's hardline policies on terrorism.

Soft on Terrorism vs. Hard on Terrorism

We actually have three administrations to compare regarding their words and actions against Islamic terrorism. The first is Bill Clinton's, the second is George W. Bush's and the third is Barack Obama's. The Republican, right-wing administration led by Bush shows a record of being hard on terrorism. Obama's record of terrorism started out as one that appeared to be soft on terrorism, but ended up taking a hardline stance when it came to certain issues. You can review the facts soon and decide for yourself the answer to a question that I asked myself during the early Obama days: To what extent did Obama's initial rejection of hardline tactics by the Bush administration reverse the effectiveness of them? First, I will include a bit of historic recollection on how jihad started here.

Islamic terrorism against the U.S. began during the Clinton administration. The February 1993 attack on the World Trade Center

North Tower, intended to bring it down and crash it into the South Tower, killed six Americans. The captured terrorist responsible, Yousef, had previously made it clear through letters mailed to various New York newspapers that the attack on the World Trade Center would occur, with more to follow, if three demands were not met: an end to all U.S. aid to Israel, an end to U.S. diplomatic relations with Israel and a demand for a pledge by the United States to end interference "with any of the Middle East countries' interior affairs." The bombing occurred just weeks after President Clinton began his eight-year long administration in January of 1993. Subsequent to this, two successful bombings destroyed the U.S. embassies in Kenya and Tanzania in 1998. Then, the U.S.S Cole naval ship was the victim of a suicide bombing in October of 2000, killing seventeen sailors.

Most of us cannot know what the Clinton Administration actually did behind closed doors to react to these attacks. However, there was never any publicly known action that he took in response to these terrorist attacks. To his credit, President Clinton did sign an anti-terrorism law on April 1996. However, this was in response to the destruction of the federal building in Oklahoma City.

Clinton did order one highly publicized targeted bombing. It was to destroy a bomb/weapons factory in a Taliban country that the CIA had scoped out as an arsenal for the Islamic extremists. Clinton ordered it bombed the day after the Monica Lewinski story broke. Political opponents asserted that Clinton chose to bomb that day to distract the public from focusing on the eyebrow-raising sex scandal. Since civilian adults and children were killed in the bombing, reaction in the Arab world was raw outrage, understandably. At this early stage in the terror war, there was no apparent link to the world that seemed to justify the bombing by Clinton. Although the bombing may have been perfectly justifiable, it would appear the action was a sloppy beginning to the U.S. defending itself against Islamic terrorism.

Consider this: In the summer of 1995, Osama Bin Laden wrote a public Declaration of War against the U.S. He called for the war against the U.S. to evict U.S. troops from Saudi Arabia and intended to launch the battle from his base in Afghanistan. Michael Scheuer, the CIA Bin Laden chief from 1996-1999 said "it was pretty clear that

Bin Laden meant what he said, but it didn't catch much attention." Scheurer and other CIA agents who were interviewed on TV sometime after the Sep. 11 tragedy admitted that "the Islamic terrorist threat was not taken seriously enough to envision a successful attack that would finally take down the World Trade Center." To me, I find this mindset incredulous since there had already been four Al Qaeda terrorist attacks on Clinton's watch, all killing Americans. All of them were known to be perpetrated by Al Qaeda. It would appear that President Clinton and his administration virtually stood by as spectators as the momentum of terrorist activity built.

There were no real publicized initiatives or plans by Clinton to address this terrorist issue. No apparent changes were made in the way the CIA, FBI and other security organizations shared information. Numerous communications coming into these organizations warning them about upcoming terrorist attacks evidently were not taken seriously. No apparent changes in our politically correct environment here in the U.S. occurred even after four terrorist attacks. (The media referred to the 1993 World Trade Center bombing as a failure because the terrorists did not achieve their goal of toppling the building.) Regardless, Islamic terrorists continued to fly unimpeded into this country on regular commercial jetliners. In fact, when American flight instructors were asked to teach the terrorists how to fly these large aircraft without needing to know how to get them in the air or land them, the flight instructors obliged. I don't know whether it was because they were naïve or that no bells went off in their heads or it was just the nature of the politically correct environment. Nevertheless, I do know that the Clinton administration scores low points for dealing with terrorism. The fish rots from the head.

Political correctness was the main ingredient in the recipe for disaster that allowed the terrorist attack on September 11 to occur. Blindly sprinkle in the usual measure of naiveté and top it off with a deep layer of arrogance, and we baked in the inevitable.

Next, we have to tackle the handling of terrorism by President Obama as compared to President Bush. I'm going to achieve this simply by listing facts and let you take score on how tough Obama was on terrorism vs. George Bush. Even though this book is designed to have a right-wing tilt, I try to be fair as possible to show my viewpoints are factually based. History will show that Obama's actions on terrorism were eventually tougher than we all anticipated from his original stance on the issue. You'll see what I mean. Naturally, I'll start with a listing of facts on Bush's administrative actions towards terrorism:

- The Patriot Act was passed a month after the September 11 tragedy. It provided authorization to use enhanced surveillance procedures, ability to counter money laundering, amend bank secrecy regulations, establish as a felony questionable practices such as cash smuggling, ramp up border security, remove obstacles to investigating terrorism, increase information sharing, improve intelligence and strengthen the criminal laws against terrorism.
- Three terrorists were water-boarded during the Bush administration: Khalid Sheikh Mohammad (K.S.M.,) Abu Zubaydah and Abdol Rahim al Nashiri.
- There are six primary sources that are on record saying that CIA water-boarding led to information that thwarted terrorist activity and ultimately saved American lives. They are:
  o Donald Rumsfeld, former Secretary of Defense
  o Stephen Hadley, former National Security Advisor
  o Leon Panetta, CIA Chief
  o George Tenet, former CIA chief
  o Michael Hayden, former CIA chief
  o Jose Rodriquez, former CIA Counter Terrorism Chief

- Two examples of specific information gleaned from their enhanced interrogation are:
  o K.S.M., who was water-boarded, provided information that resulted in the rounding up of a network of South East Asia

terrorists that Umar Patek had pulled together in order to plan the attacks that occurred on September 11, 2001.

o A captured terrorist, who was subject to enhanced interrogation by the CIA, gave information that eventually led to tracking down the compound in Pakistan where Osama Bin Laden was hiding.

Former CIA Counter Terrorism Center Chief, Jose Rodriguez, Jr. appeared on Fox News in May, 2012 to present the book he wrote substantiating the value that *enhanced interrogation* brought to the CIA in the wake of the 9-11 tragedy. It is titled, *Hard Measures* and subtitled *How Aggressive CIA actions after 9-11 Saved American Lives.*

• The last fact on the list for Bush is simply that no terrorist attacks against our country occurred for the remainder of Bush's tenure.

I don't know of any facts that would show Bush was less than tough on terrorism. I will now present you with the facts detailing the most notable actions, events and record of President Obama's administration on terrorism. I will start with facts that show when he has been soft on terrorism (mostly at the earlier part of his administration) and then reveal facts later in his administration which I would consider to be harder on terrorism. I intentionally am listing them in a brief description to remain as objective as possible:

• Before Obama was elected, he promised to end torture, and said "he will return morality to the U.S." In Obama's inauguration speech, he was critical of Bush's hardline approach towards terrorism.
• President Obama's first order of business was to sign a document committing to the closing of Guantanamo Bay within exactly one year.
• On his second day in office, Obama eliminated the tool of waterboarding from the CIA's counter-terrorism arsenal.
• Two days after Obama was sworn into office, he signed an executive order that limited some ability of the rendition

procedure practiced by the Bush Administration. It used the phrase "rendition" to refer to the transfer of terrorists outside of their native country to a location outside of the U.S. to apprehend, detain and interrogate them. Entitled *Ensuring Lawful Interrogations*, the executive order called for more oversight of interrogation by third parties. The order *did* constrain some hardline activity practiced by the Bush Administration.

- Obama chose as his attorney general someone with a history of being soft on crime.
- Obama restructured the CIA to eliminate practices he viewed as too hardline. No one within the CIA organization was chosen as their new leader under Obama.
- Obama went on an "Apology Tour," which was mostly across Europe but also here in the U.S. and made ten speeches in which he criticized America's foreign policy and mistakes of the past. These critical and apologetic remarks are detailed in the next section on "Criticisms and Apologies for America." Many of his comments spoke of needed change which espoused a softer strategy on fighting terrorism.
- The Obama administration in 2009 handed over to the American Civil Liberties Union dozens of documents from the Justice Department Office of Legal Counsel (OLC) related to torture under the Bush administration. The action was intended to boast about the new "transparency" and "morality" he would bring to the administration. The act also embarrassed the Bush administration and helped build a case for "war crimes" that supposedly were committed during Bush's war on Islamic terror.
- Obama's administration, through his Attorney General Eric Holder, (whose background has shown a liberal view towards prosecution) began and persisted with an investigation of former President Bush and others in his administration of committing war crimes. The allegations were that the Bush administration had crossed legal lines in his pursuit to detain and interrogate known terrorists. Conversely, the rhetoric from those agreeing

with Bush's hardline tactics said Obama's actions were an ugly and unpatriotic, trumped-up witch-hunt.

- The application by a group of Muslims to erect a mosque and Islamic cultural center one block away from ground zero became controversial as it was viewed as insensitive to the families of 9-11. After all, it was Muslims that perpetrated the attack. Speculation became rampant that the Islamic center was, in the eyes of Muslims, a monument claiming conquer and victory that tradition dictates be built on or adjacent to the jihadist site. It was also rumored that the new building would be financed by Middle East jihadists supporting terrorism and that nefarious activities promoting and teaching Sharia Law would also take place in the building. Obama's only public comment on the controversy, which was at a Muslim function, was "that the Muslims had every right to build it." He followed up on this by adding, when questioned, "I am not going to comment on the appropriateness" of the intent to build a mosque. These limited comments by Obama were seen as a betrayal to those that were vehemently against the building of the mosque. They felt he "looked the other way."

- As of year-end 2011, the Obama Administration has not captured and detained a single high value terrorist detainee since he became president. He did order high profile Al-Qaeda operatives assassinated, but did not keep any for questioning or gathering information.

- Obama's administration made the decision early on to try the case against 9-11 mastermind Khalid Sheikh Mohammed (K.S.M.) and four other Al Qaeda terrorists in a *civilian* court rather than a military tribunal. (Curiously enough, Obama said he let his attorney general, Eric Holder, make the decision.) A civilian court would provide this terrorist responsible for the 9-11 tragedy with the same Constitutional rights as you and I if we were convicted of terrorism. This was cited by the right as an unprecedented action of being soft on the terrorists. Alternatively, the military tribunal would treat them as war prisoners from abroad. The rationale was that they were not

American citizens. Heretofore, an enemy combatant in a war zone had never been tried before in a civilian court in the history of the United States. The left-wingers did go on record as saying the civilian court decision would prove to the world how fair we are as Americans to give *everyone* the Constitutional rights we have.

The distinct advantage of the *military tribunal* is that this more private process would enable national security information to be shielded from the hungry and often irresponsible media. The right-wing thinking was that there was no upside for the *civilian trial.* The litigation procedure and the security to hold the civilian trial would reportedly cost $800 million dollars. In addition, because the civilian court proceedings are a public venue, the defending lawyers would grandstand the event into a propaganda tool so the Islamic viewpoint would be sufficiently aired by the media. The jihadist advocates would use the press to spew their hate against Americans. This is not just popular prediction. The lawyers for the defense openly declared they intended to put the United States on trial.

The p.s. to the story is that a hot, divisive debate in the media ensued about the issue and it appeared the Obama administration was losing significant political capital because of this decision. Here's a turn of events which gave many Americans some solace: The Obama administration eventually made the decision to try the five terrorists in a military tribunal as traditional practice dictates.

- A Muslim U.S. Army Major flipped out in November, 2009 and went on a shooting rampage, killing thirteen soldiers at Fort Hood, TX. All of the details of the shooting clearly indicated it was a planned Islamic jihad. Obama infuriated at least half the country for refusing to acknowledge Islamic terrorism even had a role in the shooting, but instead used "protective" language saying the motive was still under investigation. The question that many asked was, "How can Obama protect us against Islamic terrorism if he refuses to even identify it when it happens?"

- Late in his tenure, Obama sought to negotiate with the Afghanistan Taliban by releasing five Taliban leaders in accordance with certain steps designed to further "peace talks." The traditional wisdom is that negotiating with the enemy is a position of weakness.

Okay, let's switch the set of facts from soft on terrorism to hard. I pride myself on being fair, so here is the set of the most notable, major facts on the Obama being tough on terrorism:

- As I mentioned, the Obama administration *reversed* its decision to try the terrorists responsible for the 9-11 tragedy here in the U.S. As a result, they would not receive U.S. Constitutional rights.
- Obama never closed Guantanamo Bay. Critics say he couldn't close it because he simply was never able to obtain an alternative location to detain the Al Qaeda terrorists.
- Obama authorized the assassination of many terrorist leaders, most notably Osama Bin Laden.
- Obama authorized the killing of terrorists by drones in areas such as Pakistan.
- Obama's administration did in fact extend Bush's hardline Patriot Act when the act came up for renewal in March of 2011. This legislative action did not occur completely without controversy or dissent as many liberal critics were complaining during the Obama administration that some provisions of the Patriot Act could compromise individual privacy.
- Obama extended the war in Afghanistan despite calls from the left to end it immediately. On the other hand, the generals and conservatives thought he cut back on the campaign earlier than needed. This issue has questionable weight on being hard on terrorism as Obama struck a compromise on both the number of troops in the campaign as well as with the withdraw schedule.

There are fourteen facts listed showing him being "soft" on terrorism and six listed showing him "tough," although some of these six would be disputed by conservatives as to what extent they were in his favor.

These facts are only those most notable and by no means are a complete list. Naturally, some facts have more "weight" and "significance" than others, but you can determine how much and score Obama on how soft he was on fighting terrorism.

We certainly can say the actions he took against terrorists after being the President for a year or two certainly showed a substantial turn-around in posture as compared to the days before and immediately after he became President. One of the lessons that can be learned by liberals regarding this metamorphic change in Obama's tactics on fighting Islamic terrorism is this: Most of us cannot make an accurate assessment on the morality of tactics to fight terrorism until we have an intimate knowledge about it. I contend that security briefings provided to the President on a daily basis (that we don't have as citizens) contributed to a realization about the horrors of terrorism many of us can't conceive from our sheltered worlds. Although there is temptation for many of us to sit high on moral ground about issues on terrorism, I contend it emanates from a distant, less informed perspective. I believe that the closer one gets to the devastation of terrorism (like President Bush in the middle of ground zero rubble on 9-11,) the more one realizes the moral advantage is on the side of the victims and not the perpetrators.

Critique and Apologize for America vs. Promote America

> **"We must be ready to dare all for our country, for history does not long entrust the care of freedom to the weak or the timid."**
> **– President Eisenhower**

When President Obama went abroad to reach out to other states after being elected, he conducted what conservative pundits call his "Apology Tour." Obama had little idea of the resulting reverberations that would occur in the political world back in the states. In fact, former Republican presidential contender Mitt Romney answered Obama's words with a counter strike of his own by penning a book titled, "No Apology." The book was a promotion of traditional American values in contrast to Obama's appeal to state leaders. Here's the list of "apologies" to which I'm referring, assembled by the Heritage Foundation:

1. Apology to France and Europe (*there have been times where America has shown arrogance and been dismissive, even derisive,*) President Obama, Rhenus Sports Arena, Strasbourg, France, April 3, 2009.

2. Apology to the Muslim World (*We sometimes make mistakes. We have not been perfect,*) President Obama, interview with *Al Arabiya,* January 27, 2009.

3. Apology to the Summit of the Americas (*we have at times been disengaged and at times we sought to dictate our terms. But I pledge to you that we seek an equal partnership. There is no senior partner and junior partner in our relations,*) President Obama, address to the Summit of the Americas opening ceremony, Hyatt Regency, Port of Spain, Trinidad and Tobago, April 17, 2009.

4. Apology at the G-20 Summit of World Leaders (*I would like to think that with my election and the early decisions that we've made, that you're starting to see some restoration of America's standing in the world,*) News conference by President Obama, ExCel Center, London, United Kingdom, April 2, 2009.

This next one is so egregious, I pasted in his entire, almost treasonous, criticism:

5. Apology for the War on Terror (*We Went off Course,*) President Obama, speech at the National Archives, Washington, D.C., May 21, 2009.
    Unfortunately, faced with an uncertain threat, our government made a series of hasty decisions. I believe that many of these decisions were motivated by a sincere desire to protect the American people. But I also believe that all too often our government made decisions based on fear rather than foresight—that all too often our government trimmed facts and evidence to fit ideological predispositions. Instead of strategically applying our power and our principles, too often we set those principles aside as luxuries that we could no longer afford. And during this season of fear, too many of us—Democrats and Republicans, politicians, journalists and citizens—fell silent.

In other words, we went off course. And this is not my assessment alone. It was an assessment that was shared by the American people who nominated candidates for president from both major parties who, despite our many differences, called for a new approach—one that rejected torture and one that recognized the imperative of closing the prison at Guantanamo Bay.

The next two are when he declares the U.S. will go soft on interrogation procedures:

6. Apology for Guantanamo in France (*Sacrificing Your Values,*) President Obama, Rhenus Sports Arena, Strasbourg, France, April 3, 2009

   Our two republics were founded in service of these ideals. In America, it is written into our founding documents as "life, liberty and the pursuit of happiness." In France: "Liberté"—absolutely— "egalité, fraternité." Our moral authority is derived from the fact that generations of our citizens have fought and bled to uphold these values in our nations and others. And that's why we can never sacrifice them for expedience's sake. That's why I've ordered the closing of the detention center in Guantanamo Bay. That's why I can stand here today and say without equivocation or exception that the United States of America does not and will not torture.

   In dealing with terrorism, we can't lose sight of our values and who we are. That's why I closed Guantanamo. That's why I made very clear that we will not engage in certain interrogation practices. I don't believe that there is a contradiction between our security and our values. And when you start sacrificing your values, when you lose yourself, then over the long term that will make you less secure.

7. Apology before the Turkish Parliament (*Our Own Darker Periods in Our History,*) President Obama to the Turkish Parliament, Ankara, Turkey, April 6, 2009.

   That's why, in the United States, we recently ordered the prison at Guantanamo Bay closed. That's why we prohibited—without exception or equivocation—the use of torture. All of us have to change. And sometimes change is hard. Another issue that confronts all democracies as they move to the future is how we deal with the past. The United States is still working through some of our own darker periods in our history.

8. Apology for U.S. Policy toward the Americas (*Too often, the United States has not pursued and sustained engagement with our neighbors. We have been too easily distracted by other priorities and have failed to see that our own progress is tied directly to progress throughout the Americas. My Administration is committed to the promise of a new day.*) Opinion editorial by President Obama: "Choosing a Better Future in the Americas," April 16, 2009.

9. Apology for the Mistakes of the CIA (*Potentially We've Made Some Mistakes,*) President Obama to CIA employees, CIA Headquarters, Langley, Virginia, April 20, 2009. The remarks followed the controversial decision to release Office of Legal Counsel memoranda detailing CIA enhanced interrogation techniques used against terrorist suspects. *So don't be discouraged by what's happened in the last few weeks. Don't be discouraged that we have to acknowledge potentially we've made some mistakes. That's how we learn. But the fact that we are willing to acknowledge them and then move forward, that is precisely why I am proud to be President of the United States and that's why you should be proud to be members of the CIA.*

In this last one, Obama truly put the U.S.A. on trial and declared it guilty:

10. Apology for Guantanamo in Washington (*A Rallying Cry for Our Enemies,*) President Obama, speech at the National Archives, Washington, D.C., May 21, 2009.
There is also no question that Guantanamo set back the moral authority that is America's strongest currency in the world. Instead of building a durable framework for the struggle against al Qaeda that drew upon our deeply held values and traditions, our government was defending positions that undermined the rule

of law. In fact, part of the rationale for establishing Guantanamo in the first place was the misplaced notion that a prison there would be beyond the law—a proposition that the Supreme Court soundly rejected. Meanwhile, instead of serving as a tool to counter terrorism, Guantanamo became a symbol that helped al Qaeda recruit terrorists to its cause. Indeed, the existence of Guantanamo likely created more terrorists around the world than it ever detained.

So the record is clear: Rather than keeping us safer, the prison at Guantanamo has weakened American national security. It is a rallying cry for our enemies.

When I did my research on this topic, I was shocked to find out just how extensive and how critical Obama was of our national history and our efforts to combat terrorism. Does he realize that he not only was apologizing to heads of state that he was trying to curry favor with, he was apologizing to the world and to our enemies for killing us? Think about it. It's as if he is saying, "We're sorry our foreign policies have been so bad that you had to resort to killing us."

The primary point that Obama wasn't getting is that any nation in this doggy dog world, especially the most powerful and influential one, needs as much political capital as possible to advance its agenda onto other heads of state by edifying its image and credibility, not compromising it. Whether one is selling himself, a car, a piece of legislation or one's country, the way **not** to do it is to criticize past performance and past relations; and position yourself as someone who needs to apologize for and make amends for the sins the last guy committed.

The perception on the right is that Obama suffered from the notion that being humble, likeable and making a human connection was the key to forming the relations necessary to do business. Conservatives, however, believe that school is out at this level and what may have worked for Obama from kindergarten through twelfth grade is not the strategy for dealing with the likes of Mahmoud Ahmadinejad, Dmitry Medvedev, Hu JIntao' and Kim Jong Il (who died in 2011 and was replaced by his son in 2012. The aforementioned are leaders of Iran, Russia, China and North Korea, respectively.) Here's a quick example of what I'm talking about—one that drew intense criticism on Obama's style of ambassadorship by giving away the house.

> In September, 2009, Obama decided to scrap a missile-defense agreement that the Bush Administration negotiated with Poland and the Czech Republic… to accommodate the U.S., which wanted the system to defend against a possible Iranian missile attack." (Journalists and many pundits believed that the Obama administration's) "…motive for scrapping the interceptors is that it hopes to win Russia's vote at the U.N. Security Council for tougher sanctions on Iran. Maybe the Russians have secretly agreed to such a quid pro quo, though publicly they were quick to deny it following yesterday's decision. (Wall Street Journal Review and Outlook website.)

So, Obama's strategy of being generous, accommodating and genial in his approach didn't work with the Russians this time around, and all other facts show it hasn't worked at all. Obama never even attempted to negotiate with the Russians on this issue. His attempts to placate them in advance with excessive generosity left Obama with nothing to show in return. These heads of state play hardball and are advised by the fiercest, toughest negotiators they can find. They know the U.S. is the biggest player militarily and economically and can call the shots at the negotiating table if need be. But the U.S. can only take advantage of its strength if and only if the country is led by someone who understands its power and is willing to come away with nothing less than the maximum it can obtain. You can't be the strongest leader if you are making apologies for past performance or past offenses.

Appeasement and Ambassadorship vs. Position of Strength

Obama has been a weak leader in responding to the actions of Iran, who has been a major force behind the Islamic terrorist war against this country. The following facts serve as a group of examples to underscore my criticisms of Obama's weakness in his resolve to act in America's interest. First, here's some background information on Iran (compliments of Fox News:)

- The Iranians have been manufacturing "Improvised Explosive Device" (I.E.D.'s) and providing them to their users since the beginning of the Islamic war on the U.S.
- They have been directly killing troops in Iraq and Afghanistan.
- They have been fighting "proxy" wars by funding Hezbollah (anti-Israel, anti-U.S. terrorist organization - a Shi'a Muslim militant group and political party based in Lebanon) and Humas (Islamic Resistance Movement founded to liberate Palestine from Israeli occupation) and other terrorist groups.
- They have been pursuing nuclear weapons for years.
- They have promised to wipe Israel off the face of the earth once they have obtained them.
- In 2011, Iranians were caught planning assassinations while on U.S. soil.

Now consider the following scenario: Heretofore, international sanctions have been in place against Iran, designed to punish and retard their pursuit of nuclear weapons. Here's what happened at the end of 2011 as detailed by "The Hindu" website in their Dec. 29th article:

> Apparently fearful of the expanded sanctions' possible impact on the already-stressed economy of Iran, the world's third-largest energy exporter, Mr. Rahimi (a senior Iranian official) said, "If they impose sanctions on Iran's oil exports, then even one drop of oil cannot flow from the Strait of Hormuz," according to Iran's official news agency. Iran just began a ten-day naval exercise in the area.

So Iran was sending a signal they were preparing for inevitable confrontation and that they were threatening to block the Strait of Hormuz to prevent oil barges from coming in to get oil. Here's the telling part of the story: Obama's response to this message from Iran was to cancel U.S./Israel military exercises to preclude the possibility of provoking the Iranians, according to Fox News Analyst Karl Rove. When Republican presidential contender Newt Gingrich commented on Obama's actions regarding this incident in February 2012, he said it was "beyond timid." He likened it to giving in to a bully's demands, which only results in strengthening the bully's resolve. Newt quoted Winston Churchill, who said the following in the 1930s, "If you feed the crocodiles, eventually the crocodile eats you." Presidential contender Mitt Romney said that if he were the President, he would have responded by sending anti-aircraft ships to the strait to send a message of strength. Romney said "Weakness always begets adventurism by the world's worst actors." Romney continued, "Obama asserted Obama's policies tend to be one of appeasement and accommodation. During his first year in office, he wanted to meet with Ahmadinejad [Iran's head of state] when even Ahmadinejad didn't want to meet."

Here is another example of what conservatives would consider to be both a weak and poor strategic position against an enemy: Fox News reported in early 2012 that five Taliban leaders currently residing in Guantanamo Bay are scheduled to be released soon. As of February 2012, the Obama administration was planning on allowing the release in accordance with conditional steps designed to further peace talks with the Afghanistan Taliban. Wait a second— peace talks with a group that supported the 9-11 attack? You decide what word to describe this kind of foreign policy. The presiding wisdom always has been that a strong leader does not negotiate with the enemy. Newt Gingrich said this about the latest wrinkle in Obama's ambassadorship with our Islamic opponents: "I think you have a pro-Islamic administration that is on every front trying to appease people who are enemies." I think it is also appropriate at this point to quote Romney's succinctly stated stance on foreign policy: "We want to be so strong and have a military so capable and a President so committed to American strength, that no one would ever test our resolve."

End War in Afghanistan vs. Continue War in Afghanistan

"We won the war (in Afghanistan) in 2002. We've lost the peace. And we've lost it by setting ridiculously ambitious goals by trying to turn it into a 'little America.' We have been there for over eleven years, have spent countless billions, given a lot of blood and General Allen, our commander in Afghanistan, could not walk down the street of a single Afghan city today unarmed and survive." These are the words of retired Lt. Colonel Ralph Peters, Fox News Strategic Analyst, on Feb. 28, 2012.

To me, this says it all about our protracted involvement in what I consider to be another Vietnam. Don't get me wrong. I agreed with the initial invasion, the destruction of Al Qaeda training camps and the pursuit of the terrorists who were planning on more jihadist plots. But I am in good company with objection to continued nation-building after our primary goals were achieved. Various internet sources tell us:

> The U.S. and British Special Forces ousted the Taliban regime from power in Kabul and most of Afghanistan in a matter of weeks and that most of the senior Taliban leadership fled to neighboring Pakistan. Then, the International Security Assistance Force (ISAF) was established by the UN Security Council at the end of December 2001 to secure Kabul and the surrounding areas. NATO assumed control of ISAF in 2003. (ISAF includes troops from 42 countries, with NATO members providing the core of the force.) Subsequently, the Democratic Islamic Republic of Afghanistan was established and an interim government under Hamid Karzai was created, which was also democratically elected by the Afghan people in the 2004 general elections.

And the achievement of overseeing the 2004 general election is where we should have ended our involvement there. After accomplishing the objectives stated above, it would have been prudent to make a timely exit. I know hindsight is always 20-20, but it would appear we didn't study the history of Afghanistan before we invaded it to learn some lessons. For example, did you know that Afghanistan was in a civil war involving the Taliban from 1996-2001? Did we take a close look at this to see what kind of political strife we would entangle ourselves in? Lt. Colonel Peters continued his commentary in 2012: "Ten years—We cannot get the Afghans to fight for the Karzai government and they won't fight for us...In Afghanistan, we've won every engagement on the ground. It doesn't matter. The people don't want our way of life."

Colonel Peters's sentiments are echoed almost exactly by another expert in this field, retired Colonel David Hunt, Fox News Military Analyst.

> In Afghanistan, once we took the country and it turned into
> a counter insurgency, you can't define it by win or lose and
> right now, we're not having success. (He made his comments
> also on Feb. 28, 2012.) The people are afraid the Taliban are
> going to kill them. It is not a safe country yet and it won't
> be for another ten years. It evolved into this democracy-
> building business and peacekeeping, which we don't do very
> well....We've spent billions of dollars and lost a lot of guys.
> The success rate is not good.

Can either of us argue with the experts? If a sitting President doesn't understand that the current military leadership is always going to be in favor of military involvement and skew the evidence in favor thereof, then the President is too inexperienced for the job. He has to be prepared to counter the military agenda and to lead the country in an opposite direction if need be. I speak of Bush as well as Obama, as the U.S. should have foreseen the end to our involvement long before Obama took office. But Obama could have ended the Afghanistan war much sooner, so four more years of that war are on his head. Leadership by both Presidents was weak on this issue. I'll never forget a lesson I learned in college about what Vietnam taught us: "You don't try to fix a political problem with a military solution."

Here's just one example of what I mean: "In October 2008, Defense Secretary Gates asserted that a political settlement with the Taliban was the endgame for the Afghan conflict." Now, think about this. Our defense secretary was saying that after seven years of U.S. presence in Afghanistan, the eventual goal will be to negotiate with the group that supported the Sep.11 attack on us. I don't think Americans were aware of how extreme our agenda was in Afghanistan. I know I didn't and I watch the news on TV every night. After researching Afghanistan to write this section, I became amazed at our insistence on staying in a place where death is the only certainty. The raw statistics say it all: We lost about 3,000 soldiers and will have spent about half a trillion dollars there. Wasn't our involvement in Afghanistan supposed to prevent another tragedy on the scale of Sept. 11, not re-create one of equal proportions?

I placed "Continue War in Afghanistan" in the conservative column because most conservatives view it as a war to counter Islamic terrorism. Conversely, most liberals wanted the war in Afghanistan to end years ago. My personal opinion on this issue is different from most conservatives. One of the hallmarks of conservatism is advocating a strong military. A conservative may agree with this doctrine but could be against the Vietnam War and against the Iraqi invasion. A conservative could agree with the initial invasion of Afghanistan but see the widespread, protracted nation-building there as a bad idea. They could concur it would be better to limit strikes *only* to targeted operations such as the Drone attacks against Al Qaeda operatives in Pakistan. Many of today's pundits would say such a view is embraced more by a Democrat than a Republican. This is true. But a ten-year presence in Afghanistan with a failed policy of nation building translates to more government as a tremendous amount of money and soldiers' lives are being squandered to force change in another country. More government is a left-wing philosophy. A much more limited military campaign that uses less government resources and saves soldiers' lives espouses a ***true*** right-wing philosophy. Former congressional representatives and 2012 Republican presidential candidate Ron Paul claims to be very right-wing and espouses no intervention outside of imminent threat. He believes in the formula: (conservatism) = (less government) = (spending less money on war).

I believe the conservative powers-to-be in this country would do well to recognize that excessive military intervention is, academically, a left-wing tendency. In its heyday of military intervention and expansion, the U.S.S.R.'s government was left-wing communist. Their overemphasis on putting resources into military power contributed to their economic collapse. In fact, the U.S.S.R.'s fall from power as a bi-polar military force began with *their* invasion of Afghanistan. (Is that not an omen?) The first summarizing sentence of a 1995 article from the University of Michigan supports my comment, "The Soviet Union invaded Afghanistan in December 1979. It was the last hot war it would fight and one whose failure played a leading role in its loss of the Cold War and disintegration."

A strong military will become much weaker by putting too many soldiers in harm's way and by draining the monetary and personnel resources of this country. We need to keep the military prepared to defend itself against direct threats going forward. Teddy Roosevelt said, "Speak softly and carry a big stick." This philosophy serves to keep our military strong. The limiting of military intervention is in keeping with right-wing philosophy.

> **Life is precious and it is precious equally among both the military and civilians alike.**

4.

The Legal Left vs. The Legal Right

Obamacare Constitutional vs.
Required Coverage Unconstitutional

THE LEGAL AND journalism world went into virtual shock at the end of June 2012 when Chief Justice John Roberts decided to vote in favor of upholding the constitutionality of Obamacare's mandate to require mandatory participation among all citizens. His deciding vote resulted in maintaining the constitutionality of Obamacare by 5-4. If he had voted with the 4 other justices honoring traditional constitutional beliefs, the President's signature legislation would have been rendered as virtually impossible to implement without re-legislating it. Those familiar with the Supreme Court correctly predicted 4 out of 9 justices with a history of left leaning voting patterns would vote that the Obamacare participation requirement was constitutional; as a nod in favor certainly would be consistent with increased federal government power. But no one predicted Roberts, who did not have a history of leftist opinions or creative legislating from the bench, to cast a history-making vote to uphold the legislation. Some journalists speculate Roberts didn't want the Supreme Court to be the bad guy in dismantling Obamacare. In other words, they thought Roberts decided he would let the chips fall where they may as election 2012 and the aftermath thereof would be the true democratic process to make or break the Obama tenure legislation. There is some merit in this thinking, as his actions bounced the power to decide the fate of Obama care back to the people and their representatives in Congress. But a justice has to abandon his principles when playing "king." A piece of legislation is either constitutional or not; and the politics surrounding its fate should be irrelevant in determining its constitutional status.

Here's my interpretation on how the right side sees it: The facts of the case brought before the Supreme Court is that Obamacare requires mandatory health coverage for everyone in order to generate enough premiums to pay for the additional benefits the legislation covers. Those who don't buy health insurance and remain uncovered will now have to pay a fine, which presumably will be used to help pay for the coverage. This means the federal government will be fining citizens for not buying a product offered by the private sector. Those on the right say this requirement is unconstitutional as it is an unprecedented infringement on the people's freedom to choose whether or not they wish to buy an insurance product. Don't confuse this government mandate with a requirement to buy liability insurance when you opt to exercise a privilege such as driving an automobile on government built roads. The Obamacare mandate makes you pay the government funds it needs for a certain program even if you opt out.

Here's what Roberts did: First, he re-wrote Obamacare legislation to say the charge for not buying into it was a "tax," not a fine. This action right here is in itself unconstitutional. It is not within the Supreme Court's authority to re-write legislation so it can fit it into a constitutional framework. It is Congress's job to do that. Then, Roberts used the power of the Congress to "tax" the people as the basis for casting the deciding vote. However, the remaining 4 out of 4 justices without a history of left leaning opinions vehemently disagreed with *how* he used Congress's power to tax. I say this is also an invalid twist on the word "tax." The government can tax you on the money you make and how you spend it, but never before have they "taxed" you for *not* buying something. This is not a *tax*. You might say "a rose is a rose by any other name," but Supreme Court Justice John Roberts obviously attaches legal concepts to words. He had to change the Obamacare wording from "fine" to "tax" to convert the law to a constitutional one (in the majority opinion.)

At what point do we stop becoming a country of freedoms and start becoming a socialist leaning society? This is that milestone. The line in the sand has been crossed and the word "freedom" on the right side of it has been trampled on by left feet. When I listened to those patriotic songs sung on TV by superstars and the audience alike on July 4th, 2012, (just days after this decision,) a question mark registered in my head every time the word "freedom" was mentioned. I was thinking about how the concept of "freedom" had already been watered down by leftist ideals over recent decades; and now the Obamacare Supreme Court decision had tipped the "freedom vs. government control" seesaw into what could now be graphed out as a sliding board.

The ramifications are this: If the government can tell its citizens it has to buy an insurance product from the private sector, where will this newly established precedent stop? Chapters 5 and 6 have a theme that is consistently woven among all of the analysis of Supreme Court cases; and it is this: If there is one result that proved to be consistent over decades of Supreme Court decisions, it is that established precedents continue to be stretched and mangled by creative justices so they can be used as a basis for breaking new legal ground into leftist territory. Be frightened of what can come next.

More Gun Control vs. Less Gun Control

The slogan that says, "Guns don't kill people; people kill people" is so true. If there were no guns, those intent on killing would just use another method. My first topic item is to address the fears that liberals have about the accidental deaths that could result from gun ownership.

Consider a fun fact comparison courtesy of the U.S. Department of Health and Human Services that puts this concern into perspective. We could call it "Doctors vs. Gun Owners." The number of physicians in the U. S. is 700,000. The number of accidental deaths caused by physicians per year is 120,000. That calculates to an accidental death rate per physician of 0.171, or 1.7 accidental deaths for every 10 physicians. Now let's look at the comparable set of statistics for gun owners courtesy of the FBI.

The number of gun owners in the U.S. is an estimated 80 million. The number of accidental gun deaths per year is about 1,500. Therefore, the number of accidental deaths from gun owners per year is .0000188. This equates to 1.88 accidental deaths per 100,000 gun owners. This means doctors are approximately 9,000 times more likely to kill someone than gun owners. The tongue in cheek slogan to conclude from this reality is that "Guns Don't Kill People; Doctors Do." (Physicians, please note I realize you save a whole lot more lives than those that slip through the cracks. I intend no offense.)

Gun control is a misunderstood issue because the policies that exist in our country can be either too restrictive or extremely permissive, depending on the location. Consider these scenarios:

- In Washington, D.C., a retired man living in a crime-ridden neighborhood could not get a gun to protect himself in his own home. He had to sue because of the strict gun control laws there, but won a victory in 2010 to get the rights to buy a gun.
- Contrast this with the laws in Virginia where the limit on purchasing guns is as liberal as one gun a week. Someone there could accumulate an arsenal at the rate of 52 weapons per year.
- Here is another story that is not about gun control, but about the use of guns. A few years ago, a Texan shot and killed a burglar running away outside with stolen goods, even though they were not from the home of the gun owner. The local authorities acquitted the gun owner of all charges.

These facts and stories above all have something extreme about them. Whereas I am in favor of more states rights than federal control, it seems that gun legislation varies greatly from state to state.

The liberal penchant for reducing the amount of guns that are obviously meant to be collectors' items is also out of whack. A May 15, 2012 Newsmax website flash reported:

> In a move unprecedented (at no time in U.S. history has the ownership of these firearms been illegal, restricted or banned in American history,) the Obama Administration quietly

banned the re-importation of nearly 600,000 American made M1 Carbine rifles...The M1 rifle, developed in the late 1930s, carried the United States through World War II seeing action in every major battle... The M1's caliber or capacity is no more dangerous than the millions of modern firearms owned by Americans across the country today, so there can be no rationale that the arms are more powerful than what's out there already... President Obama may be blocking as many as 300,000 1911 Colts as well.

Go figure.

I think most people believe everyone without a criminal record should be able to keep a gun in their home. I also agree with the majority of states that all citizens should have a right to carry a gun as they walk down the street to defend themselves against muggers. When I researched state laws regarding the right to carry, I was pleased to find out that all but three States and D.C. allow a permit to carry a weapon; or have policies that are "may issue" or "shall issue" carry permits with some restrictions and/or qualifications. On the other end of the spectrum; Illinois, Hawaii, and Vermont are "no carry issue" states. According to the latest 2 Supreme Court decisions upholding our second amendment, these three states are denying their citizens their constitutional privileges:

> *District of Columbia v. Heller*, 554 U.S. 570 (2008,) was a landmark case in which the Supreme Court of the United States held that the Second Amendment to the United States Constitution protects an individual's right to possess a firearm for traditionally lawful purposes in federal enclaves, (case ruled on Washington, DC jurisdiction) such as self-defense within the home. It was the first Supreme Court case in United States history to decide whether the Second Amendment protects an individual right to keep and bear arms. The decision did not address the question of whether the Second Amendment extends beyond federal enclaves to the states, which was addressed later by *McDonald v. Chicago* (2010.) (Source: Washington Post Retrieved 2010-02-19)

The *McDonald v. Chicago* case did in fact "extend the right to keep and bear arms to the states." (Source: *The Christian Science Monitor* 2010-03-01.)

For the purpose of highlighting the impact of *District of Columbia v. Heller*, I thought it was both interesting and important to note the following excerpts from the decision:

> The operative clause's text and history demonstrate that it connotes an individual right to keep and bear arms... The Antifederalists feared that the Federal Government would disarm the people in order to disable this citizens' militia, enabling a politicized standing army or a select militia to rule. The response was to deny Congress power to abridge the ancient right of individuals to keep and bear arms, so that the ideal of a citizens' militia would be preserved.

It is almost inconceivable to me that, prior to these recent 2008 and 2010 Supreme Court clarifications, many citizens in this country were being denied the right that was given to us from the outset by the second amendment which plainly said "the right of the people to keep and bear Arms, shall not be infringed." Now that the modern day Supreme Court has reinforced second amendment rights with the above 2 cases, there is currently national legislation on the table to allow states to engage in reciprocal "carry" privileges. It would establish the interstate recognition of concealed carry permits in much the same way driver's licenses are recognized. The bill titled the "National Right to Carry Reciprocity Act" was passed by the House of Representatives 272-154 in November 2011. (Source: Freedomfest news article on November 16, 2012.)

Second Amendment advocates are hoping for a Senate approval in 2012; although there is the obstacle of an anti-Second Amendment President. I believe I can objectively label our leader in the Oval Office as such as I list facts regarding Obama's record on gun control as reported by "Front Lines" website on Jan. 16, 2012:

- Voted for an Illinois State Senate bill to ban and confiscate "assault weapons," but the bill was so poorly crafted, it would have also banned most semi-auto and single and double barrel shotguns commonly used by sportsmen.

- Voted to allow reckless lawsuits designed to bankrupt the firearms industry.
- Has endorsed a 500% increase in the federal excise tax on firearms and ammunition.
- Has endorsed a complete ban on handgun ownership.
- Supports local gun bans in Chicago, Washington, D.C. and other cities.
- Voted to uphold local gun bans and the criminal prosecution of people who use firearms in self-defense.
- Was a member of the Board of Directors of the Joyce Foundation, the leading source of funds for anti-gun organizations and research.
- Supported a proposal to ban gun stores within five miles of a school or park, which would eliminate almost every gun store in America.
- Supported a ban on inexpensive handguns.
- Supported a ban on the resale of police issued firearms, even if the money is going to police departments for replacement equipment.

Regardless, we're pretty close to getting this country where it needs to be with Second Amendment rights. (At the very least, three more states need to get on board with "carry permits" and we need legislation to reverse President Obama's decision to deny gun collectors the rights to pursue their hobby.) I once had a friend who owned and carried a .38 caliber pistol. He called it his "equalizer." Hmm. Don't we all agree with the concept of "equal opportunity?"

Protect Voting Rights vs. Require ID at the Ballot Box

ID card or not—that is the name of the card game. Indeed, the democrats are against proposed legislation requiring an ID card to confirm a voter's identification at the ballot box. They contend such state-sponsored legislation is un-American in that it discourages voters from participating in Election Day. Democrats contend the cost and hassle to obtain the appropriate ID card will result in many qualified, likely voters from exercising their privilege. Predictably, a probable loss of votes for those on the Democratic ticket would result.

On the other hand, Republicans typically back voter identification laws. It would seem the push for some states to pass new legislation picked up steam during the 2008 voter registration fraud accusations toward ACORN. (The Association of Community Organizations for Reform Now was a collection of community-based organizations in the United States that advocated for low and moderate-income families by working on neighborhood safety, voter registration, health care, affordable housing and other social issues. The organization is now defunct.) Those working for ACORN were reportedly a little too zealous in getting out the democratic vote in 2008 by fraudulently registering dead people and many other voters multiple times.

> It was estimated by Project Vote that 400,000 registrations collected by ACORN were ultimately rejected, the vast majority for being duplicate registrations submitted by citizens (which is also common at government voter registration services according to reports on the National Voter Registration Act by the U.S. Election Assistance Commission.) An unknown number of registrations were fraudulent, but Project Vote estimated that only a few percent were, based on past years and samples from some drives in 2008. (Source: Miami Herald, 2008-10-24)

Regardless of how many voter registrations *were* a result of fraud, the requirement of an ID at the ballot box is a hot issue. For example, two state circuit judges in Dane County, Wisconsin blocked the ID requirement provisions of that state's law in 2012 based on constitutional grounds. Each state can determine its own laws regarding identification needs at the ballot box and evidently the judges therein can interpret them as they see fit.

The first Voter ID laws passed in 2003. As of March 2012, thirty-one U.S. states required some form of photo or non-photo identification. In the spirit of giving the liberal view on this topic voice, I provide the following quotes from those opposed to such requirements. A March

2012 website article from "The Republic" spoke of why a Nebraska bill for a federally recognized ID card didn't pass.

> Critics blasted the proposal as an attempt to keep poor, elderly, disabled and college-aged voters from casting a ballot. In the heat of the debate Tuesday, Omaha Sen. Tanya Cook likened the measure to old, southern Jim Crow laws designed to keep blacks and poor whites from voting. "This is Jim Crow light," she said. A group representing Nebraska counties also opposed the bill, saying the verification requirements could cost counties tens of thousands of dollars in each election...Regardless, sixteen states have passed photo ID laws comparable to the Nebraska proposal, according to the National Conference of State Legislatures.

A May 8, 2012 Newsmax website article speaks for the right and reported this about the issue:

> Thousands of foreign citizens might be registered to vote in Florida—a crucial presidential swing state—and could have unlawfully cast ballots in previous elections, the Miami Herald reported Tuesday night. If true, the finding would be a remarkable validation of conservative fears that undocumented aliens and resident non-citizens could be swaying elections in large, battleground states like Florida and New York. The potential problem is largest in South Florida, especially in Florida's largest county, Miami-Dade, where the elections supervisor is examining 2,000 potentially unlawful voters, Miami-based WFOR-CBS 4 News first reported Tuesday. Neighboring Broward County is examining 260 suspected foreign voters. One suspected noncitizen voter has been registered for about 40 years, CBS 4 found.

There are legitimate concerns on both sides of this issue. Objectively, 31 out of 50 states at this point require some form of identification, indicating the majority opinion on this issue is clear. In today's world of continual identity theft and fraud, the conservative view is to require some form identification to exercise the vital privilege of voting.

Unlimited Litigation vs. Tort Reform

I placed tort reform in the conservative column because those in favor of it would like to place more emphasis on individual accountability (a conservative tenet.) I also understand there are more lawyers that are Democrat than Republican, equating to more Democrats and liberals being in favor of keeping the status quo of virtually unlimited litigation. Therefore, Republicans will have to take the lead on tort reform even though I don't believe it is necessarily a partisan one.

Have you ever heard of the infamous lawsuit against the bicycle manufacturer? A car hit someone while he was riding a bicycle at night, paralyzing the bicyclist for life. His lawyer decided to sue because the bicycle manufacturer did not write into the owner's manual safety guidelines that specifically stated the consumer should not ride the bike at night without a light. The jury awarded seven figure damages, (revised downward sometime later.) The case could have been subtitled "Go for the deep pockets" vs. "Take individual responsibility." Do you think this might be why insurance is so expensive? How much more money would consumers have if rates for car, homeowner, liability and malpractice insurance were not so high? How many small businesses could not get off the ground for want of affordable insurance? I have even heard lawyers say the answer is tort reform.

Consider the following synopsis of a lawsuit that represents how tort reform has been in the offing for decades. (This will be the only one I will ask you to read. It shows how lawsuits have reached the height of absurdity.) The legal mindset of judges is now riding the pendulum away from the concept of individual responsibility towards a liberal, open-ended free-for-all grab at profiting from the blame game. This is about one of the McDonalds laws suits, compliments of the CFIF (Center for Individual Freedom.) Seriously, you have to read how lopsided our judicial thinking has become against McDonalds and in favor of people who refuse to take responsibility for their actions.

Reheating a Deep Fried Case (2010:)

The McLawsuit is back yet again. A federal appeals court has reinstated the case nearly a year and a half after a federal judge dismissed (for a second time) the class action complaint, which claims that McDonald's is responsible for the weight, girth and health of two named teenagers and countless "other similarly situated persons."

In a six-page opinion, three federal judges decided Tuesday that, at least so far as the overweight teens' misleading advertising claims were concerned, their allegations "more than m[et] the requirements" for the case to continue. That's because, according to these judges, the teens don't have to prove they actually relied on any allegedly deceptive promotions to win their case. In fact, according to the decision, the plaintiffs didn't even need to show a "'causal connection between their consumption of McDonald's food and their alleged injuries" in order to keep the lawsuit going. Instead, the three judges asserted that the teenaged plaintiffs need only prove that McDonald's advertising was "objectively misleading or deceptive" and that they "suffered injury 'as a result.'" But what injury did the teenagers suffer? And why?

According to their complaint, the teens suffered injury because their consumption of McDonald's food "significantly and substantially increased the development of ... obesity, diabetes, coronary heart disease, high blood pressure, elevated cholesterol intake and/or other detrimental and adverse health effects and/or diseases." The complaint also claims that the teens ate at McDonald's often because the company promoted the quality of its food. In other words, according to the teenaged plaintiffs, the McLawsuit hinges on whether McDonalds caused their excessive weight and poor health by inducing them to eat fast-food through allegedly misleading advertising. Thus, if McDonald's is legally to blame, logically it must be because the teenaged plaintiffs relied on those commercial messages to their detriment.

Seen this way, the three judges aren't just having it their way, they're having it both ways. On one page their decision asserts the teenagers don't have to prove actual reliance on McDonald's advertising in order to win the case, but on another the same opinion clearly explains that the teenagers must prove not only that the promotions were "objectively misleading or deceptive" but also that the teens suffered their weight- and health-related problems as a result.

It used to be that a plaintiff had to prove the defendant caused their injury in order to collect. Unfortunately, the McLawsuit has become just one more example of the rejection of this approach—and a sign post marking just how far our tort system has wandered from the age-old requirement of proving fault. According to Tuesday's decision, the case against McDonald's lives on because the teenaged plaintiffs alleged they didn't know exactly what ingredients, how many calories and how much cholesterol was in each Value Meal and because McDonald's didn't warn them. Never mind the far more pertinent and obvious fact that everyone — including the teenaged plaintiffs — knows or, at the very least, should have known: Eating a Big Mac a day will not keep the doctor away.

Indeed, Tuesday's decision — though not the first — is perhaps the most celebrated legal ruling thus far exposing the vast expansion of America's no-fault liability regime. On its face, the McLawsuit is a perfect example of a no-fault tort case. The teenagers claim they aren't to blame for their excessive size and poor health because they couldn't count every last calorie in their burgers and fries. And McDonald's logically can't be at fault because no one forced the teenagers to overeat there.

Nevertheless, more and more companies in America are learning someone has to pay. In the no-fault world where causation is no longer a factor, it is usually the one with the deepest pockets, whether there is merit in blame or not.

The above example is one that pretty much says it all about the liberal movement toward the demonization of companies providing a product and service. Moreover, it lays out how the legal pendulum has swung far towards over-protection of the individual. Many legal cases go behind the pale regarding outrageously liberal rewards to "victims" of circumstances. The truth to most of these cases is that the "victim" really is someone who did something careless, reckless and/or stupid. Rather than take responsibility for their actions, they got a smart lawyer to blame a large corporation with big pockets. Only one occupation benefits from keeping the legal system the way it is now—lawyers. The rest of us will continue to suffer while they reap the benefits until tort reform finally comes to fruition. Those agreeing with me can put themselves in the conservative column on this one.

Before I go onto the next topic, you need to know about the success story of former Governor Rick Perry passing tort reform in Texas. The state passed legislation saying that if a judge overseeing a case determines it is frivolous, the plaintiff will have to pay all the legal fees incurred by the defendant. The Public Policy Foundation reports that 26,000 doctors and nurses have fled to TX because of this tort reform. England has this policy. When Germany adopted the same law in the 1990s, frivolous lawsuits dropped by 78%. Well, that was an easy answer to this issue.

Equal Results vs. Equal Opportunity

John F. Kennedy pioneered the concept of equal opportunity and proposed sweeping civil rights legislation. However, it took three more years of promoting his vision before it came to fruition during the Lyndon B. Johnson era. At what point did the pursuit of equal opportunity evolve into equal results with quotas? Check out this condensed timetable of equal opportunity history in the U.S. to find out: (This chart is compliments of infoplease.com, although I sometimes removed excessive details to achieve brevity.)

- 1961   President Kennedy issued an executive order to ensure that hiring and employment practices are free of racial bias. His order created the Committee on Equal Employment Opportunity.
- 1964   Johnson signed the first Civil Rights Act ending legal discrimination. "No person in the United States shall, on the ground of race, color or national origin, be excluded from participation in, be denied the benefits of, to be subjected to discrimination under any program or activity receiving Federal financial assistance."
- 1965   President Johnson issued an executive order requiring government contractors to take "affirmative action" towards hiring prospective minority employees.
- 1969   President Nixon signed the Philadelphia Order, a plan that included goals and timetables, but not quotas, in hiring

minorities. The program was a result of continued discrimination by "egregious offenders of the Equal Opportunity Laws."

- 1978 This landmark Supreme Court case, *Regents of the University of California* v. *Bakke,* imposed limitations on affirmative action to ensure that providing greater opportunities for minorities did not come at the expense of the rights of the majority—affirmative action was unfair if it led to reverse discrimination. The case involved the Univ. of California, Davis Medical School, which had two separate admissions pools, one for standard applicants and another for minorities. The Supreme Court ruled that while race was a legitimate factor in school admissions, the use of such inflexible quotas as the medical school had set aside was not.

(Note: The Bakke case was the first to establish **reverse** discrimination. Some of the cases that follow bend back the newly created reverse discrimination mindset from the Bakke case and move toward a more progressive argument to achieve **equal results**. (I'll mark these cases with an **asterisk*** next to the date, in **bold**.) In other cases, there is evidence of blatant discrimination against minorities that continue to occur and the legal actions in those are **remedial** and set boundaries and goals to reverse egregious minority discrimination.

- **1980*** While Bakke struck down strict quotas, in *Fullilove* v. *Klutznick* the Supreme Court ruled that some modest quotas were perfectly constitutional. The Court upheld a federal law requiring government to set aside 15% of public works funds for qualified minority contractors. The "narrowed focus and limited extent" of the affirmative action program did not violate the equal rights of non-minority contractors, according to the Court—there was no "allocation of federal funds according to inflexible percentages solely based on race or ethnicity."
- 1986 This Supreme Court case, *Wygant* v. *Jackson Board of Education,* limited affirmative action in that it ruled the school board cannot protect minority employees by laying off non-

minority teachers first when the non-minority employees had seniority.

- **1987*** A federal court found in *United States* v. *Paradise* that the State of Alabama Department of Public Safety systematically discriminated against blacks in hiring. The court ordered a plan to correct the discrimination. The Department never implemented it, even over a 12-year period. The Supreme Court upheld the use of strict quotas in this case as one of the only means of combating the department's overt and defiant racism.

- 1989 This case of *City of Richmond* v. *Croson* involved affirmative action programs at the state and local levels. It challenged a Richmond program setting aside 30% of city construction funds for black-owned firms. For the first time, the court judged an affirmative action as a "highly suspect tool." The Supreme Court ruled that an "amorphous claim that there has been past discrimination in a particular industry cannot justify the use of an unyielding racial quota."

- 1995 *Adarand Constructors, Inc.* v. *Peña* resulted in federal programs being denied an "unyielding racial quota" just as the Croson case above did not justify it on a local and state level.

- 1995 President Clinton actually summarized in a speech the state of equal opportunity at this point as framed by the most recent Supreme Court cases above. He called for continued affirmative action to combat discrimination but called for the elimination of any programs that create a quota or preferences for unqualified individuals.

- 1996 *Hopwood* v. *University of Texas Law School:* The Supreme Court let stand a 5th U.S. Circuit Court of Appeals ruling that suspended the university's affirmative action program. The decision rejected the legitimacy of diversity as a goal. The court asserted "educational diversity is not recognized as a compelling state interest."

- 1997 California passed a state ban on all forms of affirmative action.

- 1998   Washington becomes the second state to abolish state affirmative action measures
- 2000   In February of that year, Florida bans race as factor in college admissions.
- **2000*** In December of that year, a federal judge in *Gratz v. Bollinger* ruled that the use of race as a factor in admissions at the University of Michigan was constitutional. The gist of the university's argument was as follows: Just as preference is granted to children of alumni, scholarship athletes and others groups for reasons deemed beneficial to the university, so too does the affirmative action program serve "a compelling interest" by providing educational benefits derived from a diverse student body.
- 2001   In *Grutter v. Bollinger,* a case similar to the University of Michigan undergraduate lawsuit, a different judge drew an opposite conclusion, invalidating the law school's policy and ruling that "intellectual diversity bears no obvious or necessary relationship to racial diversity."
- **2002*** The above decision was reversed on appeal, ruling that the admissions policy was, in fact, constitutional.
- **2003*** In the most important affirmative action decision since the 1978 *Bakke* case, the Supreme Court (5-4) upholds the University of Michigan Law School's affirmative action policy. The court ruled that race *can* be one of many factors considered by colleges when selecting their students because it furthers "a compelling interest in obtaining the educational benefits that flow from a diverse student body." The Supreme Court, however, ruled (6-3) that the more formulaic approach of the University of Michigan's undergraduate admissions program needed modification. It used a point system that rates students and awarded additional points to applications by minorities.
- 2006   In *Parents v. Seattle* and *Meredith v. Jefferson,* affirmative action suffers a setback when a bitterly divided court rules 5-4 that programs in Seattle and Louisville, Ky., which tried to maintain diversity in schools by considering race when assigning students to schools, are unconstitutional.

- 2008   Ballot measures proposing to ban affirmative action — race and gender based preferences by public entities — goes before voters in two states. Nebraska passes it and Colorado rejects it.

- 2009   In a lawsuit brought against the city of New Haven, CT, *Ricci v. DeStefano,* firefighters go to court. 18 plaintiffs—17 white and 1 Hispanic—argued that results of the 2003 lieutenant and captain exams were thrown out when it was determined that few minority firefighters qualified for advancement. The plaintiffs claimed that they were victims of reverse discrimination and the Supreme Court agreed, although just barely with a 5-4 vote.

The history above may seem long and hard to stay with, causing your eyes to glaze over; so I'll provide some general observations and summary. The 1980 and 1987 rulings allowed the use of quotas because they were the only solution to continued, blatant discrimination against minorities. Therefore, I would place these rulings under the category of attaining "*equal opportunity.*" The 2000, 2002 and 2003 rulings cross the bridge to "*equalizing results*" as they systematically used the factor of race in the formula. Their justification is the need for diversity. But if diversity can only be achieved through managing results, the aim of "*equal results*" is obviously being pursued. Does not such a goal violate the spirit of a Constitution that prohibits discrimination?

In conclusion, justices designed court decisions to **end discrimination** against minorities during the early stages of affirmative action. Somewhere along the way (2000,) justices began to advance the concept of affirmative action to include reverse discrimination **quotas** or other systematic methods of achieving **equal results** based on race. This is where our sense of fairness cues us to draw the line in the sand. To achieve true equal opportunity, I understand some colleges now prohibit the use of a name, race or picture on an application to prevent the admissions board from knowing the race and/or ethnic background of the student. Now, that is true "color blindness."

Race Card vs. Color Blindness

I readily acknowledge that race crimes and hate crimes persist in this country, so I do not want to diminish the need to reduce them at all costs. Moreover, I am in favor of the maximum amount of sentencing possible to punish those convicted of such. This section, however, is devoted to the trite references to race that are of no real consequence and only serve to muddy the waters for an observer who is just trying to determine if finger pointing is bogus or not.

Liberals continue to play the race card in our post-civil rights era of political correctness. The reason lies deep in the propaganda war that continually takes place between Democrats and Republicans. The downside of our two-party system is that it is subject to intense partisanship. Debating issues on merit has its place, but the use of propaganda can undermine the appearance of integrity of the opposing party. Enter the race card that many use to undermine the image of those it attacks. Here are many examples that those on the right say were an unjustified or distorted claim that racial bigotry influenced an outcome:

- Many political pundits and journalists on the left accuse conservatives of being racist because they support tough state laws against illegal immigrants, most of whom are Hispanic. I think we all can agree this is a sweeping generalization.
- Liberals were branding "birthers" as racist. A "birther" is a person who at one point believed that President Obama was not born in the U.S. because he did not for years release a copy of his birth certificate. The "birthers" supposedly were looking for a reason to constitutionally (it requires the President to be born in the United States) bar Obama from becoming the President just because he was black.
- When Donald Trump was running for President, he said Obama has to get off the basketball court and work on the problem of the deficit. Liberal-leaning news anchors responded this was a "racist" comment as accusing someone black of playing too much basketball is a stereotype and therefore racist. But Donald

Trump made it clear he was not alluding to a stereotype but meant it literally as the media had in fact reported on the large extent to which Obama did play recreational basketball.

- Fox News Anchor Bill O'Reilly was once accused of bigotry simply because he inquired about President Obama being a football fan.

- A "Meet the Press" anchor challenged former Speaker of the House Newt Gingrich that was running for President at the time: "You gave a speech In Georgia with language that a lot of people think was racially tinged, calling the President—the first black president—a "food stamp" President. What did you mean and what is the point?" Newt simply answered that "47 million Americans or one out of every six, is on food stamps (the highest percentage ever recorded) and that the President of the United States has to be held accountable." You decide if Newt was making a racial remark or a simple statement about increasing government expenditures. (If you want to determine to what extent Obama was responsible for increasing food stamp costs, please know he spent your money to advertise the availability of food stamps, presumably to increase the use of them.)

- The latest fad in racial accusations is a campaign against using the word "illegal" to describe immigrants who come here "illegally." The coordinator of the "Drop the I Word" campaign came onto Fox News on April 28, 2012 trying to convince Americans the word "illegal" is a racial slur. It is "dehumanizing" and "racist," she said. In fact, she said using the words "illegal immigrant" is a hate crime. You can make up your mind whether or not her contention is leftist propaganda—an attempt to convince us a group of people is not something that they really are. Moreover, the timing of this campaign is suspect as the election of 2012 is months away and President Obama has been steadily slipping according to re-electability polls.

Here is the test to determine if a remark is really racial—it shows prejudice against that person *just because* of his race and for *no other reason*. Politics is ugly and people do make obnoxious or inappropriate remarks. Nevertheless, that does not necessarily mean they were truly of a prejudicial or bigoted nature. Sometimes remarks are just the result of the accuser being less than sensitive or the result of the accused being overly sensitive. Fox News Analyst Bernie Goldberg stated the problem of continual racial accusations very succinctly. He made the point during a 2011 broadcast that false accusations of racism water down the word "racial" to the extent it robs the word of its true meaning. Goldberg made the on-point comparison that "racism is an attack word used by the left in the same vain they use the "terrorist" metaphor to describe the Tea Partiers. Everyone listening figured out the 'racist' accusation was all baseless, groundless, grandstanding…It doesn't work anymore when they call conservative Republicans 'racist'…it's a waste of time, nobody buys it anymore. If you're a racist because you are against Obamacare and the Stimulus and the worldwide apology tour, then what do you call the skinheads who were ***really*** racist?"

Amen. Let's preserve the meaning of words so they truly mean something when we use them.

Pardons are a Nice Tradition vs. Pardons are an Abuse

This subject is not really a partisan issue or one that fits into a left vs. right struggle, but of a constitutional nature. I believe the practice of it is an unconscionable abuse of Article II, Section II of the Constitution, which simply states this about presidential pardons:

"He shall have Power to grant Reprieves and Pardons for Offences against the United States, except in Cases of Impeachment."

Since then, Presidents have been pardoning convicted criminals by the hundreds. Our laws provide this privilege to governors as well. Although a President may pardon an inmate during the tenure of his administration, he usually exercises this privilege for a long list of inmates just before he leaves his office. This way, any political fallout from the freeing of criminals that committed the most egregious acts would not affect that executive's political standing. Does this seem right to you? Does this not make a mockery of the justice system? I believe the founding fathers placed this in the Constitution to give the President an opportunity to right a wrong.

Judicial proceedings during the time of the founding fathers were probably less than perfect. Criminal prosecutions and jury findings back then were probably quicker, less thorough and more subject to error compared to today. I suggest this because defense lawyers back then did not have the set of liberal prosecution rules that make trying suspects more challenging today. They also did not have the state of the art technology to prove suspects innocent. Consequently, I believe the founding fathers believed the privilege to pardon would be the executive branch's check against judicial powers.

However, modern day Presidents and state governors receive lists of hundreds of criminals to pardon and they fulfill the request without knowing why each one might deserve it. This is a travesty of justice to absurd proportions. The worst part of the pardon is that it legally wipes away the arrest for the crime as if it never happened. Whereas a criminal who serves his time may not legally purchase a weapon, the pardon erases the record so that the criminal is free in every way to do so. Oftentimes, a President or governor will "commute" a sentence. This is quite different in that it releases the prisoner based on the conclusion they have served enough time. I understand there are cases in which sentences may have been too harsh to fit the crime and *commuting* the sentence is a deserved act of compassion But, the *pardon* practice creates opportunity for corruption to take place along the trail that starts with the inmate's defense attorney and ends with a name written on a list. Yet, we as a people tolerate it because this practice has always been in place.

Courtesy of newsytype.com, consider some observations on modern day presidential pardons:

> The most controversial pardon was in 1974 when President Gerald Ford pardoned his impeached predecessor Richard Nixon after the Watergate scandal. Ronald Reagan also drew criticism for pardoning George Steinbrenner in 1989. The courts convicted Steinbrenner of making illegal contributions to Richard Nixon's re-election campaign. Bill Clinton likewise came under fire for pardoning Marc Rich

in 2001. Rich was convicted of cheating the government out of millions. Many believe the pardon was a result of Rich's wife's generous contributions to the Democratic Party and to Clinton's presidential library.

You can see that when I mentioned political favor or corruption, I wasn't just speculating. At what point are we endangering our society by letting dangerous criminals go free and giving them the legal freedom of a pardon? Consider the following news article that nails this issue down cold (CBS News – Jan. 2010:)

> A Mississippi judge temporarily blocked the controversial release of 21 inmates pardoned by outgoing Gov. Haley Barbour. On Tuesday, in one of his last acts in office, Barbour ordered the release of more than 200 prisoners in all, including some convicted killers. In addition, "CBS This Morning" special correspondent Jeff Glor reports the move has led to outrage. It was Mississippi's attorney general, Democrat Jim Hood, who asked Circuit Judge Tomie Green to step in, arguing Barbour's eleventh-hour pardons violated the state constitution. 'Hopefully,' an angry Hood told reporters, 'it will be a lesson to any future governors that you just don't do this kind of thing. You've gotta read the law before you go out there and do something like that.'

The reason the judge (and attorney general) assert the widespread pardon in this instance was unconstitutional is because the Governor did not abide by the rules requiring the released inmates to post (in the newspaper within 30 days) details on where they will be living. The article continued:

> Relatives and friends of Tammy Gatlin, who was shot and killed by her husband David as she held her six-week old son, are among the stunned and angry constituents who opposed the pardons. David Gatlin, who is now free after serving 18 years of a life sentence, also shot Tammy's friend, Danny Walker, who survived. "I think the governor himself will have to look me and the family in the eye and say, 'I'm going

to let this guy go.' But there wasn't any of that. I think that's
the coward's way out," Walker said."

My wrap up: Pardons put the public in danger. In addition, they
damage the integrity of the judicial process as they weaken the threat
of legal consequences.

New Policy on Gays in Military vs. Don't Ask; Don't Tell

I know what you are thinking, but you are wrong. I am not opposed to
the new politically correct program on this topic nor am I an adamant
proponent of the former policy, DADT (Don't Ask; Don't Tell.) I am
writing on this topic mostly because it is a classic example of the liberal's
aim to pursue the agenda of a minority versus the conservative's goal to
maintain tradition. First, I believe this issue speaks volumes about the
motivations of the left and the mainstream media—how they sometimes
falsely represent issues near and dear to their heart. Secondly, I will
defend the DADT policy to the extent that it did have specific positive
aspects to it. Thirdly, I will challenge the new policy as the best one
for the military. Fourthly, I will highlight the benefits of keeping one's
sexual orientation private, which is a traditional mindset that I believe
deserves mentioning. I do have to insert here that the military to their
credit did revise specific rules regarding the expediting of the DADT
policy in 2010 to achieve a less harsh and less frequent "outing" of
homosexuals. Unfortunately, their efforts to do this were a classic
example of too little, too late.

After the Obama administration passed the new legislation, it
became commonplace to hear famous actors and talk show hosts on
TV praising it by saying that it "finally allowed the gays to serve in our
military" and "wasn't it a disgrace that we weren't allowing them to do as
other countries were." In reality, these statements are factually incorrect
and fed the public frenzy about this issue. The military *had* permitted
homosexuals to serve under the "Don't Ask; Don't Tell" policy since the
early 1990s when President Clinton started the DADT policy. However,
they had simply prohibited the soldiers from announcing it.

Why would there be a legitimate need for a homosexual in the
military to have to come out and declare his/her sexual orientation?

Outside of the exception of homosexual marriages in the military, I would contend the only answer to this question is that the individual who needs to do this has a personal or political agenda to pursue and that no good to the military can come of it. Their need could be as simple as letting everyone know their sexual orientation so they could feel better about themselves. News flash—if a soldier needs to make an announcement about how different he is from his/her peers to obtain some type of a psychological boost, perhaps the military is not the place for him/her. When one enters the military, that person understands he/she will be sacrificing many personal freedoms previously enjoyed as a civilian. Among them are going where the military sends you, doing what they tell you to do, going on vacation on the military's timetable, wearing the clothes they give you, the hairstyle they permit, what to say, when to say it and how to say it. They even tell you how to think. Among their requirements (when most recruits signed on) was to keep your sexual orientation (if not heterosexual) to yourself. The military wants to be all about a group of people that are similar to one another, not different. The traditional thinking by most top brass was that cohesiveness among the military would be stronger if there was an assumption *on the surface* that everyone was heterosexual; even though everyone knew this was not the case. Theory had it that the stronger the bond, the more likely a given group will work better as a team. In addition, keeping sexual orientation private would eliminate it as a potential distraction.

The new policy adopted during the Obama administration required quite the training program as per the following January 2011 internet blurb from a page of the New York Times:

> Pentagon officials said the defense secretary's reference to a "tiering" of training referred to different levels of preparation to allow gay and bisexual troops to serve openly: one for senior administrative officials and personnel officers who need a deep understanding of what is permitted or not under the new regulations, another for commanders who will have to carry out the changes in their units and a third for all personnel.

> Pentagon officials, who planned to hold a news briefing about their plans on Friday, said the core of the training was expected to communicate to 2.2 million members of the armed forces these basic points: The Defense Department will not require anyone to disclose his or her sexual identity; local commanders are authorized to determine housing and privacy requirements; all service members are expected to conduct themselves in a professional manner and treat one another with dignity and respect; leaders at all levels are to establish a climate of tolerance in their units; harassment or violence toward another service member will not be tolerated and will be dealt with swiftly.

Did you see the various ramifications of allowing someone to declare their sexual orientation? Now the military will have to deal with possible acts of harassment and a new policy through extensive training will have to be implemented. The traditional viewpoint is that someone's sexual orientation is a private matter and that there is no real necessary reason to make it a public ordeal. Now, the military will be changing its culture from one that has always suppressed individual expression to permitting it.

Here is the ironic twist: The military ***did not*** want to make an issue of one's sexual orientation, as they had ***not*** been asking the soldiers about it. The committed left ***did*** in fact want to make an issue of it, as they wanted the soldiers to be able to declare it. So, who really is the guilty party regarding the singling out of those with a different sexual orientation? Admittedly, the advent of homosexual marriage complicates the viability of DADT. Issues related to notifying the spouse probably complicates that policy.

Regardless, I think we can all agree it is the spirit of American tolerance to treat everyone the same regardless of race, gender, creed, nationality, age or sexual orientation. Since no one was certain who was straight and who was homosexual under DADT, homosexuals had virtually guaranteed protection of equal rights and equal treatment. Use your imagination about how these individuals in the military could now possibly be subjected to either willful or subconscious discrimination.

Now some may try to make a case that they are being mistreated or bypassed for promotion because of their sexual orientation. We hope to think this would not happen, but if it does; wouldn't it be the blame of the new policy? Conversely, they may receive preferential treatment from those with the mindset that favors the advancement of gays or minorities. Now, you tell me: Which policy truly is more aligned with treating homosexuals in the military the same as everyone else?

Now that we have accepted the new "serve openly gay" legislation, it is interesting to note that our country would still be following DADT if it had not been for one federal judge. Although the Congress repealed the policy and passed the current one, here's how it happened: After it became apparent that the Senate was not going to repeal the former policy, a federal judge ruled on a lawsuit brought against the military by issuing a stay on the enforcement of its policies. This was the beginning of the end of DADT. Defense Secretary Gates allowed this decision by a federal judge to turn the military's hand in reversing their position. He decided it was more expedient to give into a political environment (now complicated by a judge's stay) to accept the new bill rather than continually defend the former policy. He campaigned for the new proposal and the Senate eventually followed his lead, narrowly passing the new bill.

Gay Marriage vs. Gay Unions

I believe most Americans favor equal *rights* for everyone regardless of their sexual orientation. Most conservatives, however, share the Christian right-wing view that strongly opposes gay *marriage*. Some Christian conservatives *are* against legal gay unions and the denial of some legal rights usually reserved for married couples, such as adoption. But it would be unfair to brand all conservatives as prudes wanting to deny gays legal unions. I believe most simply object to the re-defining of the word "marriage".

Here is *my* theory on why the conservatives are against gay marriage and how they build their argument: 1. Christians and citizens of most religions define marriage as an intimate union between one man and one woman. 2. The god (of whichever religion oversees the vows) blesses this union. It is not just a legal union, but also a spiritual union. Most religions hold marriage as a religious activity and/or spiritual milestone. For example, marriage is a sacrament in the Catholic religion. 3. Christians and citizens of most religions believe homosexuality is a sin and *not* blessed by God. Therefore, same sex legal unions cannot be a marriage by definition as it is not between one man and one woman and because it cannot be a union blessed by God.

Grant it, this is traditional belief; indeed a religious and/or spiritual one. The final religious and/or spiritual analysis is that if our country embraces gay marriage, then our children (and most certainly their children) will not only grow up believing that gay activity is *not* a sin, but observe that it is condoned by the state government. A liberal argument could question why religious folk appointed themselves the official "marriage police." On the other hand, traditionalists could ask secular progressives what gives them the right to change the definition of marriage as established by the state legislatures from the beginning. Even non-religious citizens hold firm that the traditional definition of marriage in the secular world is the legal unification between one man and one woman. The issue really comes down to what our society will determine is the definition of marriage.

The conservative mindset believes that the gay marriage milestone will water down the institution of marriage. Many conservatives make the argument that if courts permit gay marriage, the legality of polygamist marriage will soon follow. Then, "open marriages" could possibly come into vogue. At that point, the institution of marriage won't mean very much anymore. Isn't a large part of American society already on the brink of being dysfunctional with the traditional family unit falling apart?

A likely compromise would allow the courts to provide same sex legal unions with the identical legal rights of marriage but without the state using the term "marriage." Gay couples would get the specific rights they want and conservatives would preserve the institution of marriage, whose definition would not change.

What galls the right more than anything else is that judges are taking it upon themselves to award gay couples a marriage license (not just permit legal unions) when this matter has historically always been a legislative one. In February 2012, two federal judges decided that gay marriage in California would be legal in that state even though the electorate voted against gay marriage several months prior. In fact, thirty-eight states have passed legislation opposing gay marriage. Only seven states have made gay marriage legal as of May, 2012. So, state legislatures have spoken, presumably on behalf of the people. Is it right for judges to overturn their decisions? I believe most of us would rather see the people decide on the definition of marriage as it was the legislature, not the judicial system, which created the state requirements for marriage from the beginning. The mantra now utilized by Catholic groups to highlight their position on gay marriage is "reinforce marriage, don't re-define it."

The latest legal maneuver (prior to this book's publishing) regarding gay marriage is as follows as reported by a Newsmax website article on June 3, 2012.

> An appeals court in Boston ruled Thursday that a law that denies a host of federal benefits to gay married couples is unconstitutional. The 1st U.S. Circuit Court of Appeals in Boston said the (1996) Defense of Marriage Act, which defines marriage as a union between a man and a woman, discriminates against gay couples...The appeals court agreed with a lower court judge who ruled in 2010 that the law is unconstitutional because it interferes with the right of a state to define marriage and denies married gay couples federal benefits given to heterosexual married couples, including the ability to file joint tax returns.

I honestly can't completely disagree with this ruling as it returns to the state the right to define marriage. However, I reiterate the right to define the definition of marriage and issues related to gay unions such as IRS filings should originate from the legislature, *not* the judicial branch.

5.

The Constitution Less God vs. The Constitution and God

Constitution is a Living Document vs. Constitution is Unrecognizable

YOU HAVE PROBABLY heard the phrase "living document" before and it refers to the concept that the Constitution is not just the black and white document that the forefathers drafted in 1787, with amendments subsequently attached. The U.S. Constitution today is the culmination of all the Supreme Court rulings interpreting it. The need for interpreting the Constitution and expanding its effect on laws is clear. Our founding fathers could not have foreseen all the conflicts that laws would cause as our country evolved and could not write a Constitution detailed enough to determine what the outcomes of these conflicts should be. Moreover, they realized an overly thorough Constitution would have robbed the people going forward of the process of adding and changing it as they saw fit. Therefore, they kept the phraseology simple to give future generations the opportunity to mold it.

The phrase that the "Constitution is a living, breathing document" is not only metaphorical, it is literal in the sense that the Constitution really has become the living and breathing justices who interpret it. The process of changing this living Constitution occurs most often by the decision of nine Supreme Court justices. It rarely occurs through the democratic process of making amendments to it. There have only been twenty-seven amendments to the Constitution (and the first ten, known as the Bill of Rights, were original,) so only seventeen amendments have been added to the Constitution since its first drafting. In contrast, Supreme Court rulings that have changed the Constitution number in the hundreds. Arbitrary decisions made by the Supreme Court justices and lower courts are responsible for the majority of change in our prized document.

To set the stage for my argument that justices abuse their power, I want to share what I learned from a video on a discussion between current Supreme Court Justice Antonin Scalia, who has the longest tenure on the court having been there since 1986; and Stephen Breyer, who has served since 1994. Justice Scalia explained that there are two philosophies in interpreting the Constitution. A justice can be an "originalist" or an "evolutionist." Scalia said he is an "originalist," someone who emphasizes the textual value of the original words in the original Constitution written in the 1780s. An "originalist" believes they should *not* attempt to use the Constitution on a current case or law where it is vague and not clear. Rather, they believe the decision by the court should be limited to allow the democratic process of the people to fill in the blanks and change the laws accordingly. They do *not* believe they should self-assign such an authority to the courts. The example he used to make his point was about the Eighth Amendment, which bans cruel and unusual punishment.

Justice Scalia said the Supreme Court was *not* acting in an "originalist" manner when they decided the Eighth Amendment limited the use of the death penalty. Scalia said there is no wording in this amendment that would give the authority to the court to decide this, yet they did. Scalia said that if an arbitrary decision should be made as to what "cruel and unusual punishment" would include, it should be done through the legislative branch and not the judicial branch as there was no indication that the 1791 constitutional framers wished to label the death penalty as "cruel and unusual." The historical facts clearly point to the opposite interpretation as the penalty for a felony at the time of the passing of this amendment included the death penalty. By what basis, then, should modern Supreme Court Justices suddenly decide to the contrary? Hence, Scalia concluded that to make these arbitrary decisions is an unconstitutional usurpation of power.

Justice Breyer said he was an "evolutionist," one who believes the "living Constitution" must "evolve through a developmental approach." He says judges sometimes must be guided by more than the "language of laws" if the words are ambiguous or embody a value that must be applied to specific circumstances. As a Constitutional evolutionist, Breyer believes the problem of the Constitution having no words on specific issues of the day has to be solved by taking what one believes is the "unchanging value" of the original Constitution and applying it to current circumstances. He used as an example how the original constitutionalist addressed "interstate commerce." That concept, he said, has changed so much over the past few hundred years as we now have modes of transportation that were unthought-of back in the day. Evolutionists believe it is the duty of the Supreme Court to set boundaries to protect the people from the majority even if there is no historical or constitutional basis for it. However, originalists would be in favor of taking a pass on even trying to rule on such cases and let the majority rule through the legislative branch. Which process do you think is better for this country: Letting nine justices decide on an issue where there is no clear constitutional precedent or through the consensus of many hundreds of legislatures that represent the people's views?

Justice Breyer said that the courts use six concepts to decide on issues: The text in the original Constitution, history, tradition, precedents, purpose or values, and consequences. He said that the ideal scenario for the court is when these six concepts line up to point towards an obvious decision. However, he admitted this rarely happens and then the court has to decide on only some of the concepts. I was surprised to hear Justice Breyer admit that when this happens, the court too often makes a ruling based on the last two items, "values" and "consequences."

In addition to this process, Justice Breyer even spoke on how the Constitution says nothing about the using (or not using) of other countries' policies to influence decisions. The fact that Breyer would even broach such a topic suggests a legislative mindset exists on the court in that they are looking for the success or failure of laws elsewhere as information in constructing policy. (Remember, the Supreme Court's role is to rule on laws that have been already created by the legislative branch, not create new laws.)

You will not be surprised to hear that Justice Scalia said that most of the Supreme Court justices today are evolutionists. He said, "People should be able to make their own laws and that the courts have made legislative decisions from the bench." He also admitted "we don't get it right all the time."

Here's the dirty little secret that many politicians won't admit to: When a President chooses a justice for the Supreme Court, that President usually makes a decision not only on the credentials of the judge, but also on where that judge has proven to be plotted on the spectrum of liberal vs. conservative. A conservative tends to be like Justice Antonin Scalia, an originalist. A conservative/originalist favors strict interpretations of the Constitution, favors traditionalist values and most probably would be pro-life. A liberal would be like Justice Breyer, an "evolutionist." A liberal/evolutionist would take authority to make rulings without constitutional basis, favor secular-progressive values and would probably be pro-choice. Advisors points to judges that reflect the President's political agenda and the choice is made accordingly. No President will ever admit to holding any judicial candidates to a litmus test, but history has clearly shown this happens. It's a fact. Justice Scalia said, "A mini-constitutional convention occurs every time a President appoints a judge because the 'values' part of making a ruling has become the prominent reason for it." He went on to say this practice "was not intended by our forefathers." Well, I rest my case that chronic abuse of power occurs from the Supreme Court bench and you got the scoop straight from two differently opinioned current justices.

Keep God Out of Government vs. Keep God in Government

Once upon a new world, our forefathers incorporated their religious beliefs into carrying out the functions of all branches of government. They used the Holy Bible to legislate and judge the laws. They openly invoked the wisdom of the almighty through prayer. Religion and government coexisted without any objection or problem during the years in which this country was establishing itself. The best learning institutions were religiously based for centuries. Of the first 108 universities founded in

America, 106 were distinctly Christian. Harvard University was the first, chartered in 1636. In the original Harvard Student Handbook, rule number one was that students seeking entrance must know Latin and Greek so that they could study the Scriptures. The religion and government combination eventually created what most of us (at least the traditionalists) would say became the greatest country in the world. However, the God in government pendulum since that time has swung so far towards political correctness, it has resulted in governance that has achieved the goals of the secular progressives.

The following facts pertain to the point that our government's history is rich in recognizing God's place in our government:

- Emblazoned over the Speaker of the House in the U.S. Capitol are the words "In God We Trust."
- The Supreme Court building built in the 1930s has carvings of Moses and the Ten Commandments.
- God is mentioned in stone on monuments and buildings throughout Washington, D.C.
- As a nation, we have celebrated Christmas to commemorate the Savior's birth for centuries.
- Oaths in courtrooms have invoked God from the beginning. Witnesses were instructed to put their hand on the Holy Bible and asked: "Do you swear to tell the truth, the whole truth and nothing but the truth, so help you God?"
- The founding fathers often quoted the Bible in their writings.
- Every President in his inaugural address has mentioned God; even the most liberal and most non-traditional President in the history of our nation, President Obama
- Prayers have been said at the swearing in of each President.
- Each president was sworn in on the Bible, saying the words, "So help me, God."
- The Liberty Bell has a Bible verse engraved on it.
- The original Constitution of all fifty states mentions God.
- Chaplains have been in the public payroll from the very beginning.

- Our nation's birth certificate, the Declaration of Independence, mentions God four times.
- The Bible was used as a textbook in the schools.
- We still print on our money "In God We Trust."
- A prominent plaque that hangs behind the Supreme Court Justices lists the Ten Commandments.

In contrast to these historical references to our "one nation under God," traditionalists are currently suffering through a presidential tenure that plays a hard core secular progressive role. I will highlight two events during the Obama tenure to make my point. The first is about what happened (more to the point is what didn't happen) at a "God and Country" rally—an annual event that is a basically a large fair, but unique in that it is a mix of patriotism and spirituality. One secular activity that takes place is the "swearing-in" of new military recruits. The following excerpt is from an August 2009 internet account of the story:

> Obama denied a military flyover at the annual God and Country rally in Idaho, where new military recruits were inducted and all military was honored. This is the first time in 42 years that there has not been a military flyover in formation and organizers were stunned that Obama refused to allow this. When the person organizing the event contacted the Pentagon to ask why this was not allowed, as it had occurred every year for 42 years, she was told it was because the event had a Christian nature.

One would think a Commander in Chief would appreciate the pro-active support of the military by a large group of people celebrating their country is a patriotic manner, regardless of what religion they were. The fact that he actually verbalized the basis of his decision was because the event has a "*Christian*" nature is an undisputable act of discrimination against Christians. (This is something one expects in Muslim countries.) Although true patriots were shocked and angry to be denied the significant tradition of a fighter jet flyover, those who were paying attention during "Election 2008" can't be totally surprised.

During campaigning, candidate Obama let his guard down during a 2008 campaign speech and disparagingly referred to traditionalists in the area as those "clinging to their guns, dogs and religion." By the way, the same internet account above also mentions that when "Obama made a recent speech, a cross and a Christian symbol for Jesus had to be covered first."

A similar secular progressive vs. traditionalist conflict occurred just a few months earlier as depicted by a U.S. News website article published on May 4, 2009. It read:

> The National Day of Prayer Task Force, headquartered at the conservative Christian group Focus on the Family, has issued a statement criticizing the Obama administration for the way it's marking the annual event this Thursday. Though the Obama administration has announced that it will issue a proclamation marking the National Day of Prayer, it will not hold a formal White House event, as George W. Bush had done for the past eight years.

The article went on to say that George H.W. Bush (Senior) and President Reagan did host events commemorating The National Day of Prayer, although they were not as big as President Bush's (the younger) formal East Room event.

A prominent plaque that hangs behind the Supreme Court Justices lists the Ten Commandments. I wonder if it is still there for historic value or because the maintenance crew hasn't yet acted on the request to remove them. Since I'm an optimist, I'm going to say it's they are still there as recognition that they serve as a moral basis for society. At the risk of being dramatic, I'm interpreting this plaque as a symbolic recognition that these commandments represent a living branch of deity that hasn't yet been snipped by the secular progressive movement. Could it be a humble nod to the heavens above that the judges are subservient to a higher authority—the ultimate judge? The presence of the plaque is an ironic twist since the same justices sitting in front of them have ruled time and again that historic plaques of the Ten Commandments displayed in a public venue must be removed as their mere presence was deemed unconstitutional.

No Nativity Scenes vs. It Depends On Presentation

Some examples of the metamorphosis of our First Amendment are justified. Federal, state and local governments many decades ago used to be able to display a large three-dimensional nativity scene (the Supreme Court judges use the term "crèche") at Christmas in front of one of the government buildings such as the town hall. Now that we are a religiously diverse nation, I concede that there are many instances in which displaying a crèche there **would** give the appearance that the government is endorsing the Christian religion as opposed to other religions. I get that and agree with this necessary reevaluation.

Interestingly enough, one the Supreme Court's decisions regarding the presence of a crèche did in fact pass their strict constitutional muster. I chose to highlight this case to show how the Supreme Court justices make conclusions on how they see the "establishment clause" affecting holiday presentations by local governments. In Lynch v. Donnelly (regarding a Pawtucket, R.I. holiday display,) the presence of a crèche on public grounds was in fact narrowly upheld as constitutionally permissible in a controversial 5-4 ruling. Here's why: The presentation of the nativity scene was in the background amidst many other religious presentations and secular decorations. The banner in front of the presentation said "Happy Holidays." The courts decided that specific presentation, although it included a crèche, did not give the impression the municipality was endorsing a specific religion. The legal upshot of the ruling meant not all symbols of religious expression are absolutely banned (on public grounds) all the time and in all settings. It turns out there is a delicate balance to strike between allowing the freedom to celebrate one's religious observance and the "endorsement of a religion." Those setting up the holiday presentation in Pawtucket, CT got it just right in 1984 as the narrow 5-4 ruling gave them their victory.

Today, there is a lot of confusion over the constitutionality of Christmas displays on public grounds. Generally, the rule of thumb is that no apparent endorsement of any particular religion occurs if the presentation represents all major religions. However, I understand variations of this standard can occur when factors such as legal risk tolerance and local culture come into play.

> **A prominent plaque that hangs behind the Supreme Court Justices lists the Ten Commandments... Could it be a humble nod to the heavens above that the judges are subservient to a higher authority— the ultimate judge?**

Separation of God and State vs. Separation of Church and State

Supreme Court rulings have gone beyond any explicable rationalization when dealing with this next subject—prayer in school. I do agree that since we are such a diverse nation, we have to honor the doctrine of *separation of church and state*. For example, I understand and agree that there are many past religious practices that no one objected to when we were first a Christian nation, such as using the Bible in public schools, hanging crosses and crucifixes in the classroom and leading the class in **Christian** prayer. These practices all pertain to a specific religion and cannot be constitutionally practiced in public schools because they would otherwise endorse a specific religion (denomination or church.) I get that. However, justices have made rulings that arbitrarily and falsely extend the meaning of the phrase *separation of church and state*, interpreting them as a "separation of **God** and state" and "a separation of **prayer** and state." This is where their legal mechanics has gone awry.

An analysis of Supreme Court decisions will show that justices have failed to recognize (whether deliberately or not) the difference between a "religion" and "God" and "prayer." Religion is a grouping of specific doctrines that incorporates spiritual belief and reverence. "God" is a reference to a supernatural power, often regarded as creator and governor of the universe. He is the object of the belief of someone's religion. The mention of the word "god" could be a Christian God, a Jewish God, Allah, Abraham or a star in the sky. "Prayer" is an activity that may or may not be associated with religion or church. Clearly, people who are not of a specific religion pray and people who are not "religious" pray. People who believe in God may not practice or even believe in any religion. Religion involves a god, but god does not necessarily involve a religion. Therefore, there is no logical deduction in permitting the government to police "God" and "prayer" just because the First Amendment limits government authority by using the word "religion" in the establishment clause. In fact, the First Amendment specifically protects our right to pray and practice the religion of our choice. The First Amendment states:

"Congress shall make no law respecting an establishment of religion or **prohibiting the free exercise thereof** or abridging the freedom of speech or of the press or the right of the people peaceably to assemble and to petition the Government for a redress of grievances." Notice the amendment makes no mention of "God" or "prayer." An analysis of the intent of the First Amendment by our forefathers would show the word "religion" was defined in the **denominational** sense, not the "spiritual sense." (E.g.: Congress can't say we all have to be Baptist.) Evidence of this is that the forefathers practiced different religions and were highly aware that immigrants came here for religious freedom. There is no doubt they experienced the tyranny of governments that **did** establish a religion and wanted to make sure this abuse of power would never occur again. Secondly, they did not intend for "prayer" or "God" "to be included or substituted into the word "religion" in the phrase "establishment of religion." We can glean this from the fact that schools permitted prayer and even Bible reading at the time they wrote the First Amendment. Clearly, our forefathers did not want Congress to be able to ban all expressions of religion such as prayer and mention of God from all government entities, which coexisted for almost 200 years before the Supreme Court decided to change the meaning of the First Amendment. In fact, a commonly posed question by conservatives on the topic of prayer in school is this: If it is legal for a legislative body to pray before a session, why shouldn't it be legal for a school?

Prayer in school existed until the early 1960s. In June of 1962, the Engel v. Vitale case established the following prayer could not be **suggested** by the School District's Principal to be said aloud by each class in the presence of a teacher at the beginning of each school day:

"Almighty God, we acknowledge our dependence upon Thee and we beg Thy blessings upon us, our parents, our teachers and our country."

I know it is unthinkable to anyone born after 1965 that a specific prayer would actually be assigned to a student to say aloud, but the dissenting justices made several excellent points in its defense. First, the prayer is totally **generic.** It doesn't endorse any particular religion, let alone establish one. The second point is that children did *not* have to say the prayer if the parents objected. The third point is that the denial of the opportunity to pray **clearly violates** the First Amendment. (If you doubt this, go back and read the First Amendment again.)

The majority opinion in Engel v. Vitale said that the "New York authorities have established an official "**religion.**" I ask you to decide which is factually true: Was the school establishing a religion or are the children being denied their First Amendment rights? I agree with the latter statement. If you are hesitating for even a moment, go back and read the definition of "prayer" versus "religion." Keep in mind the wording of the prayer. The adoption of a policy of having **this** specific prayer doesn't endorse a religion. The prayer really just solicits God's blessings and it is about as religion-**less** as you can get.

Had I been able to be there on the court, my decision would have been in favor of defending the **right** of children to voluntarily say **this** prayer. However, I am not going to agree that school authorities should have provided a prayer verbatim for students to say aloud. I don't say this because I agree with any conclusion made by the court, but because I think that providing the prayer makes the school appear to be too controlling of a practice that I think should be reworked. I believe it is bad policy to put words in someone's mouth when it comes to prayer unless you are in church. My preference would have been for the school to allow the children to say their own prayer voluntarily and to do so silently; or very quietly to themselves. Perhaps their parents could have written it down for them. The process could have involved the administration in authorizing the student's prayers ahead of time to abide by certain guidelines of brevity and constitutionality. This alternative idea would have made it more difficult at the time for the justices to declare this scenario of praying as unconstitutional, as having the actual prayer come from the student is more defendable by the freedom of speech clause and the freedom of religion clause.

I pasted in a key part of the eloquent dissent from Justice Potter Stewart on this case. It helps to set the tone for when we will delve into other cases that violate First Amendment rights. He makes the point that, heretofore, a precedent of prayer and an acknowledgement of the supreme deity has been "part and parcel" of our government from the very beginning:

> Moreover, I think that the Court's task, in this as in all areas of constitutional adjudication, is not responsibly aided by the uncritical invocation of metaphors like the wall of separation, a phrase nowhere to be found in the Constitution. What is relevant to the issue here is not the history of an established church in sixteenth century England or in eighteenth century America, but the history of the religious traditions of our people, reflected in countless practices of the institutions and officials of our government. At the opening of each day's session of his court we stand, while one of our officials invokes the protection of God. Since the days of John Marshall our Crier has said, "God save the United States and this Honorable Court."

> Both the Senate and the House of representatives open their daily Sessions with prayer. Each of our presidents, from George Washington to John F. Kennedy, has upon assuming his Office asked the protection and help of God. The Court today says that the state and federal governments are without constitutional power to prescribe any particular form of words to be recited by any group of the American people on any subject touching religion. One of the stanzas of "The Star-Spangled Banner," made our National Anthem by Act of Congress in 1931, contains these verses: "Blest with victory and peace, may the heaven rescued land Praise the Power that hath made and preserved us a nation! Then conquer we must, when our cause it is just. And this be our motto 'In God is our Trust.'

In 1954, Congress added a phrase to the Pledge of Allegiance to the Flag so that it now contains the words "one Nation *under God,* indivisible, with liberty and justice for all." In 1952, Congress enacted legislation calling upon the president each year to proclaim a National Day of Prayer. Since 1865, the words, "IN GOD WE TRUST" have been impressed on our coins and cash. Countless similar examples could be listed, but there is no need to belabor the obvious. It was all summed up by the Court just ten years ago in a single sentence: "We are a religious people whose institutions presuppose a Supreme Being."

I do not believe that the Court or the Congress or the president has by the actions and practices I have mentioned established an "official religion" in violation of the Constitution. I do not believe the State of New York has done so in this case. What each has done has been to recognize and to follow the deeply entrenched and highly cherished spiritual traditions of our Nation—traditions which come down to us from those who over two hundred years ago avowed in the Declaration of Independence their "firm Reliance on the Protection of divine Providence" when they proclaimed the freedom and independence of this brave new world. I dissent.

I can't say anything that could improve on what Justice Potter Stewart wrote, so I will go on. The most significant modern day Supreme Court case that shapes the current status of religious prayer freedoms (or lack of it) in public schools is the Sante Fe Independent School District v. Doe (2000.) The Court ruled that students may not use a school's loudspeaker system to offer ***student-led, student-initiated*** prayer. Here are the additional facts of the case taken verbatim from the court docket:

Before football games, members of the student body of a Texas high school elected one of their classmates to address the players and spectators. The students conducted these addresses over the school's loudspeakers and usually involved a prayer. Attendance at these events was voluntary. Three students sued the school arguing that the prayers violated the

> Establishment Clause of the First Amendment. A majority of
> the Court rejected the school's argument that the activity was
> within constitutional bounds since the prayer was student-
> initiated and student-led and to a voluntary audience, as
> opposed to the school officially sponsoring it. The Court
> held that this action did constitute school-sponsored prayer
> because the loudspeakers that the students used for their
> invocations were owned by the school.

Let's take a look at the court's rationale. If providing a microphone
with a loud speaker system equates to an endorsement or promotion
of what is spoken into it, then every news station, every audio-visual
company and every private concern that ever held a microphone and
loudspeaker system to a person's mouth (to be consistent) would be
responsible for what is said as well. You and I know this simply is not
correct. Now, let's try to see if there is any legal basis for the court's
decision.

Before this case in 2000, the Supreme Court had already decided
that **school** *sponsored prayer* (as opposed to *student-led, student-initiated*
prayer) in front of a *volunteer* crowd was unconstitutional in any form.
Even though I disagree with the court's pre-2000 findings, we'll take is
as a given for now that all **school**-*sponsored* prayer is unconstitutional.
Since the facts of this case are that the prayer **was** student led, student
initiated and targeted a voluntary audience, I contend there clearly is
no school endorsement of anything said into that microphone at that
point. In addition, there was no endorsement of a specific church or
religion in the actual prayer, which otherwise **could** have arguably been
unconstitutional.

Everyone just assumes judges must have a legitimate legal reason
for their findings. However, I hope to shed light on how it is all hype
and deception. Indeed, justices often have no basis, legal or otherwise,
for rulings other than a deep secular progressive agenda that they have
imposed on us.

My next legal point is that the court has hardly considered the
religious protection clause ("or prohibiting the free exercise thereof")
and the **freedom of speech clause** ("or abridging the freedom of

speech,") when deliberating this case or prior prayer cases. They have only considered the **establishment** clause ("Congress shall make no law respecting the establishment of religion.") Shouldn't there be a debate regarding a balancing of interests in which the supposed violation of the establishment clause gets weighted on the legal scale against the religious protection clause? Moreover, shouldn't the establishment clause also be weighed against the extremely strong legal precedents of the freedom of speech clause? Why is student prayer automatically overlooked as a freedom of speech issue while all other **non**-prayer cases result in **guarding** free speech? If the justices are going to guard free speech like it was gold at Fort Knox (and they should,) then prayer should not be an exception unless it does give the appearance that schools are endorsing a specific church or religion.

At this point, you can certainly surmise I am a believer in a school-administered moment of silence. The Supreme Court actually ruled on this before the previous case. I left the "moment of silence" case until last as the order in which I'm reviewing the cases is by the amount they offend our sensibilities. The 1985 Wallace v. Jaffree case ruled that even a moment of silence administered by a school authority was unconstitutional. I am going to list their three rationales together with my counter argument (beginning with an asterick"*") to show how each are plainly fallacious. You will not need any legal understanding to see the attempt of deception by the justices, whether conscious or unconscious on their part. The facts of the case are that a school administrator required a moment of silence before academic learning began. It was presented by the teacher as an opportunity to meditate, pray or think about anything the student would like during that time.

1. The court said the First Amendment's "individual freedom embraced the right to select any religious faith or none at all." The court implied the moment of silence forces all students to participate in a religious activity." * First, prayer is not necessarily a "religious" activity as per my discussion on the definitions of prayer vs. religion. Second, the teacher had made it clear that the student may do anything they want during that time and that prayer was **only one** of the options. Moreover, the prayer would be silent. Therefore, there is no way a

student can feel isolated if he chooses not to participate because no one knows what anyone else is thinking or praying.

2. The court, prior to this ruling, had created a test for determining whether an activity in a public school was constitutional. One of the three-prong tests was that it had to have a secular purpose. In this case, the court suggested that the purpose of the moment of silence was to give the student a chance to pray, which is not a secular purpose. * However, the opportunity to meditate, make plans for their day or to think about whatever they like *is* clearly a secular purpose.

3. The court said that the purpose of the moment of silence was to **endorse religion**. But it does **not** endorse **religion**. It endorses prayer. Prayer is not religion. Here, they violate my rule that you can't substitute words and (therefore legal concepts) that are totally different from each other. Prayer can be a religious activity, but it doesn't **have** to be. Prayer *is* clearly protected by the First Amendment's religious protection clause ("or prohibiting the free exercise thereof.") The Supreme Court justices in the decision above have fallaciously substituted the meaning of words to make it appear their findings are constitutional. More importantly, they have eliminated an opportunity for a student to pray silently through an **obvious** and egregious violation of the religious protection clause. No one needs to know anything about legal jargon or the Constitution to understand this basic deduction. One just needs to understand simple English to conclude that the 1985 Supreme Court justices were denying the right to pray silently when the First Amendment says you are free to exercise your religion.

Today, students have *some* opportunities to pray, although they are embarrassingly scant in a country that claims to have religious freedom. Flagpole ministries are an example. Students are permitted to gather at a flagpole (or a similar place outside the school building) and pray. They can still whisper prayers to themselves in the hallway before a test or even in the classroom without the prayer police ushering them to the principal's office. But this is a small consolation in the battle of school prayer rights, which has been won for the most part by the secular progressives. A valedictorian still cannot thank his God at a graduation speech without school administrators literally pulling the plug. (Am I really living in the same country founded by pilgrims who immigrated here to escape religious persecution?)

I would be remiss if I didn't mention a recent victory for religious freedom pertinent to the separation of church and state doctrine. It was a no-brainer for the Supreme Court, evidenced by an unusual unanimous vote in favor of religious institution's rights. I am including the case to provide a bookend on the *right* side of religious freedom issues. The Washington Times website article from January 11, 2012 said:

> Religious organizations won a landmark victory Wednesday as the Supreme Court held that churches have the right to make employment decisions free from government interference over discrimination laws. In a 9-0 decision, the Supreme Court endorsed for the first time the 'ministerial exception' to state and federal employment discrimination laws while rejecting the Obama administration's argument that churches should be treated no differently than other employers.... We are pleased that the Supreme Court rejected the Obama administration's profoundly troubling claim of power over churches and glad to see that the Supreme Court has stayed out of the Lutheran Church's affairs and allowed its internal rules as a body of believers to stand, said Ken Klukowski, director of the Center for Religious Liberty at the Family Research Council.

As I stated at the beginning of this section, it is right to make rulings that are in keeping with the true original spirit of the separation of church and state doctrine.

In summary, I fully accept that we as Americans are a diverse nation. Except for a very small percentage, we identify ourselves as someone who believes in a higher authority, regardless of what being that might be. Why has the Supreme Court, then, gone as far as viewing the First Amendment through the eyes of an atheist? Is this not the epitome of bowing to a priority of political correctness rather than striking a fair balance for all? Are we a country of atheists or a country that is committed to tolerate the views of atheism? Conversely, should not atheists and secular progressives tolerate the exercise of religious freedoms? A true interpretation of the Constitution protects both a school administered moment of silence and a student-led, student-initiated prayer in a volunteer audience during government and school functions, assuming there is no appearance of endorsing a specific religion.

Removal of Creationism vs. Include Both Theories

The final straw regarding the movement toward pure secularism is the removal of the teaching of creationism from our schools. I don't expect public schools to divide their science lesson on evolution into two equal parts, with one espousing the traditional belief that a god created the world in five days and man on the sixth. But I would expect public schools to incorporate the teaching of intelligent design to offset the stringent theory of evolution that gives our young the impression we are just non-spiritual animals that descended from apes. The Darwinian Theory presented in science class would have the young child believe that no superior being had anything to do with his/her creation. This means public schools are directed to teach a theory to children that is misleading and incomplete according to everyone that believes in a god. This is an assault on freethinking that is guaranteed in our First Amendment by the freedom of speech clause. Doesn't the First Amendment protect all other books and publications from censorship? Where are the First Amendment advocates on weighing the value of presenting creationism?

The 1987 Supreme Court ruling of *Edwards v. Aguillard* provided precedents that laid the groundwork for many more "creationism" cases to be ruled in favor of the secular progressives. Ultimately, creationism was removed from public schools in its totality. In 1987, the Supreme Court established the three-pronged test to determine whether a school's action was unconstitutional. I quote verbatim from the ruling:

- The government's action must have a *legitimate secular purpose*;

- The government's action must *not* have the primary effect of *either advancing or inhibiting religion;*
- The government's action must not result in an *excessive entanglement* of the government and religion."

However, the court did note that alternative scientific theories ***could*** be taught: "We do not imply that a legislature could never require that *critiques of prevailing scientific theories* be taught. Teaching a variety of scientific theories about the origins of humankind to schoolchildren might be validly done with the clear secular intent of enhancing the effectiveness of science instruction."

I would argue for the point, which was made by the dissenting justices, regarding the first prong—protecting academic freedom ***is*** a "legitimate secular purpose," which means allowing creationism to be taught ***is*** a *"critique of prevailing scientific theory."* Let's look at the second prong to the above test, which states that the government's action cannot advance or inhibit religion. Isn't it clear that removing the teaching of creationism, at least in the Supreme Court's eyes, inhibits religion? Obviously, the justices made a decision that directly contradicts their own rule. Letting intelligent design ***remain*** in the classroom accomplishes neutrality on the matter (to neither advance nor inhibit religion.) After all, teaching both theories on the origin of man truly embodies the spirit of the second prong.

When a little child asks who created everything, the parents (unless they are atheist or agnostic) usually answer "god" did. I understand this answer is easy and the parents are not going to try to teach the Darwinian theory of evolution to a child. But over 90% of Americans believe in a god, so they so believe they are telling the truth to the child. Whereas it ***may*** be true that man originally looked like an ape and did go through a metamorphosis that modernized his features, most of us believe in a creator that started the process. Teaching creationism isn't an ***entanglement with government and religion;*** it is an entanglement with the belief in intelligent design. Here, the justices again were substituting the concept of god with that of religion. There is no way to stretch the separation of church and state doctrine to keep schools from acknowledging that there ***can*** be an intelligent designer (not that there necessarily *is* one.) Therefore, teaching creationism as a theory and a critique of some aspects of evolution is in fact compliant with the third prong of the test.

A book published in 1989 that accomplished exactly what the Supreme Court said it had no problem with (critiques of prevailing scientific theories) was "Of Pandas and People." The original 1989 edition espoused the theory of intelligent design and presented polemic arguments questioning the scientific theory of evolution. As you might have guessed, one of the many Supreme Court cases banning creationism material from public schools also banned the book above. Clearly, this banning is in contradiction of their academic freedom policy mentioned above in Edwards v. Aguillard, particularly because the author of the book was careful not to use the "G word" or endorse religion. The book had secular value in that it presented scientific evidence questioning another theory. It is clear that the courts are going to contradict their own findings and "twist and turn" their way into reaching their secular agenda goals, regardless of how unsound their legal basis is proven to be.

6.

Pro-Choice vs. Pro-Life

"**Y**OU ARE UNDER the influence, not me," I said to my agnostic friend, who then gave me that cynical look that I know quite well; the one with the raised eyebrow. Although we each had a beer in front of us, I was not referring to drinking. I was talking about the topic at hand—abortion. "I know you think my passion on the abortion issue is a result of my religious background. However, the reality is that *you* are the one who is under the influence from the secular worldview." I explained to him my rationale. No one in church ever *had* to tell me that abortion was wrong. Sure, religious institutions espouse the sanctity of all life and there is a high correlation between those that are pro-life and those that consider themselves religious. But children already know it is wrong to kill an unborn puppy before their parent tells them. It is intuitive. On the other hand, the tolerance of killing a fetus (which is counterintuitive) is an accepted mindset in this country by many, especially those under forty. The law of the land and the national consciousness on this issue influences *your* viewpoint, I explained; whether you are aware of it or not. My friend just looked at me with his dubious countenance.

Science and technology support my point. Centuries ago, abortion tolerance was affected mostly by how much the mother was "showing." Back then, perception was not only reality, it often shaped the course of events for the young, unwedded mother. Over time, the answer to the question of when life begins became the significant factor in shaping the morality of abortion. Today, we know from obstetricians that life begins at conception. Sonograms and other technology have increased awareness about fetuses in the womb. For example, a fetus of only five weeks already has all the vital signs for life, including a heartbeat and brainwaves. This knowledge diminishes the moral difference between early term and late term abortions as it emphasizes the same result, regardless of the fetal stage of development. Science, not religion, tells us that early term abortion is as wrong as a last minute decision to abort. I left my agnostic friend speechless with this simple argument. We agreed to disagree. If I thought these two simple paragraphs would persuade all naysayers, I would end this section here. But I know better. Therefore, I will write about this issue from every angle possible, as I believe my mission is paramount. Please keep an open mind throughout the following sections. My goal is to convince you that a pregnant woman holds another life (very much like herself) that is not a choice, but a responsibility.

I divided my material into many sub-topics. Some of it is creative. Some of it is contemporary. Some of it is historical. I get both philosophical and personal. I also may challenge your comfort level with it. I wanted to appeal to your mind and your heart; your logic and your emotions. Please have patience with my analysis of the landmark Supreme Court decision that first legalized abortion. I don't want there to be any doubt in your mind that there was absolutely no legal or constitutional basis for it.

Life Can Be an Option vs. The Foundation of Civilization

What is the foundation of civilization? What concept, reality, philosophy or truism holds civilization together? What has kept us from totally annihilating each other from the face of the earth? One could say, "The love of mankind." But why is there such a love? What is the basis for it? You might answer "trust," affirming that you can't have love without trust. One answer I might expect is "knowledge." But knowledge is a requirement for advancing civilization, not the foundation of it. Moreover, what is the motive for us to use knowledge to our benefit?

So, there is still a foundation at rock bottom that is needed in order to build love, trust or knowledge. There's a lot of other concepts having to do with contribution, helping others and charity that also require this same foundation. If you said "survival," you are very close as the will to survive must come first before love and these other noble concepts. All of these nontangible concepts are still dependent on one other foundation. They all are indeed given to us by our creator as they emanate from our free will. But one of them is required to occur first and it forms the foundation that the others are built upon.

Time's up. Make your best guess yet? Answer: The foundation of civilization is the respect for life. You can't have love, trust, honesty, charity or knowledge unless you respect yourself and each other. One first has to recognize that life deserves to exist (all life, not just yours and your loved ones.) Then and only then do we determine that we as living beings are worthy to benefit from these other noble and productive concepts. Human existence on this planet, followed by civilization, first requires respect for life. Hate, death and war all come from a lack of respect for life.

Dual Position vs. Consistent Position

Let's get out of the way a very familiar position on this topic you hear from friends and politicians. You might hear someone say in a discussion, "I'm against abortion, but I'm not in favor of forcing others that want an abortion to have a child." Former Mayor Rudy Julianni is on record (during the 2008 presidential campaign) as saying he is *personally* against abortion but recognizes the citizen's legal right to abortion, and supports the latter stance *politically*. Mr. Julianni had to say publicly that he is personally against abortion to save face as he is Catholic. But, he decided to take the politically correct stance of pro-choice to please the electorate.

When you hear someone say this, you are being asked to accept two opposing viewpoints—one is his/her personal preference as opposed to another position for everyone else. If we were to accept this thinking on every issue that *relates to vital political issues*, then we would end up going through life with two viewpoints—one for you and your family, but then another one for everyone else. Please don't get caught into this trap. The test for being honest about an issue is applying it to yourself or your closest relative. If the results are consistently the same regardless of whom you are addressing (whether or not you hold an office,) you are true to that position. If the results are different depending on whom you are speaking to, you are being hypocritical. Let me give you a few comparative statements and you'll get the idea:

- I'm in favor of Congress sending soldiers to fight this particular war, as long as they don't send *my* son.
- I'm in favor of first time violent offenders getting a reduced sentence of only three months in jail and then community service, but if he attacked *my* daughter, five years in jail would not nearly be enough.
- Communities need to understand the need for a halfway house; just don't allow one *next door.*

"No one would ever say these things," you reply. They would obviously look hypocritical. Yet, the exact same analogy applies to Julianni. Isn't it amazing that a nationally known figure such as Mayor Rudy Julianni, who ran for president in 2008 and started to run in 2012, was *not* chastised by the media with taking on one position to please his family and friends yet another position to please the NYC electorate? (I guess it's actually proof of how liberal the media really is.) The honest depiction of Mr. Julianni's position is that he is pro-life at heart, but realized he could never be mayor of New York City by publicly taking this stance, as he simply was outnumbered. This is the case with many politicians today. They shy away from standing up for the right position because a pro-life stance in their district would be so unpopular, they would never get elected or re-elected.

In conclusion, don't let someone tell you they are pro-life personally but pro-choice for others. If they do, then they need to grow a spine. That would be like saying they would never abuse their own children, but it is okay for others to abuse children. If they are okay with the latter, then shame on them. This mindset of tolerance and apathy is why we have accepted a pro-choice consciousness.

Save the Animals vs. Save the Fetuses

"We brake for animals, save the whales and protect the endangered species, including humans." This bumper sticker that goes back to the seventies speaks volumes. Here's one I saw in early 2012: "So you are for abortion but against killing terrorists?" When I first read this, I thought this one sentence had an impact equivalent to many paragraphs of what I write. How foolish do we look when we are more concerned with terrorists' lives while we look the other way as doctors legally abort fetuses from sixteen year-olds? To strike an even more extreme contrast, consider how absurd it is to substitute "water-boarding" for "killing" terrorists.

Yes, I'm going to tap into your emotional desire to save the cute little baby possum that is crossing the road, the awesome, majestic whales that accent our seas and the delicate praying mantis, especially their gentle offspring that haven't yet emerged from their soft, protective wrapping. (Ironically, it is illegal to kill even them; but not an unborn human being.) Who among us wouldn't extend this desire to also save the creature that clearly is at the top of the food chain? Aren't humans the rulers of the earth and all the creatures that dwell in it? Why doesn't the fervor for saving animals necessarily extend to the human species? I dare say it once was. After all, animals don't kill their unborn young. But our culture of tolerance, convenience and control has sadly soured our hearts and minds.

The foundation of civilization is the respect for life.

We are indeed emotional beings and a young, unwed pregnant girl making a choice is no exception. She is worried about not being able to cope with raising a child. She is struggling with obvious embarrassment. She doesn't want this new life to interfere with her plan. She is concerned about the financial burden. These are the reasons young women in this situation make the choice to abort about 97% of the time. (Statistic as per "First Choice Women's Resource Center.")

Conversely, *some* pregnant women who seek the right kind of counseling first *before* making a rash choice— make the right one. It is often based on the sonogram showing that the fetus within her is a living, active being with a heart rate and all body parts. In fact, one can go to a website (welcomehomebaby.com) and see a video of a six-week-old fetus. Even at this early stage, it has limbs formed and moves about in the sac. Many organizations help pregnant women choose life by providing them with the emotional and financial support they need to carry the unborn to full term, even if it means giving the baby up for adoption. Imagine the joy (for those who choose adoption) of meeting that adult who was once in your womb, as he/she finds you years later to thank you for giving them life. The awkward time in your life you spent allowing this human being to grow would be a small sacrifice to pay for this reward.

Life Creation is Man's Decision vs. Life Creation is God's Decision

Imagine you are the creator of the universe. It's cool to pretend this, actually. (Staunch atheists may want to skip this section.) As the creator, you are the Alpha and the Omega (timeless.) You are surrounded by blackness until you create the heavens. You spend billions of years arranging the heavenly bodies as their light show amazes you century after century. One day, nine planets around one star in the Milky Way Galaxy all position themselves on one plane, providing a unique and protective position for our Earth. You then can see that Jupiter's large mass would pull towards itself many of the large asteroids that would have crashed into this earth. Now the real fun begins. You put on your geology hat and go to work. The Colorado River carves out the Grand Canyon, volcanoes erupt to provide fireworks, rainforests create a pretty world of green, the Alps and the Rockies display your majesty, and the Redwood Forests brag how you can make trees as tall as you like. You accent your artwork with a rainbow or two.

Now it's time to crank it up a notch. You create incredibly unique and amazing living plants, underwater creatures and animals of varying size and design. Their beauty is beyond description. The polar bears on the North Pole and the caribou on the South Pole are finishing top and bottom touches amongst all the other creatures roaming the earth. The pride of the eagle that soars above the earth contrasts against the frailty of the smallest shellfish on the ocean's floor. These thought provoking and splendid creatures speak volumes about how extensive your imagination reaches. Each species will have something unique about them. Although they are awesome, you have bigger fish to fry in your laboratory. You create man. (I understand that if the history of the earth was clocked using a 24-hour time frame, man would appear on earth at one minute before midnight.)

Our intelligent designer has spent an incredible amount of time in his laboratory engineering the perfect creation of man. Is it not instinctive to realize that since he is the creator of life, he alone has the authority to destroy it? How angry would you be if someone stomped out the creation you toiled over for a lifetime? Would it not be a fair comparison for someone to kill your daughter or son? Is this not exactly what a pregnant woman does when she chooses abortion?

Not Inspired vs. Inspired

The ultimate inspiration for choosing life is someone like Sarah Palin, former governor of Alaska and former VP candidate in 2008, who carried a fetus to full term while knowing it would have Down's syndrome. If there ever would be a poster mom for the ultimate pro-life icon, it would be Sarah Palin. The devastating condition of Down's syndrome is apparently so undesirable, expectant mothers who are told the baby they carry has it will opt for abortion about 90% of the time. She simply kept the baby because she understood and believed in the sanctity of life and obeyed God's commandment to allow all life to live, not just the unblemished. Here are some of the quotes about her feelings of giving life to a special needs child in her book, *Going Rogue*:

- "I wanted our loved ones to focus on the fact that this baby, every baby, has purpose and that not only would he learn from us, but we would learn from him."
- "But when I saw him, my heart was flooded with unspeakable joy. I knew that not only had God made Trig different but He had made him perfect."

- "Special Needs community and your families—you are my most favorite people, ever. You are lucky because God touched each one of you in unique ways."

These quotes speak volumes about the preciousness of all life and I can't add anything to them to underscore their importance.

Here is what Sarah Palin told Katie Couric in an interview when Couric wanted to explore the boundaries, if any, about Palin's pro-life stance regarding various scenarios an unwed mother might face. Palin described her "no exceptions policy" this way: "…I was unapologetically pro-life and that I would counsel someone to choose life. I also said that we should build a culture of life in which we help women in difficult situations, encourage adoption and support foster and adoptive families."

Man's Love Covenant vs. God's Love Covenant

Even if you are not religious, all of us instinctively know about the love covenant. We don't call it that and we all have our own take on it. But here's the real deal: This covenant is an offer from god that transcends spirituality and religion. It is made to all those with the understanding of how a human being is created. The offer from god says:

> *You have the power to create life (with my final approval) and I give you the ideal parameters for doing so. When you share love with someone enough to trust him/her, you gain the privilege of taking part in the creation of life. I won't give you a child unless you act first (relations with your partner) in asking my permission. But understand your decision to take part in the covenant means you agree to take responsibility in receiving and caring for my gift, if and when it is given; which is un-returnable.*

With all the joy that life's creation brings, is this one caveat really unbearable? When the natural parents of a fetus have consensual sex, they take on the realization they might create another human being. The abortion process not only breaks the love covenant, it is the epitome of ungratefulness for receiving this world's most precious gift—life itself.

In most cases, couples willfully engage in the act that could, despite precautions, result in pregnancy. So, we play the game and take the risk. But some of us don't want to deal morally with the consequences when surprise hits us hard. Bypassing responsibility for a mysterious happening despite the most careful reproductive planning is not an option recognized by the love covenant. God doesn't make mistakes, only people do. He clearly calls the shots about our fate. He makes the rules, not us. If we don't agree with the obvious rules of god's love covenant, we shouldn't take part in it.

A man and a woman will sometimes assume it is they alone that create the child in the woman's body, forgetting there is a third party involved (the creator.) Couples who can't naturally have a child on their own are reminded how powerless they are without the intelligent designer to provide life. Denial can be the only explanation for a young girl or woman who thinks she alone has the right to kill something that two other parties had a part in creating. She might assume or receive permission from the natural father, but she could never get permission from the creator, who also took part in the event.

Murder is Worse vs. Abortion is Worse

Consider the following hypothetical scenarios: Two women who are forty years old live in the same neighborhood and are married to men the same age as they. The year is 1970 and abortion in their state is illegal. Mrs. Dangerfield discovers her husband has had a mistress for quite a while. So, over the next year, she methodically plots to kill him and does so successfully. Assume there was no reason she could have just divorced him instead. The other woman, Mrs. Kindermore, has three children and finds out she is pregnant with a fourth. She doesn't want a child at her age and further feels she can't afford it, either. She doesn't tell her husband because he is very pro-life and she knows he would not agree to an abortion. So, she aborts it secretly. Which crime is worse? Assume there are no other circumstances that would be significant in comparing or contrasting them. Are you ready for my answer?

I believe the woman that aborted her child committed a worse crime. Here are my reasons: First, the woman who aborted, Mrs. Kindermore, consented to her marriage and to sex. She had every expectation to believe there was always a chance she would get pregnant by surprise. She entered into the love covenant. On the other hand, Mrs. Dangerfield did not give consent to her husband to have a mistress. Score one negative point for Mrs. Kindermore, who consented. Secondly, the fetus is a totally innocent victim and Mrs. Kindermore knew it. However, Mr. Dangerfield is far from innocent. Score two negative points for Mrs. Kindermore, who killed an *innocent* victim. Thirdly, it is wrong to exclude the natural father and husband from joining in on the decision to abort. Mr. Kindermore, her married husband and father of the child, has the right to at least be informed. So, Mrs. Kindermore violated Mr. Kindermore's right to enjoy all the years of being a father to this child. That makes three negative points so far. Fourthly, Mrs. Kindermore took away approximately twice as many years of living from the fetus she killed than Mrs. Dangerfield, who killed her husband. Let's calculate. The fetus had every expectation to expect to live to be about eighty, give or take, depending on the gender. Mr. Dangerfield at least got to live for forty years, which was about half the life the fetus would expect to enjoy. So, the score for negative points is four to zero; with Mrs. Kindermore shutting out Mrs. Dangerfield. To summarize, taking away the life of *an innocent* victim that you are responsible for creating (without advising your husband) is twice the crime of taking away the life of a forty year-old that is *partially* responsible for his demise.

A very clever commercial that ran in 2008 that was produced by a pro-life Catholic organization caused quite the stir. It told a striking story about a mother who was struggling and married to an absentee husband who lived in another country. The mother's day-to-day circumstances were difficult and she was not in an ideal position to have a child. She became pregnant and could have legally aborted the child, but decided to keep it. At the end of this dramatic commercial, the person narrating reveals her child's name was Barack Hussein Obama. Since Obama was about to be elected president, the idea underscores the worth of every fetus as the mother could never know what contribution that baby, if carried to term, could bring to the world. The ironic twist is that this child went on to become a Senator in Illinois and vote in favor of partial birth abortion for that state; and maintained a pro-choice position.

Even more to the point is that *anyone* born after 1973 could have been aborted legally in the United States. Therefore, any pro-choice person must share in the same moral dilemma—their pro-choice position, *if chosen by their mothers,* would have prevented them from even existing today. If someone spared you from abortion, shouldn't you (and others) in kind spare those of the next generation? Isn't a pro-choice position a blatant violation of the golden rule: "Do unto others what you would want done to you?" President Reagan said it this way, "I have noticed that those for abortion have been born."

Potential Human Being vs. A Fetus is a Legal Person

The fetus is the same entity whether or not it is in the mother's womb. Is not every person originally one cell that has been fertilized by sperm? Did not a robin come from an egg and did not a kangaroo once live in its mother's pouch? Was there ever a scientist that said the un-hatched sparrow was not a sparrow until it was hatched? Was there ever a veterinarian that said an unborn puppy is not a puppy until it is born? Therefore, why wouldn't a living, breathing person who certainly once was a fetus also be a person during his/her fetal stage? In Roe v. Wade, the majority opinion asserted the test for whether a fetus has developed enough to be a "person" with constitutional rights is whether it can live on its own outside of the mother's womb. You can see how fallacious this argument is when applying it to a fetus that was born so prematurely, it cannot live outside of the mother's womb without modern technology to keep it living (e.g.: various tubes, such as an oxygen mask, attached to a 2 pound infant). Imagine a 1973 Supreme Court justice voting in favor of a "pre-viability abortion right" being transported through time to visit the two-pound living miracle and asserting, "this 2 pound infant has no constitutional right to live until it is developed enough for the doctors to send it home with its mother." Rather, I would hope to think that the very sight of this precious 2 pound infant would jolt some sense into his thick, misguided cranium. Moreover, what about people in hospitals and nursing homes that can't live on their own without medical science to aid them? Are they no longer people with a right to live?

Consider the scenario of a woman who murders her newborn shortly after bringing it home from the hospital. She doesn't hide the crime and is arrested in short order for committing the horrific act. We all would agree, whether we are religious/spiritually convicted or not, that this is a highly illegal crime and this mother should be sentenced with serious time in whatever institution proves to be most appropriate. Why, then, should it be perfectly legal for this mother to kill her baby three months earlier while it was in her womb? What aspect about birth changes the morality of killing this fetus that becomes a person?

Life begins at conception, not birth. I believe most fair-minded people realize this intellectually; they just don't embrace it morally. There is no **real** difference in any live being before it is born versus after the event occurs, except for the stage of development. So, there also should be no **legal** difference.

Roe v. Wade is Law of the Land vs. No Constitutional Basis

In almost every culture since the history of man, abortion had been considered immoral and illegal by the vast majority of society up until 1973 when the Supreme Court decided a woman has the right to abort a fetus. The court based this decision on a **right to privacy** and asserted the woman can abort the fetus up until the stage in which it can live on its own, called "viability."

Supreme Court Justice Harry Blackmun wrote the majority opinion. He and the concurring justices *first* decided to gather information on this topic that included various philosophies, social values, moral standards, population growth, pollution, racial overtones, medical-legal history and "what history reveals about man's attitudes toward the abortion procedure over the centuries." *Then*, the majority court made a decision on abortion based, in part, on these factors. So the 1973 Supreme Court did what legislatures do—gather information and determine law. But the Supreme Court is supposed to only determine whether a law or lower case rulings are constitutional, or not. Therefore, the Court took upon itself the authority beyond its constitutional parameters. Ironically, its *legislative activity* was unconstitutional when it ruled state laws against abortion were unconstitutional.

Blackmun ruled the Constitution provides a right of privacy to pregnant mothers, making many but not necessarily all anti-abortion legislation at the time unconstitutional. We all agree with our rights to privacy to an extent. Are the following activities legal just because they occur in private?

- Murdering someone in your kitchen.
- Selling narcotics from your garage.
- Growing large quantities of marijuana in your backyard.
- Plotting terrorist activity in your office with known jihadists.

You get the point. The argument the court used to nullify current state laws against abortion just because of a right to privacy is clearly fallacious.

At the risk of being cute, I ask: Was Blackmun acting in the capacity of speaker for the majority opinion or as the majority speaker of the House of Representatives? Obviously, this decision was a piece of legislation that the court produced, violating the balance of powers our forefathers set in place. The judicial branch's responsibility is to interpret and judge the laws, not change them. The Roe v. Wade decision clearly outlined what the state could or could not do to enforce its current abortion laws, even to the point of breaking down their authority into three sections of fetal development. The court realized they had to cite some constitutional basis for their decision. So, they based it on vague, supposedly implied rights granted to mothers from the Fourteenth Amendment, specifically the Due Process Clause. I pasted in Section One of the Fourteenth Amendment here for you to examine its wording:

> All persons born or naturalized in the United States and subject to the jurisdiction thereof, are citizens of the United States and of the State wherein they reside. No State shall make or enforce any law which shall abridge the privileges or immunities of *citizens* of the United States; nor shall any State deprive any person of life, liberty or property, without *due process* of law; nor deny to any person within its jurisdiction the equal protection of the laws.

The Spartacus International website explains the original intent of the Fourteenth Amendment:

> The Fourteenth Amendment of the Constitution was passed by both houses on 8th June and the 13th June, 1866. The amendment was designed to grant citizenship to and protect the civil liberties of recently freed slaves. It did this by prohibiting states from denying or abridging the privileges or immunities of citizens of the United States, depriving any person of his life, liberty or property without due process of law or denying to any person within their jurisdiction the equal protection of the laws.

Now I will provide some interpretations of the Due Process Clause of the Fourteenth Amendment from different sources, followed by a brief legal history. This will provide a feel for what the constitutional concept is all about. In summary, it prohibits state and local governments from depriving persons of life, liberty or property without certain steps taken to ensure fairness. This clause has been used to make most of the Bill of Rights applicable to the states, as well as to recognize substantive and procedural rights. The Free Dictionary says:

> Due process of law is a legal concept that ensures the government will respect all of a person's legal rights instead of just some or most of those legal rights, when the government deprives a person of life, liberty or property. Due process has also been interpreted as placing limitations on laws and legal proceedings in order to guarantee fundamental fairness, justice and liberty to all citizens.

The Legal Information Institute website adds this:

> Thus, it is not always enough for the government just to act in accordance with whatever law there may happen to be. Citizens may also be entitled to have the government observe or offer fair procedures, whether or not those procedures have been provided for in the law on the basis of which it is acting. Action denying the process that is 'due' would be

unconstitutional…Process was due if rights were involved, but the state could act as it pleased in relation to privileges.

The Free dictionary expounds on the legalities of the Due Process Clause even further:

> The application of constitutional due process is traditionally divided into the two categories of **substantive** due process and **procedural** due process. These categories are derived from a distinction that is made between two types of law. **Substantive law** creates, defines and regulates rights, whereas **procedural law** enforces those rights or seeks redress for their violation. Thus, in the United States, substantive due process is concerned with such issues as *Freedom of Speech* and privacy, whereas procedural due process is concerned with provisions such as the right to adequate notice of a lawsuit, the right to be present during testimony and the right to an attorney.

The Due Process Clause is rich in its historical applications. (You'll quickly see how the Supreme Court would be hard pressed in 1973 to use this clause as a basis for legalizing abortion. I promise your patience will be rewarded.) The Legal Information Institute provides a brief impact it has had on the following key cases that created precedents:

- An early case held that a state could not post a picture of a person naming them as a habitual drunkard without first providing a chance for a hearing.
- In *Goldberg v. Kelly*, NY State could not drop the enrollment of a welfare recipient without a hearing.
- In *Mathews v. Eldridge*, disability benefits could not be dropped from the beneficiary until certain procedures were followed.
- Two Supreme Court cases involving the contracts of employment for teachers at state college determined a change in procedures, e.g.: granting a hearing; before the state could decide to terminate their contract after its term expired because of some political positions the teachers had taken.

These 4 cases above are examples resulting from **procedural** due process.

- In the 1897 case of *Allgeyer v. Louisiana*, the Court for the first time used the **substantive** due process framework to strike down a state statute. Before that time, the Court generally had used the Commerce Clause or the Contracts Clause of the Constitution to invalidate state legislation. The *Allgeyer* case concerned a Louisiana law that proscribed the entry into certain contracts with insurance firms in other states. The Court found that the law unfairly abridged the right to enter into lawful contracts, as guaranteed by the Due Process Clause of the Fourteenth Amendment. (source: Free Dictionary)

I listed the summary of these decisions and their outcomes so you can see **how** the Due Process Clause applied to actual cases as determined by its original intent. But going forward, the due process clause had it powers expanded by the courts:

> By the 1960s, the Court had extended its interpretation of substantive due process to include **rights and freedoms that are not specifically mentioned in the Constitution** but that, according to the Court, extend or derive from existing rights. These rights and freedoms include the freedoms of association and non-association, which have been inferred from the First Amendment's FREEDOM-OF-SPEECH provision and the right to privacy. The right to privacy, which has been derived from the first, fourth and Ninth Amendments, has been **an especially controversial aspect** of substantive due process. (Source: Free Dictionary)

Notice the phrase *"especially controversial"* when referring to the due process clause's application to the right of privacy. I am inferring (an invite you to join me) that this juncture is where the justices assumed too much power and authority and over stepped the bounds and intentions of the Constitution.

Although Blackmun cited several cases in his majority opinion involving the right to privacy, the one that had a set of facts closest to that of Roe v. Wade was *Griswold vs. Connecticut* (1965.) The court ruled unconstitutional a state law that prohibited the use of contraception. So, the court stretched the right of privacy from permitting the use of contraception to abortion on demand. That's quite the leap.

So, we've learned from the historical case data I provided above that the courts began using the due process clause to determine **various processes** entitled to the citizen when action by the state is taken. Subsequently, the 1960s saw the Court **extending** its interpretation using its evolutionist philosophy on "rights and freedoms that are not specifically mentioned in the Constitution," specifically the right of privacy. Justice Blackmun, in need of some constitutional basis for this newfound right of privacy to pregnant mothers, decided that the Due Process Clause was the "catch all" legal bucket to uphold the court's findings. Yet, he never explained how. He literally just re-invented the concept of due process to give mothers the legal right to abort.

The justices also linked their decision to the Ninth Amendment: "The enumeration in the Constitution, of certain rights, shall not be construed to deny or disparage others retained by the people." Here's the interpretation of the legal implications of the Ninth Amendment:

> The Ninth Amendment to the U.S. Constitution is somewhat of an enigma. It provides that the naming of certain rights in the Constitution does not take away from the people rights that are not named.... Every year federal courts are asked to recognize new Unenumerated Rights "retained by the people," and typically, they turn to the Ninth Amendment.... No comprehensive list of unenumerated rights has ever been compiled nor could such a list be readily produced precisely because these rights are unenumerated. Nevertheless, a partial list of unenumerated rights might include those specifically recognized by the Supreme Court, such as the right to travel, the right to privacy, the right to autonomy, the right to dignity... the federal judiciary does not base rulings exclusively on the Ninth Amendment; the courts usually cite the amendment as a secondary source of fundamental liberties. (Source: Free Dictionary)

The short interpretation of this is that the constitutional framers didn't want a list of rights to imply those originally written down will be the *only* list of rights going forward. (You guessed it. The 1973 majority opinion in Roe v. Wade decision decided this amendment is part of their basis in that abortion rights *are* suddenly one of *those* rights that were never enumerated in the Constitution.) In other words, the justices arbitrarily and officially decided to add the right to abort to the list. There were no legal mechanics to justify the decision.

In conclusion of the legal analysis of Roe v. Wade, I just wanted you to see with your own eyes there is nothing in The Fourteenth Amendment, the due process clause and its case precedents, or the Ninth Amendment; that provides any constitutional basis for the Roe v. Wade decision. Rather, they were cited as a device to provide some legitimacy (in the justices' minds) to their grand scheme. After studying every detail of Blackmun's opinion, I summarize with the following ten points about the court's decision. Phrases in quotes are Blackmun's words verbatim:

1. Blackmun began his legislative tear by discussing all the issues of the day, including historical and religious attitudes that affect the current mindset. He even spoke of over-population and pollution as influential factors in the court's decision.
2. Blackmun wrote on how a large part of the court's decision was based on the social and psychological ramifications of this issue (not a constitutional or legal basis.)
3. He said himself "The Constitution itself does not guarantee a right to privacy."
4. He also admitted the cases he cited to support the Roe v. Wade decision demonstrate some rights to privacy, but "formulate privacy rights that are much different than the issue of a woman carrying a live fetus."
5. He claims *without explanation* that the due process clause of the Fourteenth Amendment is the primary constitutional basis for his decision. He also cites *without explanation* that the Ninth Amendment is a secondary source of fundamental

liberty—that the right to abort is one of the un-enumerated rights in the Ninth Amendment.

6. He states that is not necessary for the court to determine when life begins, but in a contradictory twist, decided the court will determine at what point life can legally be ended.

7. Blackmun creates the concept of "viability," which is that point of fetal development in which a fetus could theoretically sustain itself outside the womb. Blackmun determines a "compromise" of allowing mothers to abort up until the state of "viability." He allows the states to regulate abortion after that point. He provides no rationale to his decision other than that he sees it as a likely compromise.

8. Blackmun decides a "fetus in not a person" and bases this decision on the fact that there is no previous ruling or legislation that says it is. (There also is no precedent that says the fetus is *not* a person.) It is obvious he makes this claim to prevent the states from saying the fetus *is* protected by the Equal Protection Clause of the Fourteenth Amendment.

9. The court goes to tremendous lengths to balance the interest of the mother to abort against the interest of the state to protect late term fetuses. It is a highly thought out process. The court calls it a compromise. Regardless, it is clearly "legislation," not "interpretation."

10. After deliberating in length about the state having a right to protect late term fetuses, (after the stage of "viability,") Blackmun throws in a loophole at the end saying that a mother can choose to abort after the first trimester for "health" reasons. The court then broadly defines the mother's health to include her psychological well-being.

I submit that these ten observations regarding the 1973 majority opinion determine their decision to be totally arbitrary, without constitutional basis, and the product of legislation from the bench. The court undoubtedly overstepped their bounds of **only** interpreting the laws (and case precedents.) In addition, the court loses credibility when it contradicted itself in these areas:

1. The relevancy of previous privacy rights cases: In the beginning, they used them to form a precedent for a legal basis. Later in the opinion, they admit the privacy rights of abortion are "much different."

2. The decision to create the concept of viability: The court asserted it didn't have to determine when life ***begins*** but decided to determine when life can ***end*** (a mother can abort prior to the viability stage of the fetus). This is a contradiction as the court ***did*** determine when ***legally protected life*** begins (which is the same in their view as "when life begins.")

3. The creation of the ***psychological well-being loophole***: The court constructed limitations on when a mother can abort in accordance with the age of the fetus, but threw it all out the window with a very liberal "out" for the mother to claim a right to late term abortions based on "psychological" issues.

4. A different type of contradiction (let's call it an "unsubstantiated reversal on legal mechanics") can be inferred from the court's (supposed) long standing practice to "hold" firm in rulings by honoring legal precedents and historical findings. Despite the fact there was no legal precedent for holding that a fetus is a not a legal person and despite the fact that a history of abortion laws imply that a fetus is in fact a legal person with legal protections provided to it, the 1973 majority opinion decided a fetus is ***not*** a legal person.

Associate Justices Byron R. White and William H. Rehnquist wrote emphatic dissenting opinions in this case. Justice White wrote:

> I find nothing in the language or history of the Constitution to support the Court's judgment. The Court simply fashions and announces a new constitutional right for pregnant mothers and, with scarcely any reason or authority for its action, invests that right with sufficient substance to override most existing state abortion statutes. The upshot is that the people and the legislatures of the Fifty States are constitutionally disentitled to weigh the relative importance of the continued existence and development of the fetus, on

the one hand, against a spectrum of possible impacts on the mother, on the other hand. As an exercise of raw judicial power, the Court perhaps has authority to do what it does today, but in my view, its judgment is an improvident and extravagant exercise of the power of judicial review that the Constitution extends to this Court.

Here are the various points that White made in his minority opinion (quotes are his:)

- White asserted that the Court "values the convenience of the pregnant mother more than the continued existence and development of the life or potential life that she carries."
- He wrote that he saw "no constitutional warrant for imposing such an order of priorities on the people and legislatures of the states."
- White criticized the Court for involving itself in this issue by creating "a constitutional barrier to state efforts to protect human life and by investing mothers and doctors with the constitutionally protected right to exterminate it."
- He would have left this issue, for the most part, "with the people and to the political processes the people have devised to govern their affairs."

Rehnquist elaborated on White's points, by asserting that the court's historical analysis was flawed:

To reach its result, the Court necessarily has had to find within the scope of the Fourteenth Amendment a right that was apparently completely unknown to the drafters of the Amendment. As early as 1821, the first state law dealing directly with abortion was enacted by the Connecticut Legislature. By the time of the adoption of the Fourteenth Amendment in 1868, there were at least 36 laws enacted by state or territorial legislatures limiting abortion. While many States have amended or updated their laws, 21 of the laws on the books in 1868 remain in effect today.

From this historical record, Rehnquist concluded that:

> There apparently was no question concerning the validity of this provision or of any of the other state statutes when the Fourteenth Amendment was adopted…the drafters did not intend to have the Fourteenth Amendment withdraw from the States the power to legislate with respect to this matter.

At the risk of reiteration, I need to make Rehnquist's paramount point crystal clear. When the drafters of the Fourteenth Amendment wrote it in 1868, there were at least thirty-six laws enacted by state or territorial legislatures limiting abortion. Rehnquist makes the solid, undeniable point that it was clearly ***not*** the drafters' intent to have the Fourteenth Amendment eventually negate the current laws on the books at that time, as they had let them stand as is. How, then, can the 1973 majority opinion change the legal conclusions by these drafters who wrote the Fourteenth Amendment 105 years earlier? They can't, but did so anyway.

Constitutional Decision vs. What Really Happened

Here's my take on what ***really*** happened in 1973: The laws against abortion were becoming increasingly unpopular and there obviously was much debate about the benefits to women to abort at will, especially if the abortions were early on in the pregnancy. Since allowing late term abortions would be more blatantly offensive to casual observers, there was a lot of thought clearly given to protecting the rights of fetuses that were in their final trimester and then about half way through their development (as evidenced by the content of the Roe v. Wade decision.) It would seem that there was a growing demand for a woman to at least have the convenience of disposing of a fetus that is in its first trimester, as this could be done confidentially without anyone besides the mother and the doctor having to know. Here are reasons why the national consciousness back in 1973 was different than it is today:

- There were many anecdotal stories of young girls and women whose attempts to self-abort had gone awry.

- The embarrassment of getting pregnant out of wedlock stigmatized the mother, which was much less acceptable in the early seventies as compared to today when tolerance is at an all-time high.
- Contraceptives for young girls and boys back then were not as readily available as they are today. In addition, the vasectomy procedure for men was not as much in vogue back then as it is today.
- Since there were no anti-abortion rallies or pro-life educational pamphlets at the time, there was less emphasis on the morality of aborting early term fetuses.
- Scientific and medical knowledge about early term fetuses was not as advanced, so unwedded mothers facing a decision didn't have the benefit of today's technology to make them as emotionally aware of their choice.
- The sixties brought us the sexual revolution and the bra-burning feminists who wanted equal rights and more. The early seventies saw Gloria Steinem, a celebrated advocate for women's rights, highlight the need for legitimate issues such as equal pay, child care, etc. In fact, the magazine "Ms." founded in 1971 instantly became a success, carrying the message of the "second class citizen." The table had been set for more women's rights in 1973.

All of these facts about this time period created a mindset that supported giving women the ultimate right—legal abortion on demand. In his majority opinion, Blackmun unabashedly discussed all of these issues as a means for supporting his opinion. So, it would appear that the Supreme Court justices *first* decided arbitrarily that the interest of the woman to have the ability and convenience of a legal, safe abortion was imperative (at least for the first trimester.) ***Then,*** they went to work looking for a constitutional basis to back their decision. The end game was that seven men negated what hundreds of legislators in all fifty states have debated and decided. In January of 1973, all but four states had laws on the books restricting abortion. The majority opinion even noted how controversial the topic of abortion was at the time. In fact, the

Roe v. Wade decision and other similar decisions on abortion are held by constitutional experts to have a legal basis that is more questionable than any other landmark decision by the Supreme Court.

A postscript to my argument is a comment from Justice Antonin Scalia speaking on how the "abortion right" is not in the Constitution: Justice Scalia debated with Nadine Strossen, president of the American Civil Liberties Union (ACLU) on a one-hour television program on 2006-OCT-15. Justice Scalia said that unelected judges have no place deciding politically charged questions in areas where the U.S. Constitution is silent. He said that liberal judges in the past had established new political rights, such as abortion access. He warned: "Someday, you're going to get a very conservative Supreme Court and regret that approach...On controversial issues on stuff like homosexual rights, abortion, we debate with each other and persuade each other and vote on it either through our elected representatives or a constitutional amendment."

We Are Sophisticated vs. We Are Still Evolving

Those who are pro-choice think we have finally evolved as a nation promoting equality among all. However, if you ask one of them about the minority rights of the fetus, they will make them an exception to their policy on equality. Is this not a huge inconsistency in their ideology? The fate of the fetus often is in the hands of young teenage girls who at the time feel they have every reason to do away with the problem. What kind of a society lets girls aged thirteen through seventeen make life and death decisions? Do you realize a child can get an abortion at any age in California without parental consent? Many states have similarly liberal laws regarding parental consent, although not as extreme. Would we give teenagers power of attorney in charge of making bedside life and death decisions regarding the care of a dying grandparent? Would we put them in the judge's seat to preside over a conviction that could involve capital punishment? Would we let them determine if a court will accept an appeal case involving a death row prisoner? Of course not. Are minors any more mentally, emotionally, intellectually and morally equipped to make a choice on a life inside of them than they are in these examples? Do we as a society recognize that teenagers are not morally or spiritually developed yet at such a young age? Why, then, do we as a society permit what we know goes on inside an organization like Planned Parenthood? The reason is because we still, as a nation, have not fully evolved our moral and intellectual consciousness about this issue.

Many other countries still hold abortion as illegal. While we look askance at other cultures that condone and arrange the marriage of children, we condone and arrange the abortions by our children, although by proxy. In most cases, we don't even know our children are aborting babies. As a society, we have given the ultimate power to the state to control what happens to our precious offspring. We don't even have the freedom to know that our children are having abortions behind our backs.

When the Roman Empire reigned as the largest power in Europe, the Caesar that presided over the Coliseum games authorized life and death to loyal warriors with the direction of his thumb. He did so just for sport. We've come a long way since then in respecting life, but still have a way to go. In the U.S. Civil War, over 600,000 men died on principal over the issue of slavery. Afterwards, there were rumblings about the excessive death of young men, so our national consciousness was jolted. To end World War II, the U.S. dropped two atom bombs on Japan. This sparked debate over the annihilation of such a vast majority of civilians. I am not taking a position here as to its justification either way, but am saying the debate of its use was healthy. During the Vietnam Era, our country became divided because many of us observed the reckless disposal of our country's young military men for what was deemed an unnecessary cause. Our national consciousness regarding the preciousness of life was now continuing to make healthy strides. When I was growing up, euthanasia was a controversial practice, although partially accepted. Middle-aged people were pulling the plug on their aging, debilitated parents with long trials of suffering before legal solutions came to fruition. Now, we've solved that problem with living wills. During the sixties and seventies, we resolved the equality issue. During the last two or three decades, we thought we truly arrived when we achieved political correctness. However, I have to disappoint the reader that thinks we have reached our final level of sophistication.

We currently tolerate a nasty barbaric habit. In terms of unborn life, we are living in the dark ages.

The national consciousness on abortion has its own cycle. When the Pilgrims landed, fetuses enjoyed solid respect. During those days, life was precious for no other reason than so many babies died through natural causes. As time passed, self-induced and physician-assisted abortions became frequent enough for 46 states to pass laws against it. That changed in 1973, quite the time span since the Mayflower docked at Plymouth Rock. Since then, the nation peaked with being pro-abortion sentiment sometime after the Roe v. Wade case. But the last few decades have brought us poll results showing pro-life fervor is making a comeback.

The pendulum was skewed very much against life in 1995 when Gallup Poll surveys found only 33% were pro-life versus 56% pro-choice. Only six years later on August of 2001, a dead heat was struck with 46% of those claiming to be pro-life with a matching 46% saying they were still pro-choice (the remaining 8% had no specific opinion.) Pro-life citizens took the lead in 2008, taking the chart from a dead even survey to one where the chart lines crossed each other for the first time in Gallup Poll history. Then a Gallup Poll conducted May 7-10, 2011, found 51% of Americans calling themselves "pro-life" on the issue of abortion and 42% "pro-choice"—an astonishing 9 point lead. This is the first time a majority of U.S. adults have identified themselves as pro-life since Gallup began asking this question in 1995. Why? Overall, the subject of abortion over the last couple of decades has generated more press, information flow, and education than ever. (A subsequent Gallup Poll taken in May 2012 showed the same 9 point lead, with 50% holding as pro-life and 41% favoring pro-choice.) Here are some specific reasons why pro-life awareness and sentiment has increased:

- The medical community has prompted young mothers facing a choice to be more aware of the life inside of them by the use of sonograms and other modern devices. One fact of interest to a young mother, as an example, is that a fetus of only five weeks has all the vital signs of life, including a heartbeat and brainwaves. (Providing such facts would be relevant to over 99%

of mothers facing a choice, as only about 1 percent of mothers are quick enough with their decision to abort prior to the five week stage.)

- Pro-life organizations have offered services and counseling to young mothers facing a choice, providing them with the realization of how precious the life inside of them really is; that it *is* in fact a human being like themselves at the earliest of stages.
- Many religious-based as well as pro-life organizations have programs to assist the young, unwed mother financially and psychologically to enable her to carry the fetus to term for the purpose of adoption, assuming the mother doesn't want to keep and raise the child.
- Infertile parents who wish to adopt find they have to fly half way around the world and incur tremendous expense because the supply of babies to adopt here in the U.S. is so low.
- The internet has been used to provide knowledge and information about fetuses and abortion. Many facts on the subject can be found quicker than ever before. As an example, one can read on how some economists have calculated how much more robust our economy would be if there had not been so many *millions* of abortions in the United States.
- Pro-life journalists and politicians have utilized more airtime to speak on issues related to abortion. Perhaps this practice is becoming less hush-hush and less frowned upon. Two of the related issues which have received mainstream coverage are:
  o The House of Representatives voted to cut funding to Planned Parenthood back in February 2011. (The effort did not progress in Congress from there.)
  o Many leaders in Washington, D.C. claimed early in President Obama's tenure that our country should outlaw water-boarding to legitimately claim moral leadership in the world. I have observed some politicians counter argue with the comment, "How about outlawing abortion as a path to moral leadership?"

I would encourage everyone to be bold and speak about the sacredness of all life in a non-offensive way whenever the opportunity presents itself. Here's an example I observed of someone who had a golden opportunity to impact millions (more or less depending on that show's ratings,) but blew it. An accomplished actress who recently published a tell-all book about her life was interviewed on a talk show in spring 2012. She spoke openly about her past and how she kept some stories of her life secret for decades. The interviewer's first question about the book was on the abortion she had when just a girl. The actress briefly spoke about the effort to keep it secret, her psychological trauma and the counseling she received sometime after her decision. She then changed the subject to the regimented manner in which she was raised and shared some insight on how she currently raises her teenage daughters. Yet, she never took the opportunity to say that the decision she made was morally wrong or that she would have made a different choice if she could go back in time. There was no reference to the realization of what she had done. She only spoke about how the event affected her. When speaking of her teenage daughters (currently at a vulnerable age,) she never said how she would teach them anything she may have learned from this experience. I found this to be extremely disappointing, yet typical of the glib manner in which the crucial *morality* issue is glossed over or avoided altogether when the opportunity to address it arises, especially on TV. Conversely, high profile stars could project untold amounts of pro-life influence on young watchers if they just chose to.

Regardless, the trends over the decades show light at the end of the tunnel regarding our move toward recognizing the preciousness of all life. In fact, they prove that the abortion issue can be influenced. A nine percentage point spread favoring the pro-life viewpoint is a huge success for the movement—a very rewarding one based on their vigilant attempts to educate those willing to listen. My question at this point is, "What will be the political process to eventually free the fetus from us from the 1973 decision by seven justices in black robes?" My answer: Our Congress passes a bill citing that they conclude "a fetus and embryo is in fact a legal person from the moment of conception;" and then get this bill signed by a pro-life President. Fetuses would consequently be protected with the same rights to life as stated in the Fourteenth Amendment. Such a bill is currently in the planning stage among some conservative politicians. In the meantime, 56 million babies have been aborted since Roe v. Wade.

Protect Minorities vs. Protect the Fetuses

Minorities have received legal protection over the last several decades. Courts have made many rulings against racial discrimination. Laws have been passed providing equal rights to all U.S. citizens regardless of their race, sex, nationality, creed or sexual orientation. The problem in the interim was that the minority didn't have the power to prevail over the policy dictated by the majority. The minority needed people outside of their group to help push their agenda. Martin Luther King, Jr. and other black leaders were not able by themselves to get the relevant legislation passed to provide equality. Many whites marched down Main Street in Montgomery, AL side-by-side with the blacks to back the cause. Legislators (mostly Caucasian) had to pass the laws giving minorities equal rights.

The fetus is today's minority that is being brutally discriminated against. They need *us* to back *them*. The fetus itself is completely powerless. They have no way to defend themselves. They can't hire a bodyguard. They have no venue for making their case. They can't appeal their case to the Supreme Court. They cannot group together and march peacefully down Main Street. They cannot script brief but pithy sayings on signs to flash at the news camera. They can't pick a fearless leader to be spokesman for their cause. They cannot organize. They cannot appeal to the masses. They can't caucus. They can't strategize. They can't riot. They can't vote. They can't sue. They can't even speak. They need an advocate to speak for them, act for them, vote for them, organize and strategize for them, appeal to the masses and to affect change. Hence, the fetus is in a politically unique position. They remain the last minority without equal rights. Who among us will take up their cause?

Google "counseling for unwed mothers" to look up organizations to support those faced with a choice. One such organization is "First Choice Women's Resource Center" at www.1stchoice.org

Conclusion

More than a conclusion, I have summarized the contents herein on behalf of conservatives. Along with it, I mixed in my personal vision for this country in the following eighteen ideals:

- **Our religious freedom is precious.** Obtaining it was the number one reason tens of thousands of Europeans immigrated to the United States. Since then, our country has fallen from the mindset of taking it for granted to letting it become diminished by the secular progressive agenda. Today, unconstitutional court decisions robbing us of First Amendment rights have remained unchallenged.

- **Our personal freedom is all-important.** The expanse of government intrusion and control over our lives has grown to annoying and sometimes unbearable proportions. Most citizens today prefer freedom over freebies. We need less government, less law and less regulation on the federal, state and local levels. State control is better than federal control and local implementation is better than state law whenever possible. Since we are a large, diverse nation, localized versions of law allows for differences of culture and preference. It is more likely for the average citizen to have more influence (freedom materialized) with local legislation instead of state or federal.

- **Self-reliance is the key** to American success and the health of America as a country. When the existence of government-funded programs is excessive enough to minimize the necessity and urgency for every individual to continually strive to be the best that he/she can be, we have entered into the downward spiral of the nanny state. If necessity is the mother of invention, then excessive government aid is the big brother of personal failure. (Read that again.) I want to share a story with you that I think has deep symbolic meaning that underscores the importance of self-reliance, a conservative tenet.

It's a beautiful spring day and a little girl prances about the backyard. She finds amidst the garden a thin silky pouch attached to the underside of a leaf. It has an insect inside. The creature is nearing the end of that beautiful metamorphic stage just before it emerges with beauty and grace, ready to flap its colorful wings. She observes how the little butterfly-to-be is struggling to get out from its protective pupa. It obviously wants to break free and begin its new life, but is having trouble doing so. Excited, she takes the creature to her Dad. She asks him to help the butterfly, as it can't seem to escape. She is afraid it will die trying to get out and doesn't want this to happen. Seeing how important this is to his little girl, the Dad takes his Swiss knife and very carefully cuts a slit in the lining of the butterfly's protective environment, being careful not to hurt the insect. It then crawls out. The little girl leaps for joy to see it is now free. But she then observes it won't fly. Her adorable smile that is the joy of her parents now turns upside down. She asks her Dad why the butterfly can only crawl, but this masculine hero doesn't have the answer. She put the little creature in a jar with a porous lid and shows it to her Grandfather the next day. He grimaces as he explains to her what happened. "Sweetie, the butterfly builds muscles from the struggle to free itself from its wrappings. By the time it breaks through on its own, it will have built up enough strength to fly. But now it can't because you have altered the course of nature. If you had let it alone, it would have developed naturally and learned to fly."

- **Capitalism works best here**. Our political and economic system needs to reflect who we are as a people. We need to stop comparing ourselves to countries that are not outperforming us economically, militarily and politically (how much democracy and freedom they have.) A system of government may work for one nation, but not for another because of the history, culture, mindset and the DNA make up of its citizens. We can't take over an uncivilized, rogue nation and expect our democratic process that works here to work there. The same idea holds true for our economic system. We can't expect the socialist leaning or government-run economic practices of Europe to work here. Capitalism, not "tamperism" or "nannyism," has proven to work best for this country. Part of it is due to the very fiber of Americans who work hard and want to make something of themselves. Part of the reason is because we have always had a group of fortunate individuals with large amounts of capital to invest. I don't speak of unbridled capitalism, but correctly regulated capitalism. We want to protect the consumer, but business and environmental regulations have now stifled economic growth and sent it overseas. The Congress has been guilty of over-tampering with banking regulations that rubbed against conventional banking practices. The Federal Reserve has been guilty of artificially adjusting the availability of money. We are still trying to get it right. The process in regulating it is slow, reactive, subject to corruption and always one step behind the constantly changing business and investment environment. The process needs to be swift, pro-active, free of corruption and one step ahead of those that aim to run around it. Most importantly, the process of regulating needs to be free of political pressure that originates from leftist ideology.

- **The role of government is becoming too large.** We affirm we would like the government to provide certain levels of protection to its citizens as well as economic regulations that will provide a fruitful and fair business environment. Today, however, government wants to control specific outcomes on issues that in the past would be relegated to the private sector, the local community or to bankruptcy courts.

The ideal role for government to play is to limit itself to a system of regulations that will incentivize the private sector to take risks in spending capital. Ideally, this will increase the quality and quantity of products and services. If this happens, the byproduct will be an optimized economy with the maximum potential for jobs and business opportunity. At this juncture, the executive branch needs to roll back excessive regulations to jumpstart this strategy. History has taught us that government overreach can create more problems in the long run than the actual benefit from programs that might be realized in the short run. The answer is to strike the right balance between using tax money prudently to provide programs that provide broad benefits in a fair way versus an overabundance of policies and programs that unfairly benefit only certain groups of people. Americans are a generous people and pride ourselves on taking care of the needy, but the question is "where do we draw the line?" The answer is the point at which the government: 1. Has to borrow money or go into debt to expedite the program as the current tax revenue flow is insufficient to pay for it; 2. Has to further redistribute income and wealth to pay for it; 3. Creates programs with benefits so substantial, it discourages the pursuit of employment or profit making that generates tax revenue.

- **Eliminate the annual deficit and decrease the national debt.** We can't conceive of how much sixteen trillion dollars is and how impossible it would be for us to pay that off. To realize the urgency of reducing the national debt and eliminating the huge deficits we face annually, review these events that have *never* occurred before. They mark the beginning of the end of our prosperity.
    o The U.S. federal government had to borrow 36 cents for every dollar it spent in 2011. Can you imagine running your household finances that way?

o   That national debt is now more than the entire gross national product of our country. When foreign countries stop lending us money, nobody will be able to bail us out at that point since the size of our debt is already larger than the GNP of several countries.

o   The feds started to print money (create it out of thin air) in October 2008 during the credit crunch and added about $850 billion to cash reserves through March 2012. Although only about $300 billion of this amount filtered down to consumers, the threat of inflation occurs when they print money as the unearned fake stuff artificially bids up the cost of goods. The fed's decision to do this reflects on their limited capacity to borrow, which is dwindling. This gives new meaning to the phrase "red flag." (Compliments of History News Network website.)

o   The dollar has been continually falling in value against other major world currencies for many years. As a result, the major international players in the world have determined the dollar is too unstable. In fact, they had a meeting without us in 2011 to decide how they will replace the U.S. dollar as the reserve monetary unit. When this happens, the resulting repercussions will make the banking/Wall Street meltdown in 2008 look like child's play.

o   President Obama appointed a commission in 2011 to make recommendations on how to get our federal deficit back to sustainable levels. The recommendations that followed were quite sobering and drastic. Obama didn't follow them. Now, the country and the world have no confidence we will resolve our issues.

o   The Republican-dominated House of Representatives and a strong minority Republican presence in the Senate still wasn't enough to affect negotiations on the deficit for us to observe a *realized* decrease in spending (not just a slight decrease in *budgeted* spending) as of mid-2012.

o Agencies that rate organizations for credit worthiness has downgraded the score for the U.S. government in 2011 for the first time in history. Part of the reason for the drop in rating was due to the political stalemate in Congress, as it is not resolving the issue. This literally is the writing on the wall.

o There is a clock on the internet that shows the constant increase of the national debt. In early 2012, we were averaging an increase to the debt of 4 billion dollars a day or 167 million dollars an hour. This is not what we are spending, but *what we are borrowing in addition* to what we are taking in! Getting the clock to reverse—to show our national debt is lessening—has to be our number one goal if we are to even maintain our current economic state of affairs. The only way to do this is to reduce all federal spending. This means entitlements such as government employee benefits, payroll and pensions, welfare, Medicaid, Medicare, the military, discretionary spending—everything. We all will have to live with less. But the President and Congress (all administrations, not just the current one) don't have the resolve to do this. They care more about their careers and their compensation then the country. It's that simple. Our only choice is to elect candidates who will have the resolve to drastically cut spending across the board.

• **Tax Reform is still needed.** It takes the average person about half a year of work to pay for all the taxes levied against him/her. The anecdotal fact was that it used to take the average American until the *end of July* to accomplish this, but admittedly federal income taxes are now lower than they have been in decades. Regardless, federal taxes are only part of this as most of us pay state taxes and municipal taxes in addition to sales taxes, especially products and services with additional taxes attached to them such as gasoline, cigarettes, imports, your phone bill, etc.

There is merit to the argument that many corporate tax loopholes are affecting overall revenues into the IRS coffers. Corporate tax reform is needed. Regardless, many economists assert one of the leading reasons that businesses are taking their capital overseas is to improve their tax liability. Therefore, corporate tax policy has to be adjusted so that U.S. can better compete in the global market going forward.

The myth that Warren Buffet and other investors pay less *income* tax than their secretary is democratic propaganda. It is the comparing of apples to oranges by comparing capital gains tax to income tax. Here's what the Democrats don't tell you when this debate comes up—the money that a wealthy person has in a taxable investment has already been taxed 35% (assuming the top bracket was applicable) *when they earned it.* Now, they are paying an *additional* 15% on its investment profits. In actuality, they are paying taxes on it twice, which indeed results in a much higher percentage.

Another misleading issue that Obama and the Democrats have trumped up during 2012 is the call for the wealthy, particularly the top one percent of earners, to pay more in taxes. I'm not going to argue the merit of this idea, but just want to put the dollars into perspective. I have seen estimates from those crunching the numbers that as much as $5 or $6 billion more could be squeezed from the upper crust. But let's give the democrats the benefit of the doubt and say substantial tax legislation was passed that would put as much as $10 billion more into the coffers from those that could afford it (by lowering the income bar to include more taxpayers.) Consider that the deficit will definitely continue to shortfall by over a trillion dollars over the next couple of years. (The 2012 budget deficit is $1.3 trillion.) Get this: The newfound tax revenue would only equate to paying for less than 1% of the deficit (because 10 billion is only one percent of a trillion.) This means the remaining 99%

plus of the problem needs to occur through the reduction of spending (and this is *after* tax increases to the wealthy!)

- **Discrimination** against any individual based on their sex, age creed, color, language or sexual orientation is wrong. Conversely, a government policy or action that gives preferential treatment to someone decided on the basis of any of these attributes is also wrong. No difference in policy should be made because any of these attributes pertain to a majority versus a minority of people. Our moral target should always be equal opportunity, not equal results.

   Tolerance is a two-way street. I will tolerate your choice not to be religious, but you need to tolerate my choice to be religious. Someone of a particular religion should not be exempt from the ideals of equal rights and political correctness that we use to defend minority groups.

- **Get angry.** I spent a lot of time talking about the wrong kind of anger. Attacking the arguer, unveiling personal dirt on the opponent, spewing vitriol, carrying hate speech on signs, using violence, destroying property and showing utter disrespect for those you disagree with are actions that are counterproductive in the political discourse. Here, I refer to the right kind of anger. There is valor and nobleness in appropriate, controlled anger at actions that are unacceptable. I'm talking about using verbiage in the political arena that appropriately and accurately describes the problem (not the person) without concerning ourselves with political correctness. Getting angry should include the use of emotion and illustrative use of inflection and tone to make our point. Change often requires protest, and you can't have an effective protest without some degree of dramatic expression. Our congressional representatives will hopefully listen to their constituents when they sense they are angry.

- **Perspective—keep one that is personal, logical and real.** Many of us have high ideals when it comes to holding up the importance of morality and second chances. A good rule of thumb in judging what should happen to someone that committed an act of violence, destroyed someone's life because they were driving drunk, were caught in a jihad or even molested a child is to ask themselves, "What if this happened to my wife, son or daughter? How would I feel then?" This is the only way to think because the victim was in fact a loved one by *someone's* family. True light is thrown on an issue when we personalize it as close as we can. What if *you* lost *your* job because the environmental regulations for the company you worked for were so extensive that they had to go out of business? What if *I* was the fetus and my sixteen year-old mother had to make a choice?

The logical perspective is the only way to go. Those who pride themselves on taking the high road about the role of our government need to look at facts as well as feelings. We are a compassionate people and emotional as humans, but we must take a step back at times to analyze the costs of a policy or program to the majority in order to justify the benefits to the minority.

Keep it real. Stick to the facts. Question a viewpoint if it is presented using only emotion and feelings. Avoid getting sucked in to unfairly defending or criticizing a particular group of people just because it is in vogue to do so. Ask yourself if an opinion is a result of merit or political correctness. Anger and emotions can be a force to implement positive political change, but can also be abused and therefore harmful. Use wisdom to discern the difference between the two scenarios.

- **Who's right?** Political discussions on any law, program, policy, executive decision or court decision must be based on merit if the argument is to be valid. Any attack on the individual/group defending their position or a blind allegiance to a group of people/political platform/party/ideology does not make for a valid argument. We need to shun hateful vitriol and insist on respectful dialogue so we can pinpoint the real issue and not disguise it with smoke and mirrors. If a person is a member of an organization with a specific goal or agenda, we need to take into account their viewpoint is going to be subjectively skewed toward that organization's agenda. Anyone who is advocating a position because they are catering to special interests or rewarding those who have contributed to their campaign also lacks the legitimacy of having an argument with merit.

- **Protect citizens**: The most important function of our government is to protect us and our property from harm. The only way for government to do so is for all of its branches to thoroughly legislate and enforce laws. The judicial branch on all levels needs to mete out sentences needed to deter the first offense from ever happening and prevent second offenses from occurring. If any American does not feel safe or feel his property is in jeopardy, we have failed to accomplish this. We would then need to re-double government laws, enforcement and sentences until we *all* can live without fear, not just the privileged. The biggest problem in keeping repeat offenders off the street has been judges who have taken it upon themselves to hand out extremely lenient sentences to violent criminals without explanation. This is why we have "Jessica's law" in 42 states—to ensure vicious child molesters receive appropriate, uniformly meted out sentences. Ideally, all fifty states should have a similar law, either through state legislation or a congressional one to protect all children regardless of where they live.

- **We have to protect our country** from the onslaught of immigrants who are entering our country illegally. In recent decades, the illegal entry has brought with it the criminal element, resulting in Americans being killed or harmed. Our country is divided over how to deal with the criminal issue becoming so prevalent, with a huge percentage of authorities refusing to take part in implementing justice for political advantage or political ideology. Sanctuary cities are places that are unsafe in that they virtually provide illegal immigrants a license to break the law and get away with it, resulting in repetitive rapes, robberies and death that occur needlessly. There are many documented cases of repeated offenders being let go simply because they are illegal immigrants whereas American citizens would have received the full force of the law if they had been the perpetrators. There has been no resolve by leadership on the highest levels to take command of this out-of-control problem.

- **Citizens have the constitutional right to protect themselves with arms**. Now that state governments have gone out of its way to protect criminal illegal immigrants and the federal government has kept states from enforcing laws to protect its citizens, we need Second Amendment rights now as much as we ever have. If we are in danger of being harmed by walking down an inner city street at night, we should *all* have the right to carry whatever weapon we need to protect ourselves.

- **National security is paramount.** Terrorism knows no moral boundaries. Likewise, we cannot be concerned about the welfare of terrorists who have already engaged in the ruthless slaughter of innocent Americans. Those advocating softness on captured terrorists in the name of keeping high moral standards are misguided. It is a nobler, loftier goal to do whatever it takes to protect our citizens from harm. If this means allowing enhanced interrogation of a sub-human monster with only hate in their heart and the intent to kill Americans at random, then so be it.

  Political correctness was the main ingredient in the recipe for disaster that allowed the terrorist attack on September 11 to occur. Blindly sprinkle in the usual measure of naiveté and top it off with a deep layer of arrogance and we baked in the inevitable. Political correctness breeds the mindset of tolerance, which converts into a practice of letting our defenses down. The commission that investigated 9-11 confirms that bureaucratic failures of carelessness and sloppy errors have been identified as reasons why the terrorists responsible for the Sep. 11 tragedy entered the country. However, it was the naïve and politically correct mindset that determined the obviously low level of concern, urgency and resolve. After all, (read with sarcasm) this is America. Everyone is welcome. Therefore, terrorists simply flew in unheeded. Finally, the arrogance among all the powers-to-be sealed the deal. They thought we were too militarily strong to be taken down by a radical group of towel heads that lived in the desert. After all, we had been openly, specifically and repeatedly threatened by these terrorists. Yet, we virtually ignored it (with our nose high in the air, along with our oversized, vulnerable butts.)

Regarding the release of classified information that could compromise national security, the interest of protecting citizens and our military supersedes the public's right to know. Homeland security and life is more important than the free, unedited distribution of information.

- **Life is equally precious for both military and civilians.** A strong national defense is important, but this doesn't mean military intervention can be exercised because trigger-happy generals can't wait to solve a political problem with a military solution. "Walk softly, but carry a big stick" (Teddy Roosevelt) is the best military strategic plan. Deterrence is the answer. Achieving foreign political goals with minimal military engagement is the way to go if possible. The fine young men and women in our military are people, too. Their lives should not be considered any more expendable than mine or yours. Life is precious and it is precious equally among both the military and civilians alike.

Here's the best formula to determine when we should consider putting our military in harm's way when our country is threatened: If the number of troops in the field that are likely to give their lives exceeds the number of American citizens at home that the enemy will likely kill if no military intervention takes place, then don't intervene. We must make the decision based on which option will likely preserve the most Americans. Looking back at history, this means the Korean War, Vietnam

War, Iraq War and Afghanistan wars should never have been waged *in the prolonged fashion* in which they were fought.

> **Wasn't our involvement in Afghanistan supposed to prevent another tragedy on the scale of Sept. 11, not re-create one of equal proportions?**

Far more American lives were lost in these wars than anyone could theorize would be saved if those wars were never fought. Conversely, if a small number of soldiers' lives had to be lost in killing known terrorist leaders who were planning more terrorist attacks on the scale of the September 11 tragedy, then this particular extent of intervention can be justified.

- **We need leadership, not apologies.** Anyone that studied American history will agree that our country has proven itself as exceptional among all others not just from a standpoint of economic prosperity, but from its adherence to the freedoms and values that originated from our founding fathers. Granted, pride and arrogance have no place in influencing foreign policy. We realize our country is not perfect. However, verbalizing unpatriotic sentiment or taking a position that diminishes the image of our country, especially to foreign leaders on their soil, does not does serve us well. We strive to be looked up at, not down at, by foreign heads of state. A leader walks in front of others. He does not follow them. He speaks from a position that others look up to. He cannot lead if he places himself among others. A leader doesn't brood over the past and apologize for it. He sets a positive vision for the future and seeks to obtain it.

  For this country to survive the next hundred years, we need to work together, not against each other. We need to be cohesive, not divisive. We need to find a way to exclude politics from decision making, not use it to our advantage to get our way. We need to stop being so loyal to our political party and start being more loyal to our country. We need to understand our limitations regarding the lives and treasure that we can afford to dedicate to achieve a foreign policy goal. We cannot act as if our supply is limitless. We need to be brutally tough at the negotiation table, not congenial and agreeable. We need to stand by our convictions and act unilaterally if necessary. We cannot retreat from the plan or water it down if consensus cannot be reached among other potential international players.

- **Preserve the Constitution.** Are Presidents really abiding by it? Here's some examples during the Obama Administration to show they often do not.
  - o In January 2012, President Obama declared on his own authority that the Senate was in recess and then proceeded to make four appointments without the required Senate confirmation. This is an unarguable breach of the Constitution. (Source: The Heritage Foundation newsletter March 2012.)
  - o In June of 2012, President Obama announced that he exempted about 800,000 illegal aliens from being subject to possible deportation if they met certain age requirements, had a clean record, and had obtained either a high school diploma or served in the military. Whereas most those on both sides of the aisle did not disagree with this fair policy adjustment, Obama's actions were an unarguable breach of the Constitution in that he altered legislation on immigration policy without involving the Congress.
  - o The Obamacare mandate to require Catholic-based institutions to insure for contraception and sterilization, and the general requirement to purchase health care, have been argued as unconstitutional by many judges and many states. However, the Supreme Court has ruled to the contrary by a 5-4 vote in a highly questionable and controversial ruling.
  - o Presidents often skirt the intent of the Constitution when they send our military into battle without consent from the Congress. There is an allowance of 90 days given to the President to gain consent from the Congress after authorizing military intervention, but not all Constitutional experts

have agreed that President Obama and his predecessors have abided by the specific rules checking the Commander-in-Chief's powers.

Have we allowed the Constitution to evolve into a purely secular document? Since the first Pilgrims landed, our values, ideals, morals, ethics and civilized behavior have been rooted in the Judea-Christian beliefs of our forefathers, who incorporated them into the architecture of our government—the Constitution. This document states that our freedoms come from God and not the state. Secular progressives need to be reminded of this as they sometimes seek to change society in a way that traditionalists view as ungodly. Separation of church and state does not mean separation of god and state, or even separation of prayer and state; although our secular progressive justices have ruled it does. Change to reverse decisions that are in actuality "legislation from the bench" still needs to occur.

The problem has been that Supreme Court Justices have taken it upon themselves to change the meaning of the Constitution. The "evolutionist" justices do in fact legislate from the bench. Put simply, justices don't necessarily make decisions based on the Constitution or case precedents, but what they would like them to be—period. Courts should refuse to make a decision and yield to the legislature in cases which have no Constitutional precedent. Many court decisions, laws and policies continue to rub against the true spirit of the Constitution. The most egregious are the presidential abuse of the pardon privilege, permitting the release of national security secrets, policies requiring equal results instead of equal opportunity, laws restricting the Second Amendment, laws obstructing religious freedom, and laws related to abortion.

- **A fetus is a human being** that hasn't been born yet and needs to have the same government protection from harm that you and I enjoy. The current law of the land does not recognize this. Every politician needs to advocate the need for passing legislation to provide such protection. Every person that votes needs to ensure their candidate declares himself as pro-life. Society has rendered the fetus the last minority to be provided equal protection. If only it could speak, it would be screaming out for us to champion their cause and save them from peril.

> Imagine the joy (if you had made the adoption choice) of meeting that adult who was once in your womb, as he or she finds you years later to thank you for giving them life.

- **Vote.** When deciding on a candidate for office, we need to weigh their past behavior and achievements more heavily than feelings of inspiration we may get from hearing him speak. It may be just a result of empty rhetoric from a skilled politician. After all, hasn't history taught us that a politician is most likely to do what he has done in the past and not what he says? In addition, if he doesn't have a past filled with accomplishments, do we really want to merely hope he performs as well as he promises? Regardless of our conclusions on a candidate, the most important thing for every American is to learn about a candidate for office and vote according to their merit. Remember when voting that the next president we put in office will likely be selecting one or more Supreme Court Justices whose contribution to decisions will have an enormous impact on our lives.

Bottom Line

When preparing to cast your vote for the 2012 election, consider this list regarding the Obama tenure. Our 44th President:

- Is responsible for increasing the national debt by an amount more than all other Presidents combined.
- Has seen more negative economic milestones (see section above on debt in Conclusion) that have occurred during his administration than any other President in modern history.
- Has presided over an unprecedented increase in entitlement spending (re-visit section on income re-distribution if you have any doubt about this.)
- Has the most liberal voting record of any President in history.
- Has been more anti-oil exploration than any other President.
- Has presided over the most aggressive regulations against businesses in modern history.
- Is the most pro-choice President ever.
- Has been more anti-Christian than any other President (based on the number of bigoted remarks and discriminatory acts against Christians.)
- Is the most anti-religious rights President ever (as determined by the number of legal challenges against him re: religious rights.)
- Is the most anti-Second Amendment President in recent history.
- Has created more constitutional challenges and debates over his actions more than any other President in recent history.
- Has been the most apologetic President ever when addressing other heads of state.

- Has been the most divisive President in history regarding black vs. white, Hispanic vs. non-Hispanic, Muslim vs. non-Muslim American, Democrat vs. Republican, secular progressive vs. traditionalist, and liberal vs. conservative.

Questionnaire
(to see how conservative you
are on the issues.)

First of Two Categories: Social and Philosophical Viewpoints
Check off each statement if you agree

*We have too many annoying laws in this country on the federal, state and local levels which impinge on our freedom, providing too much government control.   _____

*Our government is over-involved militarily in world affairs and needs to recognize that our uniformed personnel are not anymore expedient than civilians.   _____

* Every law-abiding citizen has the right to bear arms and carry an appropriate weapon on the street to defend themselves against an attacker.   _____

*Jessica's law needs to be passed in the remaining eight hold out states or the Congress should pass a similar bill for all states.   _____

*States having problems with excessive crime committed by illegal aliens should have the power to enact laws to help them identify and deport those endangering the public.   _____

*Releasing criminals who have been arrested and/or convicted of a felon just because they are illegal immigrants has to stop.   _____

*Presidents and governors abuse the pardon privilege and should only exercise it when it genuinely appears there has been a judicial error or sentence unfairness.   _____

*Laws and policies should reflect equal opportunity, not equal results.   _____

*Many Supreme Court justices unconscionably legislate from the bench. Presidents need to select justices with a record devoid of legislative and/or creative decisions.   _____

*Since we are a nation founded on godly principles and recognition of a supreme deity, we should tolerate and even promote references to god in the public sector.   _____

*A valedictorian at a High School graduation should be legally permitted to thank his/her god during their speech as per the First Amendment.   _____

*The theory of intelligent design (without mentioning god) should be taught in schools as an alternative one in addition to the evolutionary theory.   _____

*I need to be keenly aware of how the mainstream media slants their presentation of news and omit certain stories to promote left-wing ideology and protect liberals.   _____

*Politicians can't be trusted to do what they tell you they will. The best way to vote is to judge them on their record and their accomplishments.   _____

*Political correctness is over-rated, especially when it comes to identifying and preventing criminal and terrorist activity.   _____

*I don't believe water-boarding is torture and should be permitted in circumstances when its use will most probably save American lives going forward.   _____

*Children belong to their parents and not the state. School boards, state and local laws regarding supervision of children should reflect this age-honored philosophy.   _____

* I am in favor of strict laws requiring parental notification when a minor reports to a medical or counseling professional that she is pregnant.   _____

*I am opposed to government funding of abortion, both here and abroad.   _____

*Congress should pass a law entitling fetuses to Fourteenth Amendment equal protection and then the Congress or the states should pass anti-abortion legislation.   _____

Now add up your check marks for your social and philosophical conservatism score. Where are you on the liberal to social conservative spectrum?

Hopeless Liberal	0 to 4
Middle of the Road/Centrist	5 to 12
Conservative	13 to 16
Very Conservative	17 to 20

Second of Two Categories: Fiscal Viewpoint
Check off each statement if you agree

*The ideal America is when every individual is as self-reliant as he/she can be.   _____

*We need to drastically reduce government spending, including entitlements.   _____

*Stimulating the economy through the government is not the best use of our money. I'd rather see it invested directly to the private sector or taxpayer.   _____

*I am in favor of a constitutional amendment stipulating that under no circumstances can the federal government spend more money than it takes in.   _____

*The solution to increasing tax revenue is not to tax by further redistributing income. It is tax reform through the elimination of unfair loopholes.   _____

*Our country cannot afford Obamacare. The tax money needed to fund it and the additional cost of premiums far outweigh the benefits it yields.   _____

*We need to roll back business, banking and environmental regulations to stimulate growth and get the economy (and job creation) back on track.   _____

*We all love clean energy. In the meantime, we need to optimize opportunity here in North America to drill oil, decreasing our dependence on the Middle East.   _____

*We need to seal the borders and institute immigration reform that will reduce the excessive state spending of funds on illegal immigrants, which we can't afford. _____

*I believe *limiting* military intervention (when imminent threats are not present) coincides with the conservative fiscal view of reducing unnecessary military spending. _____

*The feds or all states should pass a tort reform law like that of TX requiring plaintiffs to pay all legal costs for a frivolous lawsuit when determined as such by the judge. _____

*I would forgo "freebies" from the government if I knew I would have the freedom from having to pay for them. It's less expensive for me to buy them directly. _____

Now add up your check marks for your fiscal conservatism score. Where are you on the liberal to fiscal conservative spectrum?

Hopeless Liberal	0 to 3
Middle of the Road/Centrist	4 to 6
Conservative	7 to 9
Very Conservative	10 to 12

For your ranking on the overall liberal to conservative spectrum, add your scores for both the social and fiscal conservative questionnaire and plot them below.

Hopeless Liberal	0 to 7
Middle of the Road/Centrist	9 to 18
Conservative	20 to 25
Very Conservative	27 to 32

Since one obviously doesn't need to read this book in order to take the questionnaire, you can give it to your friends and family to see where they score and have fun with it. Challenge each other on the merit of agreeing vs. disagreeing with each statement. Just remember to attack the argument, not the arguer. No vitriol, please.

Acknowledgements

I owe a debt of gratitude to the person who edited this book. He provided the objective, straightforward feedback I needed, which ideally should come from someone you know and trust. That person is my son, Aaron. He has a B.A. in English from Liberty University, a Christian institution. Aaron has been one of my political sparring partners, usually playing the devil's advocate role. Although he has had the advantage of attending both a fundamentalist Baptist Church and a Baptist High School, any conservative influences resulting from his schooling were certainly balanced by a typical young adult's liberal view of politics. You can guess he was always ready to correct his Dad about a thing or two. I was extremely lucky to have him as a partner in publishing this book.

I have to unabashedly list Fox News as the default source for factual information and statistics collected by their team wherever the origin of facts or statistics are not provided. It is obvious I am a loyal fan. It was clear I did mention individual credit throughout the book to all Fox News contributors and analysts that provided the benefit of their reportage.

The book *The Beginners Guide To Conservative Politics* by Dan Nagasaki provided concept ideas to me on the topics of "determinism," "macro vs. micro goodness," "feelings vs. logic," and "altering human nature." In one section, I quoted him verbatim and listed his book as a credit.

I thank my lovely wife, Veronica, for putting up with my political discussions at family parties and social outings, especially at times when I should have kept my opinions to myself.